Apostles Of The Last Days

The Fruits Of Medjugorje

The Bible tells us you can tell a tree by its fruits.

This is the story of the fruits of Medjugorje and more.

By Thomas Rutkoski

Published by Gospa Missions

200 Wilderness Trail

Evans City, PA 16033

412-538-5700

Third printing, ISBN: 0-963366 7-7-7

Table of Contents

Dedication

I dedicate this book to:

The Father,

The Son,

The Holy Spirit,

and to ... The Blessed Mother,

who gave birth to The Son.

Acknowledgements

Patricia Beharry   Florence Jaskey

Melinda Brierton   Lorraine Mutschler

Judith Doerr   Susan Mutschler

Charles Gaffney   Mary Rutkoski

Donald Gaus   Valerie Spence

Ann Gould   Elaine Taft

My dear friends,

To simply say thank you for your sacrifice of time and talent to aid in the production of this book, would be inadequate. I will pray for you the rest of my life. My hope is that by working on this book, you know how much I believe in prayer. So, believing that my prayer will be answered, my appreciation is best expressed in prayer. I pray that God will bless you for your effort and the Blessed Mother will wrap Her mantle of love around you and intercede on your behalf. May the blessing you receive for your participation be not once, but every time a life is changed for the good because someone has read this book.

In the love of Jesus and Mary,

Thomas Rutkoski

Introduction

My name is Thomas Rutkoski, the founder and director of a non-profit foundation called Gospa Missions. For twenty years, I was a well-paid photojournalist for KDKA Television in Pittsburgh, Pennsylvania. On March 22, 1991, I walked into my supervisor's office and boldly stated, "This coming Friday will be my last day of employment here." To say the least, he was shocked, as was everyone who knew me. Realizing the mistake I was making in the direction of life, I altered my course in this drastic fashion to go out into the world to evangelize. I was proclaiming my belief in God with my mouth, but making a mockery of that proclamation with my actions. This is the story of the supernatural events that led me to quit my job and the subsequent effect it had on me and those with whom I've come in contact.

This is the story of my profound conversion.

Chapter 1

We All Start Out the Same

As members of the human race we all start out the same, with free wills, souls and bodies. That is where the similarity ends. So equipped, we are then fractionalized into many degrees of wealth and religious beliefs depending on the family into which we are born. We do not get a choice in either. I was born a Catholic. Most of what Catholics are taught to believe is contained in a prayer titled, "The Apostles Creed." I probably recited it as a child; I just can't remember doing so. It goes like this:

I believe in God, the Father Almighty, Creator of Heaven and earth; and in Jesus Christ, His Only Son, Our Lord; Who was conceived by the Holy Spirit, born of the Virgin Mary, suffered under Pontius Pilate, was crucified, died and was buried. He descended into hell; the third day He arose from the dead; He ascended into Heaven, sits at the right hand of God, the Father Almighty, from thence He shall come to judge the living and the dead. I believe in the Holy Spirit, the Holy Catholic Church, the communion of saints, the forgiveness of sins, the resurrection of the body and life everlasting. Amen.

As a Catholic child with minimal training I was left wondering, does God really exist?

The premise of Christianity is this: God created this world. God then created a man and a woman to live in it. He placed them in a beautiful garden called Eden. In the

Garden of Eden, Satan, the snake, tempted Eve with forbidden fruit. After Eve's first bite of this forbidden fruit, original sin was introduced to the world. The snake had made his first inroad into leading us all astray. His second victim Adam, quickly fell with Eve's help. Satan's deception, by working through Eve, convinced Adam to taste this forbidden fruit.

Curiosity masks a pure heart, opening the door and allowing the entrance of evil. This curiosity has continued to plague us through the centuries. The shrewdness of Satan is almost always hidden in the attractiveness of an apple, making the evil seem appealing.

God in His infinite mercy, seeing us founder in sin, with no hope for salvation, sent us the first sustaining pure heart, Mary. She was a young woman born without original sin, who answered with a humble "yes" to Her Father in Heaven. Mary, the new Eve! When asked by the Angel Gabriel, to be the Mother of God, She consented.

A Savior was born and He is named Jesus. He was to give us an example of how one could, through the grace of God, live a pure life in this world, despite the influence of Satan.

The last three of Jesus' thirty-three years on this earth were spent training twelve men to carry on His teachings. After the tremendous example of His life, the crescendo occurred; Christ's ultimate sacrifice. He suffered and died so our sins could be forgiven. He was crucified to bring us triumph over Satan. He became the most glorious gift from God. By surrendering His life, Jesus was showing us what sacrifice is.

Jesus, while He suffered and hung on the cross, was forgiving those who were killing Him. Then to prove He was God in the second person (God being three Persons in One; the Father, the Son and the Holy Spirit) Jesus came back to life on the third day after His death. He was confirming to His twelve apostles, and the world, that the word He spoke to them was true.

After His resurrection, Jesus brought His work on this earth to fruition in forty days. He then ascended unto Heaven, leaving these instructions for His apostles: *"Go into all the world and preach the good news to all creation,"* (Mark 16:15). Through the gift of His death and resurrection, we could be forgiven for our sins.

This forgiveness would come to us through confessing our sins, feeling sorrow for having committed them, and making a firm commitment to follow, The Ten Commandments. Then, if we hold onto this grace until the end, we may join Jesus in Heaven to live eternally, without the influence of Satan. What then would happen to this Satan? He would be cast into a place called hell and chained there forever.

My God, what a story! Do you believe it, or do you need proof? For forty-four years I acted as if I didn't believe. I might have *said* I believed in God, but I *acted* as if I didn't. I think that is probably similar to the relationship most of us have with God.

If this fantastic story is true, what does God expect from us? To what length is He willing to go in proving to us that He exists; or is that the problem? Have we placed God in the position of having to prove to *us* that He is real? These are the same questions that have been asked by many through the ages. I also asked these kinds of questions; but now I'm getting answers. I would like to offer to you the answers given to me.

The premise of Christian faith tells us there is a Heaven and a hell. If there is a God and we have paid little or no attention to Him, then we are going to hell, unless we change! God tells us to love Him with all our hearts, all our minds, all of our souls, and all of our strength; to proclaim Jesus Christ as our Savior; and we will join Him in Heaven. If we love God, in the way He asks, we will obey the rules He gave us to live by, The Ten Commandments.

We all start the same. It is ultimately up to each individual to decide whose side he or she is on. It's Good or evil. When reduced to the basics, there are no gray areas involving salvation. The bottom line is . . . Heaven or hell!

With this book, my hope is to take you full circle, as the Lord did with me.

As little children we are born with a clean slate, except for original sin. The foundation that is laid for our lives, religious or otherwise, generally represents our parents' beliefs. The start we get in our religious life depends on that foundation. I had an average start. My parents were not unusually holy people, but they did go to church regularly. The foundation they tried to lay for me did not appear to take hold.

When we enter the real world, we are responsible for ourselves, for our own actions. That responsibility starts at a much younger age than most people realize. The Blessed Mother was fifteen when called to be the Mother of God.

We can't even legally drive a car at that age. So much for tradition!

As we start making our own decisions, God is watching, testing our motives, drawing us to Him. As God draws us closer, Satan sets his snares and traps to distance us from God; almost imperceptible at first; then as blatant as rape, abortion and murder! Good or evil? We all get to choose every day. In all of life's decisions, consciously or not, we can and do choose Good or evil, God or Satan.

God is always creating examples for us to follow. Jesus Christ is the greatest example of all time. He trained the twelve apostles to carry on His teachings. Those twelve, in turn, taught many others and for almost two thousand years, they have followed the teachings of the original twelve.

Jesus said to them, *"Go, therefore, and make disciples of all the nations."* (Mark 25:19) This became their life's work, and through it, the one, holy, Catholic and apostolic Church has remained intact. God's Holy Spirit still works in and through His people today.

If we were in a theater and I shouted FIRE, would you know what I meant? Of course you would! If we were standing in a church and I shouted REVELATIONS FIRE, would you know what that meant? Hopefully you would, because the fire is right at the door. The sword is still wet from the sharpening and the bow is drawn. The Blessed Mother is calling us by Her apparitions throughout the world. Through the fruits of these many apparitions, She is recruiting the "apostles of the last days."

Who are these "apostles of the last days"? Great religious philosophers? Learned men hidden in an abbey in southern France for years, waiting for just the right moment to be sprung upon the earth? Apostles readied to make the last, swift, evangelizing effort before God sends the FIRE?

Well, I believe the last part is right: the last swift evangelizing effort. To play with words, *"The last shall be first and the first shall be last,"* (Matthew 20:16), in this instance, the last shall be *just like* the first. The apostles of the last days, just like the apostles of the first days, will no doubt be of questionable character; called by God from the ranks of average people like you and me to become Apostles of Light, to help the Blessed Mother in the battle against Satan. We are all called to do the task. Who is going to say 'yes'?

If God was calling me, no, *when* God was calling me, before 1987, I had Him turned off. I just wasn't listening. As I wandered aimlessly in my blindness, God, infinitely patient, merciful beyond understanding, was perfectly placing the pieces of His mosaic of my life.

For the last twenty-five of my first forty-four years of life, I fell into the category of those who paid little or no attention to God. My first sixteen years were controlled by my mother and father. You know how that goes. When I was old enough to make my own decision, I stopped going to church on Sundays. I guess I fell into the 'prove it to me' class. Prove to me that I have to do more than I am doing to go to Heaven.

I believed that God existed, but did little to acknowledge it. For over twenty-five years I did not go to church or pray. I made up my own rules as I went along, never realizing that all of the correct rules were written for me in a book I had never read, the Bible.

In August of 1987, I had a profound religious experience that changed my life. I want to tell you about that experience, but first you need to know what there was to change about me. I would like you to look at my life: what I was, how I lived, where life took me. I am not going to place before you all the details, just enough to let you know that I was not an angel. You may find that you and I had a lot in common, to a point. I have told my story to thousands of people and many of them write or call to tell me how it changed their lives. Christ's intervention into my life changed me and now I am praying that it will change your life also.

It would be easy at this point for you to say, "this is just another person saying Jesus saved me. Ho hum!" Don't be as foolish as I was for more than forty years, playing Russian roulette with my soul.

Please read this book cover to cover and then judge for yourself. If you put it down and do not read it, you will miss the redeeming grace of God at work, for this really is God's work. It has nothing to do with me other than He came for me; I said, "yes"; and now He is using me. I am His instrument. I did nothing to deserve it and certainly I am not worthy of this grace. It is a gift from God and now He wants to give the gift to you.

"Our Father in heaven, hallowed be your name. Your kingdom come, Your will be done on earth as it is in Heaven. Give us today our daily bread, and forgive us the wrong we have done as we forgive those who

wrong us. Subject us not to the trial but deliver us from the evil one. Amen." (Matthew 6:9-13)

I offer this prayer as I begin this new endeavor. My desire is to convince you, through this book, that prayer works. I pray that the Our Father you just read, the way Matthew wrote it, will be the start of the grace that will open your mind to this work of Jesus Christ.

I don't mean to be repetitive when I say, "this work of Jesus Christ," but I would not want you to be misled for one second. I have done nothing in my life to be worthy of this blessing. I am simply a most grateful recipient of God's divine grace and mercy. I know now what we must do when we hear the call from Jesus Christ . . . surrender.

The following chapters will show you how patient Jesus was in waiting for me to do just that, surrender.

"Come after Me and I will make you fishers of men." (Matthew 4:19) Our Lord wants our help in changing the world, but first we have to change ourselves. This could be the beginning of *your* story, *your* conversion.

Chapter 2

Growing Up

To understand my surrender to the will of Christ, it's important to review my childhood and look at all the things, good and bad, that God allowed me to experience through my free will.

It is interesting to note that in 1943 the Catholic Church made a dramatic change in policy. Holy Scripture was opened to new forms of investigation and interpretation, inspired by the Holy Spirit. It's not that I was going to read any Scripture that year; I was just a baby! I was born on, August 4, 1943, in the town of Butler, Pennsylvania. My parents were Anna and Frank Rutkoski, both deceased. I have two older sisters, Elizabeth and Mary Jane.

Recalling my early childhood is somewhat difficult. I have never had a very good memory, but I will do my best. The first event that comes to mind is when the apartment house in which we lived caught fire on Christmas Eve, 1949. I was six years old. I recall running back into the burning building to retrieve my train, then I disappeared to our neighbor's house to play with it and left everyone wondering where I was. Not a very bright thing to do! Like Mary and Joseph's pain when Jesus was missing for three days, my parents must have been in agony when they couldn't find me that night. They eventually discovered my whereabouts; maybe that was the first miracle in my life. They didn't kill me!

In 1949, I started school. What a tough time I had! I was classified a slow learner. In reality, I have dyslexia and back then no one knew what that was or realized how difficult it made learning. Second grade was no better. To gain points with my teacher or to get her to like me more, I picked some flowers on the way to school that weren't mine to pick. I saw some tulips in someone's yard, thought of giving them to my teacher, pulled them out of the ground and ran. The flowers seemed to help, but her smile turned to anger when the owner of the flowers called the school. It got worse. I lied and said they were flowers from around the new house my father was building. How does a little boy learn to lie at such an early age?

Around the age of seven, I learned from my sisters how to pick up some extra spending money. If Mom and Dad couldn't attend Mass on Sunday for some reason, let's say Mom was sick and Dad was working, the three of us would go to church alone. Sometimes we would rifle the money that was in the envelope meant for the church. We would occasionally skip Mass altogether, take the money out of the envelope and go to the Hotdog Shop to eat. Great kids, huh?

When I was eight, I got into some real trouble. In Highfield, the neighborhood into which we moved, the community was putting in a sewer system. A game of sorts developed among my friends and me. The object was to see how many colored wires each of us could collect. The wires were left over from the blasting that was necessary to do the excavation. Unbeknownst to us, the wires originally had blasting caps attached to them. The caps, via the wires, connected to a battery box. The box had a plunger switch and when the plunger is pushed, an electrical charge is sent to the cap. The cap, filled with nitroglycerine, then explodes. If the cap is inside a stick of dynamite, it makes the dynamite explode.

One day, two friends and I were walking past the construction site. The gate, normally locked, was open. No one was around so we went in. There was a whole box of wires, so we took them; no we stole them. The wires had caps attached to them. Not knowing what they were, we didn't want the caps. We wanted to find some way to separate the colorful wires from these things on the end, the caps. Rocks seemed to do the trick. We placed the wire on a flat rock and hit the wire with another rock. Presto! The thing on the end broke off. (Maybe I'm not too stupid, I figured out how to do that.) What I didn't anticipate was the explosion on the next try, when the rock hit the blasting cap. You've probably heard the expression, if brains were dynamite, he wouldn't have enough to blow his nose? Well, I had just enough to blow the ends off two of my fingers and blind myself. Thank God my blindness was only temporary!

This was Satan's first attempt to take me out. My body looked like someone fired a shotgun at me a couple of times. I was a bloody mess. The blindness came from all the blood in my eyes caused by some cuts. An eye doctor told me, considering the depth of the scars on my pupils, he didn't know how I ever regained my sight.

My two friends, injured slightly and frightened immensely, ran home, leaving me to stumble around. I don't remember any pain; I assume that shock suppressed it. How I found my way out onto the street is beyond me. A neighbor recognized me and tried to get me into a car, but I resisted. I didn't want to get blood on his car seats. He lost no time in forcing me into the car and driving me home.

Instantly my father grabbed me and rushed me to the hospital. I remember my mother screaming as we left. At that point she didn't know what had happened. She only saw her son covered with blood from head to toe.

I eventually healed, minus the tip of my left index finger and the top of my left thumb.

How does a little boy learn to steal at such a young age? The fear of stealing was there; I knew it was wrong; but I still did it; and I paid for it dearly.

My childhood was punctuated with accidents. I was so overactive, there was no way to slow me down. I spent most of my free time in the woods, building shacks. I always preferred being by myself more than being part of a group. Being with two or three friends was okay, but being alone was better.

My parents, I thought, were good parents. But they both worked and to me, that was not so good. When they were able to spend time with us as a family, we had a great time. We did very basic things for entertainment, although I did not realize at the time that they were basic. I thought the things we did together were the best times anyone could have. We would all go to Thorn Creek to swim. It was just a plain old swimming hole, but what memories! I loved going there.

Another place we frequented was a summer cottage on Lord's Pond (how appropriate!). My Aunt Olga and Uncle Walter owned this little piece of heaven. Their's was one of only three cottages on this beautiful lake buried in the hills of northeastern Pennsylvania. One year I asked and was granted permission to spend a summer there.

I have a short attention span for most things in life and I am sure that contributed to my not doing well in school. I definitely didn't have a short attention span for Lord's Pond. All during the school year, I would daydream about it. I could hardly wait for summer to come so I could go back to Lord's Pond.

My aunt had three children, Ellen, George and Walter. George and Walter were afflicted as youngsters with muscular dystrophy and confined to wheelchairs. Their disability had no bearing on my love for these two guys. I enjoyed doing things for and with them!

Once I got George into the rowboat. I attached a blanket to the oar as a sail and started sailing around the lake. My aunt had a fit. Her concern was, if the boat capsized, that George would not be able to swim. But I had taken precautions. I had put a life vest on him and was confident of our safety. I said to my aunt, "Let him live a little." She relented and we had a ball. The two boys took turns. George, then Walter, in the boat and out of the boat, up and down the lake. I never saw my cousins laugh so much.

Sometimes we would fish and other times we would shoot the boys' B-B gun. I loved to shoot or do anything with them. George had a mouth on him. I still can hear him yelling, "son of a 'bleep'. . . Mother! I have to pee. Hurry!" He would get clobbered for saying that, but the kid had to go! It brings tears to my eyes thinking about all the wonderful experiences at Lord's Pond.

Even with all this fun, I still got a little bored. To broaden my horizons, I got a job with the farmer whose property was adjacent to the lake. I fell in love with farming. Donald Williams, the owner, taught me many new things. I particularly cherished the moments on the tractor. I felt big, good, and in charge. When summer ended it was hard to go home.

The saving grace of returning home was that my father was a hunter. He taught me to hunt and I loved that also. Being in the woods with a real gun hunting for food was like living out a fantasy. I felt like Daniel Boone.

I really messed up there, too. My dad told me never to touch the guns when he wasn't around. Well, naturally, I did. Once I got a 16 gauge shell stuck in the barrel of my dad's 12 gauge shotgun. Too frightened to tell him, I said nothing about it. I could have sent him to Heaven early. If the 12 gauge shell he was trying to put in the chamber had fit, the gun would have blown up when he pulled the trigger. Fortunately, it didn't fit. Unfortunately, I got my butt kicked when he got home!

The only religious event I can remember from my childhood is my First Holy Communion. A photograph of me standing with my mom, behind our house, refreshes my memory. I can recall a candle with some fancy decorations on it. My mother saved this candle but I can't find it now and that makes me sad. I wish I still had it. The picture makes me think about how I felt then about church and God. It was mind-boggling to me. The Masses then were in Latin so I understood nothing. It made God seem distant, not real. By the time I was sixteen, church became something I could do without.

Thinking back, there were only two things I wanted to change about my childhood. First, I would have eliminated school. (Ugh!) I really disliked it, especially sixth grade, since I had to repeat it. The second thing would be that my childhood would have never ended. I wished I didn't have to grow up at all. You know what I mean. It's like having a puppy. Wouldn't it be great if it could just stay that small? Besides, I had never met anybody that I would have wanted to be like when I grew up. Now there is a third thing I wish I could change about my childhood; with all my heart, I wish I would have known then what I know now . . . that God really does exist!

In my high school years, I had an even tougher time trying to learn. However, it was not a miracle that led to my graduating from high school; it was a lie. I was failing my senior English class. My teacher gave me the opportunity to write sixteen book reports to get a 'B' in our last report period. Getting that 'B' would enable me to achieve a 'D+' average and graduate. I asked a friend, who was a teacher, if he would have his class write book reports so I could copy them and turn them in as my own. He did, I did, and there I was, a graduate and a liar.

Graduation brings me to a point in time in 1962. I was in love. I was dating a girl in my last year of high school, and it led to those big words, "Will you marry me?" Wow, was this a difficult process! To get married, one needs a job. In 1962, there was a recession, and jobs were hard to come by. But we were so in love, or was it lust? I think we all have trouble making that distinction.

I think I was willing to do almost anything to get a job. Uncle Sam was the answer! I joined the Air Force so I could have a job, in order to get married, just so I could satisfy this lust. In March of 1963, I left for six weeks of basic training at Lackland Air Force Base in San Antonio, Texas. The plan was to get married after basic training and military school. The projected date for this great event was in September, 1963.

Basic training was to be my first real experience away from home. I would finally be on my own. Isn't that what we all crave when we are young? I never realized how lonely I could get until I was removed from the atmosphere where everyone loved me. Words of love gave way to shouts of, "I CAN'T HEAR YOU," a familiar cry of the drill sergeant.

As if it wasn't bad enough having someone yelling at you all the time, for some unknown reason, everyone was getting mail except me, and I was devastated. I thought the whole world had abandoned me. Worse than that, my drill sergeant picked up on it. "Whatsa madder, Rutootski, doesn't anybody love you?" My only reply was, " My name's not Rutootski, it's Rutkoski."

Day after day I wouldn't get any mail and there he was, "Whatsa madder, Rutootski?" I wanted to kill him! Three or four weeks went by . . . still no mail!

I was standing outside the roller rink one afternoon, looking through the window, watching people skating, when a girl came over to me and introduced herself. That was the first sign of affection I had experienced since leaving home. Oh, hearing a female voice! I thought I died and went to Heaven. And out of the blue, in the middle of our conversation, this girl asked me if I would like to come to her house and have a home-cooked meal.

"I'd love to," I said, "but I'm in basic training and I'm not allowed to leave the base." She smiled and said, "That's not a problem. I have a car with a military sticker on it. I can drive on and off the base anytime I want. No one will even know you're gone!"

It was ironic that our squadron had been given a day pass to go anywhere we wanted, as long as it was *on the base*. Like she said, who would know? It was nice just to be out in the free world again. We arrived at her house, and she introduced me to her mother. Now don't get the wrong idea here. I wasn't cheating on the girl I was going to marry; I was just after a home-cooked meal. And there, standing in front of me, was the wonderful lady who was cooking it. What a delight to meet her. My friend, whose name I can't remember, said she would introduce me to her father when he got home. I didn't much care about meeting him since he didn't have anything to do with preparing the dinner. Weeks and weeks of Air Force food can alter one's mind.

When the great moment arrived, we all sat down to eat, without her father. He was a little late. When he did show up, I almost passed out! This young lady introduced me to her father and he said, "Do I know you? You look familiar." I said in a very military voice, "YES, SIR!" This was my first sergeant! " I'm in your squadron, Sir." He said, "Well then, you're not permitted to be off the base, are you?" "NO, SIR," I said, choking on my food. Suddenly, this treasured, home-cooked meal and the pleasure of this young lady's company didn't seem so appealing.

I seem to remember a quotation that fits nicely here. Something about being up some kind of creek without a paddle. Well, I didn't even have a canoe. I was in it deep, right up to my ears! My first sergeant said, "Relax, son, my daughter does this all the time. She feels sorry for you guys away from home." This *had* to have been God's grace at work.

Thrilled to be returning to the base alive, and with nothing else to do, I decided to go to the post office to see if they solved the mystery involving my mail. Certainly there was someone out there who loved me enough to write to me, especially the girl I was going to marry. BINGO! I found out, in my fifth week of basic, that there was a problem, and my mail had been piling up. They couldn't give it to me right then and there; I had to get it at a mail call. Regulations!

The next day at mail call, I heard: "Rutootski! . . ." then a little louder . . . "Rutootski!" and then really loud, "RUTOOTSKI!   I GUESS RUTOOTSKI DOESN'T WANT HIS MAIL!"

The drill sergeant passed out everyone else's mail, and I was the last one standing there. He walked up to me and yelled in my face, "Whatsa madder, Rutootski, don't you want your mail?" And I replied, "My name is not Rutootski, it's Rutkoski. If you have mail for Airman Rutkoski, I'll take it." I think he actually smiled when handing me my mail, the first crack in the armor of this man of stone. He was trained to break me and I wondered if I hadn't started to break him.

Oh, to have mail . . . especially love letters!   Of course they didn't replace the real thing, but they made my heart beat faster! All I knew was I had my girl back, even if it was just in a letter. I was not abandoned after all.

It took most all of my last week of basic training to read the letters. Then, basic was over! Leaving Lackland was like getting out of hell. It is only now I realize it was more like getting out of purgatory. My next assignment was six months of schooling at Lowry A.F.B. in Denver, Colorado.

There must have been a lesson to be learned in my close call with the girl that took me home for dinner, but at the time, it escaped me completely. The very next time I had an opportunity to be favored by the presence of a young girl, I grabbed it. You see how Satan works here? He gets you burning the wick at both ends. There I was, at Lowry Air Force Base in Denver, Colorado, out with the guys. We were drinking beer, and we met some girls and talked. Maybe one of them took me by the hand. Before you know it, I'm in love with two girls!

Meanwhile, back in Pennsylvania, plans are being made for a September wedding, and I was having second thoughts. My fiance was the first girl I ever loved. Then there was that girl from Texas. I was so young and impressionable and she was so sweet, I could have fallen in love with her if I'd had more time.

Now there was the girl in Denver that I really felt good about . . . and I was about to say, "till death do us part" to the girl back home! I was learning a lesson about burning the candle at both ends. If there was any angel left in me at all, my wing feathers were starting to singe.

One day a letter arrived from my sister, Betts. In the letter, she explained that there were problems with the marriage plans. Was there any possible way that I could come home and straighten out the mess? Well, I looked at this development as a blessing in disguise, because I had some strong second thoughts about my upcoming wedding.

My reasons for getting married in the first place no longer were an issue. Joining the Air Force had achieved for me what most children desire, getting out of their parents' house. Now with two girlfriends, the lust I had for women did not have to be a problem. The only thing that convinced me to go home was thinking how nice it would be to see everyone, so I went home.

I arrived back in Pennsylvania only to find that the parents of the girl I was going to marry did not allow her to see me anymore. That didn't bother me, it was just good to be home. I heard through the grapevine that her parents thought that their daughter could do better than a stupid polack! The thing about that was . . . they were right. Again through the grapevine, I heard that even though she wasn't allowed to see me, she wanted to. We arranged a meeting through mutual friends.

My best friend, John Fediaczko, picked me up one day and we headed for the rendezvous. It was really nice to see her again. It brought back many warm moments we had shared. We ended up double dating with John and his girl and ultimately back at my house. I really wanted to be alone with her, maybe to talk, or more. (I think it's time to stop calling my fiancee she and her. I don't want to use her real name and hurt feelings, so I'll call her Sue.) Oh, to be alone with Sue! I didn't know if John would allow me to borrow his car so I figured the best solution was not to ask. I just took it. Boy, was he ticked! It didn't matter, I got my wish. Alone at last! But I found that the fire wasn't as hot as it once was.

Our visit ended with Sue and I agreeing that maybe marriage in September was not such a good idea; that perhaps we should put the wedding on the back burner for awhile. I don't know if part of the agreement was our mutual consent for dating others; all I remember is that I was relieved not to be getting married, to say the least.

The next day, I was at home packing, getting ready to return to Colorado and begin dating the girl in Denver, without any guilt. The phone rang. It was Sue, and she was crying uncontrollably. It was almost impossible to understand her. She explained to me that her mother found out that we had seen each other, and threw Sue out of the house with all she owned. All her clothes were sitting on her front porch. Her mother told her not to come back.

Sue cried, "You have to come and get me." I said, "Come and get you, and do what? I'm leaving for Denver." "Take me with you," she pleaded. "We were going to get married anyhow, why not just get married in Denver?"

Talk about guilt! Can you imagine what was racing through my mind? I didn't want to get married, but I was responsible for her situation. What could I do? I went to get her. I thought the situation with my first sergeant was bad, but this was the worst situation of my entire life . . . so far.

Indeed, Sue's clothes were piled up on the porch and she was sobbing pitifully as we loaded them into the car. Her mother was screaming from the porch, "Get her out of here, you no good g.d. hunky!" Sue's mother was a card-carrying Catholic and went to church every Sunday. This was Christian?

With that, Sue and I drove off to be married and live happily ever after. No, I don't think so. It just wasn't to be. It's not that it went downhill from there, because it couldn't.

Well, we did it. I called the air base and told them I might be a couple days late on my leave, because I was getting married. They explained to me that it was necessary for me to get their permission to get married. I said, "Well, can I have permission?" Their answer to that was, "You have to have marriage counseling first, and it would be very difficult for the two of you to make it on your salary."

I said, "I don't have any other choice." I think they took it the wrong way, because they gave me permission to get married. My parents took us out and bought us a Ford Falcon as a wedding gift. Pretty good "hunky" parents! That was the only bright spot of this whole episode.

Off to Denver with my bride-to-be! On the three day trip, living like we were married, I bent the valve lifters in the Falcon. I was speeding to get to Denver on time and the car just couldn't take it. With the car repaired, I continued speeding. I passed a state trooper who had his lights already flashing. He pulled me over, and said if he had time, he would give me a ticket. Thank Heaven he did not have time; he was on his way to a bad accident. This was only the second bright spot in five of the worst days of my life. I think all of this was worse than when I blew off my fingertips with the blasting cap.

When we arrived in Denver, we went right to the courthouse. There was no waiting period for marriage, just a blood test. After the blood tests, we were in front of the judge. He asked us who our witnesses were. We explained

we didn't have any. He yelled down the hall for some people, and they were the witnesses. Some guy whose name I
can't remember, and Roxie. There we were, Mr. & Mrs.
Thomas Rutootski, I mean Rutkoski.

Then off we went to find a place to live, an apartment. There we were, eighteen years old, and we didn't
have a pot to . . . put in an apartment. You want to talk
about a struggle? I was making sixty-four dollars every two
weeks, and now that I was married, the government was
going to give me ninety-eight dollars a month housing allot-
ment. It was just awful!

There was no joy in our lives, or in the city of Denver. There was a series of murders, and everyone was
paranoid, including Sue and me. About our third week of
wedded 'bliss', there came a knock at the door at about 3:00
a.m. We knew no one in this city; who could it be? I went
to the door with my only prized personal possession, my
handgun. I opened the door and stuck it in a man's face
and asked, "What do you want?"

He said nervously, "Don't shoot! I'm Sue's cousin."
Well, we invited him in. He stayed that night and the next
night, and the next night, and he was eating with us. We
couldn't afford to feed ourselves, and her cousin wasn't
making any financial offers. I eventually got bold enough
to say, "Why are you here?"

He finally admitted, "Sue's mom sent me out to
make sure you two were married." At that moment, I could
have shot *her*. I was livid.

Sue's mom also had a message. As I recall, the gist
of the message was, "If you're going to stay married, why

don't you at least get married in the Catholic Church?" I accepted the message from him and said, "Well, you have to leave. I can't afford to keep feeding you." And he did. But he had stayed almost a week. Maybe I *should* have shot him. (Just kidding.)

Eventually, the military insisted that I enroll in the marriage classes that should have been attended before I got married in the civil ceremony. Sue, wishing to make her mother happy, pushed for the Catholic ceremony, and I agreed to go along. I never considered it anything other than an attempt to make this bad situation a little better and satisfy all parties concerned.

I attended the classes in which they explained to the potential brides and grooms the pitfalls of being married and living on such a small salary. This was not a revelation to me. But you know how kids are. You can't talk them out of anything, and everyone there was about to make the same mistake Sue and I had just made. I thought to myself, oh, what awful times lie ahead for them!

After the classes, Sue and I repeated our marriage vows in the Catholic Church. Unfortunately, it did nothing to improve our circumstances and we spent a total of two years on this rocky road in the Rocky Mountains.

In 1965, I was transferred to my permanent assignment at Westover Air Force Base, Chicopee Falls, Massachusetts. There we proceeded to a mobile home dealer to buy our dream home for twelve hundred dollars. In reality it looked like a nightmare. It was old, it was ugly, and it burned down that night . . . taking with it our clothes, our money, and our dignity, because now we had nothing. The tragedy of it all was that the insurance papers were not signed. Remember, when I told you I thought we were at the bottom? I was wrong. *This* was the bottom.

As devastating as the whole tragedy had been, it introduced me to how wonderful people can be when they want to be. Help came from everywhere. Even the people that sold us the original mobile home got us into another one much better than the original, and made it financially possible. One would think this would have been a good time to turn to prayer, but I didn't. We didn't.

To try to dig myself out of a financial hole I took on an additional job with the permission of the Air Force. I worked about sixteen hours a day. Still battling debt, Sue took a job and slowly we were climbing out.

If that wasn't bad enough, my wife had many physical problems, one of which prevented us from having children. None of our attempts were fruitful. This led to added frustration, but more than likely this was another blessing in disguise.

After six months at Westover, I received a top secret government clearance and was sent back to Denver to be trained in an entirely new career field, precision photographic processing. Sue's job was at the local Sears and we were not in a financial position to have her quit to join me in Denver. She had to remain at Westover.

There I was, all alone again. But not for long. You see, I got awfully lonely, awfully fast. Several other guys, who were sent with me on this assignment, felt the same way. So we sought some female companionship. At first, that's all it was, just friendship. We would go out, have a few beers, maybe go back to the girls' apartments, have a few more beers, listen to records, talk, play cards. It took the pressure off trying to learn all the things in class that seemed beyond my comprehension.

I knew I was in deep trouble from the first day of my classes when the instructor said, "As you will recall from your trigonometry classes . . ." at which point I interrupted him. I said, "Trigonometry? I flunked out of algebra in high school." His response to me was, "Then you will have to try harder than everyone else."

He went on to explain that the alternative was Vietnam. People who quit this class, washed out or failed, went to Vietnam. What an incentive to learn. As I explained earlier, I have dyslexia. Now imagine trying to learn trigonometry with dyslexia. I transpose numbers, so 28 looks like 82 to me. The only place that numbers don't present a problem is when they are numbers like 11, 22, 33, if you get my drift. And the instructor was telling me that if I didn't learn this stuff, I was going to Vietnam.

This opened my mind to a totally new concept. I had this knack for remembering the lyrics to an enormous number of songs, and I sing all the time. Off key, but I sing. Sometimes I would create my own words to songs to make them funnier than they originally were, or make them really off-color. A thought struck me. Why not take these stupid rules of trigonometry and put them to music that I already knew? Instantly, I knew could learn; I could remember; I could get the right answers on a test, simply by singing a song with the answers in the lyrics.

I don't know if you're familiar with Mel Tillis, a country western singer, who has a profound stuttering problem, but sings like a bird, without stuttering. It must have been the Tillis principle that ironed out my problem for me. Whatever short circuits our minds to cause these difficulties, is somehow, while singing, temporarily set aside.

This secret weapon made school seem like a breeze. There was still pressure, but the relaxing times with the girls helped that. A friendship grew between one particular girl and me. Once again, I found myself in a familiar situation. I loved two girls again. Girl number one is married to me, but doesn't know I'm dating someone else. Girl number two is dating me, but doesn't know I'm married. Some of you know exactly what I mean.

I tried to keep the passion part of this at arm's length. I just wanted a friend; but something was pushing me on. I didn't know the exact definition of adultery, but there I was one night, at my girlfriend's apartment, going about as far as you could go without committing actual adultery. Then someone opened the door on my partner and me, and we raced to get dressed before we were seen.

Rethinking in technical terms about the manner in which I was married, I was wondering . . . was I really married? The thoughts were running through my mind at the time, but were they my thoughts or Satan helping me to justify my actions?

Let's not forget that the Lord says it isn't necessarily the act alone that commits the sin, but the thought itself is a sin. And you know what I was thinking. So, was I an adulterer? I hope you understand how Satan was laying traps before me; but I had the option to say no. But I didn't say no. I was a willing participant.

My masquerade of footloose bachelor was uncovered by none other than myself, by mistake. My friend and I were at our girls' apartment one day, and while playing cards we got into a discussion about a record. It led to an argument of the date when this record had been released. In an effort to prove that I was right about the date, I blurted out, "I know exactly when it came out, because my wife bought it for me."

I felt the temperature rise in my cheeks, instantly realizing my mistake, and quickly tried to cover up my error. Seeing the shocked look on their faces, I said, "I'm just kidding!" My friend, in an effort to keep *his* relationship intact, squealed that I was married. Needless to say, my girlfriend was no longer any kind of friend. Fortunately for me, I was headed back to Massachusetts and was feeling lucky to get out of Denver alive.

I had been gone several months, but on returning to Westover, life didn't seem to go any smoother. Absence didn't make the heart grow fonder. If the blame should be placed anywhere, it should be on my shoulders. I was the one making the bad decisions and continued to make them.

One bad decision was that, despite our precarious financial state, I thought it justifiable to buy equipment for my new hobby, scuba diving. Mostly, my experiences in diving were exhilarating.

My friend, Tom Bednadz, and I would go to various lakes, diving; then we advanced to the big time, the Atlantic Ocean. In our many trips to the shore, we gained experience and confidence. We were so confident of our skills that when we went to the Watch Hill Lighthouse Station on the coast of Connecticut, we got a little too cocky. The U.S.

Coast Guard warned us about a bad riptide in the area and advised us not to dive there. We explained that we were aware of the situation, and were positive we could avoid the riptide.

A riptide is water coming into the shore from two different directions and returning out to sea in one direction forming a very dangerous underwater river. This underwater river current can reach speeds of up to twenty miles an hour at times. That doesn't seem fast until you try to swim against that type of current. A cardinal rule of diving is: if you ever get caught in a riptide, never try to swim against it. Swim with it, and gradually work your way out of it. Unfortunately, I was about to learn that this rule was far easier said than done.

I was engulfed in an enormous school of fish! Enchanted by this mesmerizing experience, I lost track of Tom. My mind wasn't now on the riptide, but on the fish. That's when it happened. I was sucked into, and consumed by the treacherous riptide. I fought it and in moments I was exhausted. I found myself in a state too weak to resist, and I became just another piece of rolling debris, bouncing off rocks, literally being cut to ribbons. The air tank felt like it was being ripped from my back, and the mouthpiece that supplied my air was torn from my mouth. I couldn't get my hands in a position to replace it, and in gasping, I began to take in water! As this was happening to me, I felt a sort of peace come over me. The next thing I knew, someone was pulling me out of the water.

The someone turned out to be a member of the U.S. Coast Guard, the one who had given me the warning. Fortunately, they had kept an eye on us from the lighthouse and when they saw air bubbles from my air tank nearing the riptide, they launched a boat to check things out. It was my good fortune that they did, for I was a mile or more out to sea. For all intents and purposes, I was a goner! But the Coast Guard pulled me out and saved my life, foiling Satan's second great attempt to do me in!

As my hitch in the Air Force was ending, I had the opportunity to reenlist with a ten thousand dollar reenlistment bonus. I turned it down, opting to go back home in hopes of finding employment that would provide Sue and me with a better standard of living. We packed up all our belongings, which fit in a small U-Haul trailer, and headed for Butler, Pennsylvania in March of 1967.

With no place to live, we moved in with my sister, Betts, and I tried to secure a job. The best I could find was work with a roofer. A friend of mine was a subcontractor. We worked together week after week. It didn't provide much money but it was something. Sue didn't believe I was out working on roofs. She thought I was out cheating on her. I believe these thoughts were instilled in her by her family, but as I have previously demonstrated, I wasn't beyond messing around.

However, neither Sue nor her family ever knew that I was seeing another girl when I was in Denver. That was the only time I really did cheat on my wife and I had no plans to do so in the future. Because of all the anti-Tom propaganda that her family generated, it took my sister Betts, driving Sue to my work location and pointing to me up on a roof, to convince her that I was actually doing what I said I was doing.

The final blow to this extremely fragile relationship was dealt when Sue went to stay with her sister for a week.

Her sister lived in Pittsburgh, in an upper-class neighborhood. I believed the week apart would do us both much good, but I was wrong. When I went to retrieve my spouse at the end of the week, her sister explained to me that she wasn't there and that we had a problem. People were always trying to explain to me what I already knew. We didn't have *a* problem, we had *lots* of problems. To my surprise, Sue's sister introduced me to a new one.

She said, "The two of you can't continue living with your sister, and here's what we worked out. There is a house just down the street, and Sue wants you to buy it. If you don't buy it, she is going to leave you."

Don't you just hate ultimatums? I do. I fired back an ultimatum of my own. "You tell Sue to get back here right now, or she won't have anyone to leave." She called Sue to tell her what I said and Sue replied, "Then it's over."

What you have to understand is that we didn't have the money to buy a house in that neighborhood. We didn't have the money to buy a house in *any* neighborhood. It was explained to me that Sue's family would loan us the down payment and that would solve one problem. Now, if we could only find someone to make the monthly payments, we could save this marriage. It just wasn't meant to be. I left with the thought in my mind that it, indeed, was over.

Two weeks later, Sue returned to my sister's house with an apology on her lips, which I refused to accept. "You said it was over, so it's over," was my only response, and she left crying. It was around September, 1967, that I became what I considered a 'free man.'

I acquired a job at the Warren R. Smith Motion Picture Laboratory in the Oakland section of Pittsburgh. From this point on, in relation to the laws of God, my life went downhill rapidly!

I purchased a Honda motorcycle as an economical means of transportation from my home in Butler to Pittsburgh. The motorcycle probably represented freedom to me, and only secondarily, transportation. However, buying a motorcycle for transportation turned out to be a terrible idea. More often than not, I got caught in the rain. The pitfalls of this open-air mode of travel forced me to find a place to live in Oakland.

At first it was just moving in with a friend. This came about when a party at his house went well into the night, and he invited me to stay. During the evening, I went outside to get a bit of fresh air, and to just be alone for awhile. I knew virtually no one at the party, and I never did function well in large groups. While outside, two girls were walking down the street, and they stopped to say hello. That was the closest I'd come to warmth or companionship for weeks, maybe months. The conversation was friendly enough so I invited them into the party, and they accepted. This led to a relationship with one of the girls. It also opened the door to an entirely new lifestyle.

I was almost single at this time, since my wife had begun the process of getting her divorce. My attitude toward the divorce was that I didn't start it and I'm not going to participate in it. I told Sue, "You do what you have to do." I considered myself single.

One relationship led to another, then another. Sex became a means of entertainment to me. I always had low self-esteem, which was probably attributable to my dyslexia. I never seemed to do well at much, but now I felt in charge. I didn't have a clear cut attitude about women, all I knew was we were all willing participants in a new social attitude.

Women were becoming more aggressive and at times, I didn't even have to initiate the idea of sex, they would. Even with what I thought was my liberal attitude, women were making bold advances to me, and I was shocked! One woman I dated was so aggressive, I wouldn't even date her again!

It finally occurred to me that maybe I wasn't cut out for life in the fast lane. Maybe I had a hint of some morality, or was it just male ego? It is at this point that I want to introduce to you the ultimate trap. Satan had me convinced as he did many others in the '70s, that babies were not babies until they were born. What I find now too repulsive to commit to paper, back then, was just a form of birth control. Abortion, the ultimate lie and he had me believing it wasn't sin.

One thing that always amazed me is that, despite buying into much of life in the fast lane, I never got involved in drugs. Alcohol, yes! My friends did drugs, and from my observation of them, I realized that wasn't the life for me. The term 'fast lane' was two-fold for me: I was involved in a demoralizing life style; and I had always liked fast things, fast cars. I also liked the outdoors: camping, fishing and hunting, simply being outdoors. I was active, with a zest for life. What I witnessed in my friends' way of life was lethargic and stagnating. They just sat around and smoked dope. Good name for it! I do recall attempting to smoke one joint, and I got so sick from it, that just the smell of grass made me run. Dope! You've got to be a dope to do it! I wonder now why I didn't look at the rest of my life with that same vision.

God had His plan for me. He allowed me all the leash I wanted to make my mistakes. Well, maybe not all. I believe He intervened, in His own way, to stop me from killing myself or allowing Satan to take me to that point.

Chapter 3

Settling Down

In 1968, I struck out on my own. I started a home remodeling business and found myself working on the home of Bill Kelly, the sales manager of WTAE TV. Bill and I became friends and in our conversations he learned of my Air Force training and my photographic background. In early 1969, Bill asked me if I would be interested in employment at a new television station in Pittsburgh, WPGH TV. I was elated at the thought. Bill had some influence with the management. He told his friends at WPGH that he knew a hard-working man with a background in photography. I interviewed for the position of Director of Photography and got the job. Without Bill's intercession that wouldn't have been possible, but, in reality, I also had to lie to get it.

They assumed, on Bill's recommendation, that I had all the qualifications needed for the job. When they asked about my experience in an interview, I led them to believe I was a proficient still and motion-picture photographer, which I was not. For the most part, my background was in the scientific end of photography with little experience in still or motion photography. After being hired, I quickly purchased some books on photography and tried hacking my way through them. With my dyslexia it was not an easy task and I didn't get very far. Most of my knowledge was obtained by asking questions of the people at the photographic store where I made the purchases for the TV station. They guided me well, but not well enough!

I was called into the manager's office and asked how to spell, 'Auricon'; this was the name of the motion picture camera I was attempting to use. I told him I didn't know how to spell Auricon. He asked me if I knew what it meant, and I said, "No, I don't." One would expect a proficient motion picture photographer to at least be able to spell the name of his camera, or know what the name meant. "Exactly how much training did you have in motion picture photography before we hired you?" he asked me. "None," I replied.

"That's obvious. If you had lied to me again, I would have fired you. But I think it takes a brave person to accept a job in hopes of training himself before his deficiency is discovered. Also, you have been improving, so I'll let you stay." Then he added, "Oh, two more things: one, just in case someone else asks you, "auri" means over a wide spectrum, and "con" means continental; auricon meaning a wide spectrum covering the continents. And two, leave the women alone." My reputation had preceded me.

In the fall of 1969, I met Mary, who is now my wife. I saw in Mary enough of what I wanted in my life to ask her to marry me. We dated from 1969 to 1972. I don't know what it was that drew me to the point of being able to ask anyone to marry me after such a bad experience in my first marriage. Mary was the first girl that I had to try to convince to go out with me. Finally, I'd met a woman that was a challenge and I really had to work at convincing her to be interested in me. If you ask Mary, she'll tell you that I sat on her doorstep many nights, and just refused to leave, although she asked. (You don't necessarily have to believe her!)

What is it that I saw in Mary? Well, for one, she has a pretty face. The first time I ever saw her was at The Casbah in Shadyside. Shadyside was the "in-place" in the outlying area of Pittsburgh. The first time I saw Mary there, I was attracted to her. We didn't even speak that night at the bar and there was no way to know that she was acquainted with the club's regular singing act, David & Anthony. I came to know them through the possibility of doing a TV documentary for WPGH, my employer.

There was a party at Anthony's townhouse that evening, to celebrate the release of their first record. I was invited and went to the party alone. Hey, guess who was there! It was Mary. Not having a date, and noticing that her situation seemed the same, I made my move. I don't remember what slick line I used, but it didn't work. She actually did have a date, but it wasn't going well! We'd spent some time talking and it turned out that she asked me to take her home. We still didn't seem to hit it off, but I did manage to finesse her phone number from her. Even though she purposely gave me the wrong number, I tracked her down!

Alright, so maybe I did sit on her steps a couple of times waiting for her. We did eventually go out. One of our first dates was to see Peter, Paul and Mary in concert, by Mary's special request. The concert was at the Syria Mosque in Oakland. Before arriving at Mary's, I had been drinking a bit, well, a lot. I guess I had been drinking to the point of being impervious to pain, because when we got to the Mosque, on my way in, I pushed on the door a little too hard. Being just sober enough to realize I pushed it too hard, I grabbed for the door to keep it from smashing against the brick wall. Instead of the door doing that, it smashed my fingers into the wall! Later I was sure I'd broken a few fingers, judging from the pain and swelling but, then, I couldn't feel a thing.

I had so much fun at this concert! I loudly sang every song with Peter, Paul and Mary from my seat in the balcony. I was miffed because Mary wasn't enjoying herself, and even more miffed when she got up and walked out! But that didn't stop me from singing . . . "I'm leavin' on a jet plane . . . " The next time I saw her was during intermission. "You're embarrassing me," she said, "and you sing off key!" She insisted that I take her home. "Are you kidding me?" I said. "I'd rather give you cab fare to go home yourself." I wanted to finish singing with Peter, Paul and Mary!

I somehow convinced her to return to our seats for the second half of the concert. I was overjoyed, and somewhat vindicated, when a few songs later, Peter, Paul and Mary insisted that the audience participate in a whole medley of their hits. Mary *glared* at me the entire time.

With my drinking, dating and keeping late nights, it's a wonder I kept my job. My work must have been pretty good, since I wasn't fired.

I spent three years at WPGH-TV and felt proud of what I had accomplished. I mastered well the art of still photography and won awards and I shot all the station's locally produced television commercials on film. In addition, in late 1970, I was chosen as one of the cinematographers to work on a new concept in television, called "Music Connection!" My task was to put pictures to the words and music of popular songs. No one bought this concept then, but what foresight! Now they're called music videos and dominate an entire network called MTV!

In August, 1971, KDKA-TV, the granddaddy of Pittsburgh TV, called me and asked me to work for them. They had seen for themselves, and had been told by others, about my abilities in motion picture photography. They offered me a job as photographer for two new shows that were soon to begin in Pittsburgh. These shows were the result of a recent Prime Time Access rule by the FCC, to attempt to limit network power. One of the shows, "Some of my Best Friends", succeeded only marginally. The other, "About A Week", was a big success both critically and in the ratings. It was the pilot of a Westinghouse Broadcasting, nationally syndicated program called "Evening Magazine" in the affiliate markets, and "PM Magazine" in syndication. I rejected their offer. I explained I was happy doing what I was doing at Channel 53. They informed me that they knew what I was making at WPGH, and they would double my salary. I said I would think about it. That conversation took place at 9:00 a.m. on a Wednesday morning, in August, 1969. At noon that very day, the management of Channel 53 called all the employees into the studio and announced that as of 5:00 p.m. that day, they were closing their doors, and going off the air. I instantly called Channel 2 and said, " I decided to take your job offer." They told me that they were well aware of the announcement my company had made, and were more than glad to have me on staff, but now they were not going to double my salary; in fact, they would pay me exactly what I was making now. Welcome to the world of big business!

The idea of having someone from KDKA in the family might, I thought, soften the cool reception I got from a real hardliner, Mary's dad! Meanwhile, our relationship, with its rocky start, more one-sided than not, somehow blossomed into love. We discussed marriage and when Mary addressed it with her family, her mother was all for it, but her father . . . well, I think he wished I'd just go away. He explained to Mary, "This man has been divorced. How can he possibly have any respect for women?" But between Mary's mom and her seven brothers and sisters, they somehow convinced their dad that I wasn't as bad as he thought I was.

As we were arranging for the marriage, a problem arose. Her parents were Catholic and wanted their daughter to be married in a Catholic church. I was a divorced, non-practicing Catholic. In 1971, we went to a priest at St. Patrick Church in Canonsburg, Pa., Mary's home parish. We discussed applying for an annulment and he was to initiate the process with the Diocese. Time was a problem for us because Mary's mother was terminally ill with cancer and wasn't expected to live more than a few months. Because Mary wanted her mother to be at her wedding, we just couldn't wait for the annulment. It wouldn't have mattered if we had waited; the priest never got back to us as he promised he would. To this day I don't know why; but the end result was two Catholics getting married in a Baptist Church by Dennis Benson, a protestant minister who was also a radio evangelist.

The wedding was special, though I admit, it was the first one I ever saw where the bride carried metal flowers; silver roses or something. Mary was always a forward thinker. She wanted to be able to have her wedding bouquet in its original state forever. Everyone remarked how touching the ceremony was. Our wedding bands were absolutely beautiful, with interlaced olive branches carved in gold. We passed them around at the service for everyone to see and touch and give us their prayers and blessings before we put them on. But something about that wedding band on my hand made my finger hurt! I did not wear it for sixteen or more years. Every time I would put it on my hand, that finger would swell up and the joints would ache.

We lived in an apartment in East Liberty for the first three years of our marriage. As we tried to make the adjustment to each other's personality, there was some friction between us and we argued a lot. Mary tried to explain to me that it was just normal, and it probably was. The difficulty I had with it was that after an argument, I carried the hurt, angry feelings around for days. Mary, coming from a large family, learned early on that to survive in a houseful of people, you couldn't hang onto hurt feelings for very long. So when Mary would argue with me, her anger only lasted as long as the argument. This infuriated me, even to the point that, once, I slammed a bowl of spaghetti against the wall in frustration. I didn't understand how anyone could get over anything that quickly! She couldn't understand how anyone could react to something she considered so trivial, so violently.

In early 1975, we started looking for the perfect house, on the perfect property. I remembered the days at Lord's Pond, working at Donald Williams' farm, and dreaming of owning my own farm. In April, I realized my dream. We found a farm and although I wished it had been on Lord's Pond, it was in Evans City, Pennsylvania. As we worked through the mortgage application with the bank, it became apparent that it wasn't financially feasible for us to buy the farm. We were a few thousand dollars short.

Soon afterwards, Mary and I were visiting friends in Indiana County, Pennsylvania, Fred and Ellen Musser. Fred is the owner of Musser Forests, the world's largest producer of evergreen trees, (20,000,000 a year then, 80,000,000 now!) I was always in awe of the great freedom that Fred's wealth seemed to provide him. Fred was a go-anywhere, do-anything you want, anytime you want, kind of guy. I often wondered why he even considered me a friend; I didn't have two nickels to rub together. I'd often do stories for KDKA with him and we did enjoy each other.

Fred asked me if I found a farm yet. I explained that I did but it was financially out of reach. He said, "What do you mean by 'financially out of reach?' What kind of money are we talking about here?" I told him I was $2,000 short of the down payment. He said, "Two thousand dollars! You would let two thousand dollars come between you and the dream of your life?" I said to Fred, "From your perspective, two thousand dollars isn't a whole lot of money. To me, it's the difference between owning a farm and not owning one." He whipped out his checkbook and wrote a check for two thousand dollars and handed it to me. I said "Fred, I can't take this." "You'd be a fool to refuse!" he responded. Our discussion went back and forth with my trying to keep my pride intact. I ultimately accepted his offer, and promised to pay it back in a year. He said he didn't care if we ever paid it back. We bought the farm! Actually, we ended up paying it back in a year, as promised.

Our dream turned into a nightmare the very day we took possession of our home. The only access to our twenty-eight acres was on a private road through a neighboring farm on which five families lived, all related. We had a right-of-way, by our deed, to use that road. The deed had an attachment giving us legal right to uninterrupted ingress and egress. This appeared to be no problem to me, because it seemed so clear and all encompassing. Mary wasn't nearly as sure.

Mary was the first one to come down the driveway, which was a half mile long. Driving past one of the neighbors' houses, she was stopped. The owners of the property wanted to explain to her how the right-of-way was going to work. They informed her that she and I were the only ones allowed to use this road. No visitors, no delivery trucks.

When I came home, I found Mary crying. She looked at me and said, "What did you get me into?" She then related what had happened. I said, "Surely there was a mistake. I'll go and talk to these people." And I did.

In trying to determine why their greeting to us on our first day in our new home was one not of welcome, but rather of warning, the owner explained that her husband had just passed away and that it was his death bed wish that no one use this road. I said to her, "How can you try to force us to live here with no visitors? And most certainly, delivery trucks have to come!"

Our winter heat was an oil furnace that required truck-delivered oil. We were to cook, heat our water and dry our clothes with truck-delivered gas. There stood this woman telling me that we should have considered that before we bought the property. Trying to control my anger, I said I did consider it, and showed her the right-of-way agreement. It had her signature on it, granting us "ingress and egress uninterrupted." She said, "Well, you have another road you can use."

Well, sort of. I did have another access. It was only a tractor path cutting across someone else's property. We had a right-of-way there also, with the same terms and conditions, but it wasn't a road . . . it was also a half-mile long.

I left my neighbor's house dismayed, but with a conviction to make this work. In fact, I was very friendly with the son-in-law and most everyone who lived on the road. Unfortunately, they began to stop all visitors and deliveries, telling them it was a private road, and they couldn't use it. We tolerated this constant harassment for more than two years. This kind of situation causes extraordinary stress on individuals and relationships. Mary, with a smile, now admits that she was not above saying, "I told you so, hundreds of times." We were constantly worried about our neighbors' habit of detaining visitors and admonishing them for attempting to use *their* road.

Then something happened that only caused the situation to worsen. One summer a drought caused the collapse of our well. We had no water. I frantically called a well-drilling company. They informed me that many people were having well problems due to the lack of rain. He advised that it would be about a week before he could get to me. I explained to him the seriousness of the situation; that I had cattle and their only source of water was from that well, other than carrying it for quite a distance from a neighbor's house.

My sad story didn't change his mind. So for a week I carried water from my closest neighbor, a half-mile away, to keep my cattle alive. I was excited coming home from work on the following Friday, knowing that the well-driller was there punching me a new watering hole!

Imagine the frustration upon my arrival home when there was no sign of a drilling rig! I called the driller immediately. He explained that he had come to the property, but was turned away by my neighbors. Now I would have to go on the back of the list, and it would be another week before he would get to me!

Never knowing I was capable of feeling that kind of rage inside me, I was virtually pushed to the brink of an emotion beyond my understanding. Racing to my neighbors' house, I started to unload my anger on this woman, who was the source of all the problems, yet called herself my neighbor. I berated her with every profane word I could bring to mind, but it didn't seem to make any difference. She didn't want anyone using this road causing dust and she was also quite upset at the kind of language I was using.

I remember the reaction to my tirade of all the other families on the road. The friendships I once had with some of the families fell apart. It turned a bad situation into a nightmare. Blockades went up. Too often that summer to be pure coincidence, our cars suffered flat tires from nails that appeared along the part of the driveway only Mary and I used. Within a few weeks, gates went up on both ends of their property. The gates were the last straw. We decided to sue because our lives were being toyed with through a situation that couldn't be controlled any other way. Legally, the letter and the spirit of the agreement for the right of way (uninterrupted ingress and egress) were being blatantly violated.

We retained an attorney in Butler, who immediately got an injunction against the gates. He took the case on contingency, rather than on a fee basis. He explained that he would be happy to settle for a percentage of the damages, because he was convinced that we were in the right.

In his opinion, the court would order the gates permanently removed and assess sizeable damages against the families involved. We were well prepared for the hearing on the date the court had set and we had taken time off from our jobs to be there. We had arranged for a witness from Florida to be present and several local witnesses had also taken time from their jobs to help us tell our story to the court. Unbelievably, the defendants appeared that day and told the court they had fired their attorney. They asked for a continuance to allow time to find a new one. Even more unbelievably, the judge granted their request with no consideration for the time, effort or money expended by us to present our case that day.

When the big day finally arrived, I was truly excited. I was finally going to see justice in action. We arrived at our attorney's office early that morning, nervous, but excited. As the attorney prepared me on how and what to answer, he said to me, "We are going to nail these niggers to a cross." (What I haven't told you yet is that the five families on the farm in question are black.) I couldn't believe my ears. We'd had many disagreements with our neighbors, but never had it been concerning anything remotely racial.

"Why on earth would you use words like that?" I said. "This has nothing to do with ethnic descent, and I am neither a racist nor a bigot. All I want is my right to uninterrupted ingress and egress as provided for in my deed. If I get a cash award on top of that, well, that would be great. I'm not getting involved in any racial attacks on these families!" My attorney was stunned at my response to him. We shared very few words after that.

The courtroom sequence was short, but not so sweet. I couldn't understand what my attorney was doing . . . or not doing would be more like it. I tried to say something to the judge, but he cautioned me about contempt. The judge eventually ruled that they could keep the gates, but couldn't stop anyone. No damages were awarded. I was mystified! What happened to all the confidence in our winning? We lost! I asked our attorney what happened. He said it was the judge's decision and that is what he ruled. He seemed cold and unconcerned about the whole thing. I was shell-shocked!

Within a few days the gates were closed again. To make matters even worse, the neighbors put a lock and chain on the gate closest to my house and presented me with a key! This meant we now had to unlock a gate every time we left the property and all visitors and delivery trucks were *locked out.* So much anger was building up inside me, that I literally could have killed someone.

It almost came to that point one day when Mary and I, my sister, Betts, and her husband were going out the driveway. We rounded the bend and my sister yelled out, "Oh, my God, he's got a gun!" There was the owner's son standing in the middle of the road with a gun held in two hands across his chest, in a military halt position.

At that particular time in my life, I had a permit for, and always carried, a handgun. I took it from my holster, and felt that if he moved that gun one inch toward us, I'd kill him.

Fortunately, he lowered the barrel to the ground and waved us through. My heart was pounding knowing how close I had come to pulling the trigger of a gun pointed at a human being. There was no doubt in my mind I would have done it, if his gun had moved in any direction but down, for it was my intent to protect my family. I forget at what point I put the place up for sale, but I know that I eventually did.

Those events represent the worst of times. This is not to say that there weren't great times on the farm, so many that at one point in my life, I considered writing a book just on the events that filled our life on the farm. A good name for the book would have been "Farming: A Comedy of Errors."

Just days after we signed the papers on the farm, I bought myself a small tractor. This was the first one I'd ever owned. I painted it red, white and blue. On the hood was the American flag! I was going to be the All American Farmer!

One of my fondest memories of early farm life involved a horse-drawn one row corn planter I had purchased. I attached it to the back of the tractor with chain. Picture me (Pa) on the tractor, and my wife Mary (Ma), with her hands guiding the corn planter . . . planting our first row of corn.

I quickly learned not to push the starting button on the tractor while the tractor was in gear if I wasn't sitting on it! I did that once, and as a result the tractor took off across the field by itself, almost running me over. I tore after it in hot pursuit! Running as quickly as I possibly could, I caught up to the tractor and jumped aboard to gain control.

Often friends would come to visit and I would end up putting them to work on the farm. I recall one day asking one of those friends, Rich Senopole, if he ever drove a tractor. He hadn't, but said he'd like to try. The tractor had a hay bailer attached to the back of it. After I explained how it operated, I told him he might as well try to aim it at a long line of hay laying on the ground. You don't have to be a rocket scientist to bail hay, just be able to keep loose clothing and body parts away from the moving machine parts. After only one pass around the field, Rich was proficient at it!

I was so impressed in Richie's ability, that I left for my job in Pittsburgh, allowing him the pleasure of riding on the tractor all day. To my surprise, he liked it so much he was one of the few that came back for more! Rich was learning a lot about farming from a man who knew almost nothing about it! One thing we learned together was never to pull the pin that keeps the tractor and bailer connected . . at least not when you're positioned on a hill. I was on the tractor and Rich was pulling the pin and the bailer lunged forward trapping Rich against the tractor. Thank God, he wasn't hurt!

A lesson I learned all alone was to never feed green corn to the cattle. I bought some prime beef on the hoof that needed a few months of good grain to be ready for the dinner table. No matter how much they were fed, they kept getting skinnier and skinnier! Fearing for their lives, I called in a veterinarian. He was astonished to see the condition of my cattle!

He said, "What have you been feeding these poor animals?" I said, "If you are accusing me of not feeding them, you are wrong! I give them all the corn they want to eat everyday." The vet said, "Where do you get the corn?" I said, "Right there, out of that field, fresh everyday." "Green corn!" he shouted, "You feed them green corn? That will give them diarrhea! No wonder they look this way!" So, if you're thinking of raising cattle for the first time in your life, take it from me, don't feed them green corn! It took them about a year to reach their pre-green corn weight.

Then there was the time I almost drowned. It had rained every day for the first two weeks of November, and constantly for the last three days. The ground was saturated and could not absorb any more water. I was returning from a hunting trip in the mountains of northern Pennsylvania. Nearing my farm, I decided to take the back road. The back road crossed a very small stream. Not a problem for me. I had a four wheel drive Jeep that could go anywhere! Being smart enough to know that the rain over the past three days would have increased the size of this tiny stream, I built up a little more speed than usual to carry me across.

A small bend just before the stream blocked my view. When I turned the bend and saw the stream, I choked. It wasn't a stream any longer. It was more like a raging torrent! What used to be six feet wide and six inches deep, was more like fifty feet wide and, as I found out, over six feet deep! I was unable to stop and the momentum carried me to the center of the rapid waters! I learned one thing, Jeeps float! Not for long, but they do float!

I remained nautical for about three minutes, but to my astonishment and horror, I found myself trapped inside this Jeep in water about chest high and rising. The Jeep was rapidly turning into a submarine! The doors would not open and fear engulfed me, but the grace of God must have been with me! I managed to open the window and the water gushed in. If I climbed out of the Jeep, I would be swept away by the tremendous force of the water!

For a man who didn't pray, I sure said, "Thank God," often! This time I was thanking God that I'd ordered a roof rack on the Jeep. The roof rack gave me something to hold onto, so I was able to pull myself out of the Jeep window and up onto the roof. Standing on the roof we were moving downstream, the Jeep and me! A tree appeared just ahead. What a glorious tree! It was going to be my salvation! Just as I had hoped, the Jeep hit the tree dead center. I breathed a sigh of relief! If the water rose higher, I figured I could climb higher up the tree. Basking in my salvation, I discovered you can't count on anything in this world. The tree was succumbing to the pressure of the water pushing on the Jeep, and very slowly the tree uprooted and fell. Off we went into the murky depths of this "stream" again. The day before, the stream was too small to have a name. Now, it was big enough to take my life!

At that point, the strong current of the water was hitting the windshield and blasting over the top of the Jeep. Any higher, and it would knock me off! Then the Jeep hit a pile of rocks and ground to a halt. Thank you, thank you, thank you! Again I found relief and rescue. Although I owned a boat and loved being on the water, that was more water than I could take! There was a limb of a tree about three feet out of reach. I saw hope in that limb. If only I could muster up enough nerve to leap for it. Under normal circumstances, I don't think I could have jumped that far, but I made an "Evil Knievel" attempt, and it must have been a world's record in the "leap-for-life" category! Success! I reached the limb! A moment later it broke, but not completely, thank God. It just dropped me down into the icy water. I climbed along the limb, and grabbed onto other growth at the water's edge, and pulled myself to shore. I looked back at my brand new '85 Jeep Cherokee and didn't even care that it was submerged! I was just so happy to be alive! That was the third time I had a near death experience, and it still didn't turn me to prayer.

Now, don't get me wrong, I wasn't a total loss to God. Despite my attitude and problems, I did some good things. I probably did as many good deeds as the next person, once even rescuing two people from drowning in the Atlantic. I also got involved with the Hands Across America project. Getting my friends at the yacht club to join me, we made a day of it. It was a lot of fun and we raised money for the starving people of the world. My group of about thirty was asked to fill some empty space in central Pennsylvania as thousands attempted to form a human chain across the entire USA. The place we were specifically assigned was called Noah's Ark! *Was this a coincidence?*

As you follow along with me in my life, you will have to be the judge. Were these little scenarios put in place by Our Lord or did they just happen through coincidence?

Chapter 4

The Lord Is My Tour Guide

In 1982, I was just starting to feel financially secure, not rich, just secure. Mary and I both had great jobs that paid well. I had been employed by KDKA - TV for almost ten years. I was the union steward and I had been made chief cinematographer. Mary was employed by the General Nutrition Corporation, as the national director of advertising.

The income from KDKA made me happy, but the working conditions there did not. The management was not very compassionate about personal problems and mine were mounting. The equipment that I carried in doing my job as a news photographer was very heavy. At its heaviest my camera gear and accessories weighed eighty pounds! I started to experience much pain in my joints and attributed it to the weight of the equipment. The problem got so bad that I started seeking medical answers about how to deal with it.

While doing a story on the Pittsburgh Steelers I made an inquiry of Chuck Noll, the team's head coach. What did he do for his players when they had aches and pains? Chuck explained the different solutions he had for various problems. The advice he gave me was to go see the team's orthopedic surgeon, Dr. Paul Steele. One appointment with him, on October 2, 1980, turned into years of treatment. Dr. Steele diagnosed my problem as inflamed tendons and strained muscles caused by the constant heavy load at work. He placed me on various types of anti-inflammatory drugs. The drugs seemed ineffective and the problem only got worse. I had to continue to work despite the pain, to support the lifestyle to which I had become accustomed.

In September of 1982, Ray Tannehill, one of our anchor reporters, Jay Newman, our news director, and I were sent by KDKA to Beirut, Lebanon. Our assignment was to follow Senator Arlen Specter and his information gathering tour of this civil-war torn area. The Senator's objective was to analyze the effect that U.S. support had on this area and to determine whether that support should continue.

While in London, en route to Lebanon, we learned just how volatile the situation was in Beirut. The U.S. Marines had pulled out of Beirut because a car bomb had been driven into their military compound killing many Marines. To continue meant to be on our own, without any U.S. government protection. We talked it over and decided to proceed, despite the uncertainty about what lie ahead.

We had to change our plans dramatically. Originally we were to fly from London to Cyprus, pick up our U.S. military escort and chopper to Beirut. Minus the military escort, the whole itinerary had to be revised. At the ticket counter of El Al, the Israeli airline, we exchanged our tickets to Cyprus for tickets to Tel Aviv, Israel. This, unknown to us, sent up a red flag in the Israeli security system and we were instantly detained. While the other passengers were loading, we were being interrogated. "Why did you suddenly change your plans from Cyprus to Tel Aviv? Why now, why not yesterday?" a military officer asked.

Being Americans, I guess we were naive in thinking we should not be treated this way, but there wasn't much we could do about it. We were finally taken, at gunpoint, to the runway level of the airport, escorted outside where we found our luggage sitting next to a bus. A guard ordered us to open our luggage. We opened the luggage. Were we intimidated? Yes! The armed soldiers were Israeli. And as often as I had heard the word Uzi, an Israeli automatic weapon, I had never experienced looking down the barrel of a loaded one.

Looking back I realize why the Israelis were so cautious. We were getting on an Israeli aircraft. Israel, constantly in danger from terrorism, had security measures at its airports that far surpassed anything that we could have envisioned. Finally, we passed the security check, boarded a bus and traveled a long way to our plane. After boarding, armored personnel carriers escorted the plane to the take-off point and we took off. Welcome to the world of living on the edge.

Going through immigration after landing in Tel Aviv was much easier than getting on the plane in London. Not that it wasn't intimidating, just easier. This was my first experience traveling outside the United States. What a way to start our overseas travels!

Life seemed normal at the Tel Aviv Hilton where we stayed. Well, almost normal. The Hilton was very similar to a hotel in the United States. Looking out the window, Tel Aviv might be any large city. Down on the street, however, the atmosphere was not quite what we were used to. There were people carrying automatic weapons. That certainly wasn't normal to us!

After a good night's sleep, we awoke early to begin a day that would give us new insight into the meaning of living dangerously. That day introduced us to experiencing Beirut first hand. Believe me, an entire movie could be written around the drama about to unfold.

Our news crew met with Senator Arlen Specter and his entourage outside the hotel. We obtained our rental cars and headed for the Lebanese border with one Israeli soldier as our escort. The border crossing was uneventful. The countryside was intriguing to me. There were banana trees, the Mediterranean Sea and buildings with three-inch black circles all over them. I never dreamed that they were bullet marks left by an Israeli military assault.

We came upon a village that was literally leveled to the first story of all the buildings. Senator Specter wanted to investigate, so we stopped. I was amazed to find empty 223 caliber shell casings everywhere. Although I was not a religious person at the time, I found the sight of a half-destroyed church heart-breaking. To see a holy place attacked and left in ruins, pressed my mind for a reason that made some sense. Although I didn't act it, I did believe there was a God, and I was moved by what I imagined He felt about all this destruction.

All of us, even the senator, were taking pictures. The others, with their still cameras, were taking pictures for memories. I, with my 16mm film camera, was recording the senator's every move. It was my job to provide the viewers of Eyewitness News in Pittsburgh a first-hand look at what this war really looked like. Ray Tannehill, the reporter, did a 'stand-up', (that's TV jargon for standing in front of the camera with a microphone to explain the filmed story, or a part of it.) When we finished with the stand-up, I noticed a hillside and decided to climb part of the way up to get a general view of this village. I set my camera on the tripod and ran off sufficient footage of the panorama to satisfy my needs. The second I clicked the camera off, I heard gunfire. I was instantly excited to think I could possibly have the drama and sound of actual gunfire added to my story. I quickly turned the camera back on. Nothing! Once the camera was off, I heard the shots again. The same sequence occurred again. I seemed to be out of sync with the shots. Persistence did pay off, and finally, I had recorded the sound of gunfire.

The next thing I noticed was sand flying in two or three spots about thirty feet from me . . . then, gunfire . . . then sand flying . . . this time closer! I have already admitted that at times I am a bit slow, but how dumb could I be! They were shooting at *me*! I realized I had to get out of there quickly. Feet don't fail me now! If the folks at KDKA could have seen me then, they would have expected this kind of performance all the time. I might have broken a record with that run . . . the fastest escape time carrying the most weight! Who would have believed I could run that fast with all that camera gear? Not me!

Back in the little village, all were piling into their cars. Our solitary soldier escort was yelling for everyone to hurry, while waving his Uzi. Where did he get *that*? He must have had it hidden. The situation was deteriorating rapidly, but we escaped with no one hurt. Thank God, again!

The speed with which we traveled to Beirut might have been more dangerous than the gunfire we had just escaped. The guy with the gun was not a great shot so we'd at least had a chance back there!

At one point we ran into a traffic jam but this did not stop our escort from driving into a field at 70 mph to go around everyone. This was fine for those in the lead car; they could see! Jay Newman, driving the second car, with me as a passenger, was in their dust trail, blinded! Jay, in his excitement, shifted the automatic rented Volvo into reverse. Right then, I would have been receptive to turning back, but we went on.

Soon we came to a beach resort, or what had been a beach resort. There were about twenty soldiers just hanging around talking. I attempted to take their picture and one stuck the barrel of his gun in my face and said, "Don't take my picture." It's amazing how obliging one can be in a situation like that.

Once back in Beirut, the lead vehicle stopped at each intersection, slid back its door and pointed the Uzi at the cars waiting at the traffic light. This was so that no one would attempt to ram us.

We stopped at the hotel where the CBS crew was supposed to be staying, but it had been bombed out, and no one knew where they had gone. Between all these episodes, we were filming the senator.

As we were preparing to depart, Jay backed the Volvo into someone's Mercedes Benz. I couldn't believe he wanted to try to find the owner. "Jay," I said, "these people settle things with guns here. Don't you think we should just leave?" We did. 'Hit and run' in this place meant survival!

I can remember the rush hour traffic, or rather the rush hour chaos! The highway leading into Beirut was four lanes, two in each direction. Except during rush hour, the traffic flowed in only one direction as the drivers ignored the law and drove by their own rules. The person with the biggest car won! It's hard to imagine living in a country without any traffic laws. We witnessed rush hour traffic commandeering the entire highway. Worse than that, they jammed the sidewalks and at one point they were even driving through people's yards!

After finishing in Beirut, we went to Jerusalem to obtain an interview with Prime Minister Menachim Begin. We thought we had enough guns shoved in our noses in Beirut, but it happened again at the prime minister's palace, a very security sensitive place. It seemed that having a camera with me made it even tougher.

We arrived without Senator Specter and approached the palace to find out if he had arrived before us or if we would have to wait for him. Not being familiar with protocol, we assumed we could just knock on the door. Wrong! A voice shouted from above, and it wasn't God! "Put the camera down and go across the street." I looked around to see where the voice was coming from. High above the sidewalk was a little stone structure that looked like the corner of a castle wall. Two walls met at the turret. When I looked up, the voice repeated, "Put the camera down and go across the street!"

"But, Sir," I replied, "we are a TV crew from the United States, and . . ." I didn't get a chance to finish my statement before there was that, by now, familiar sound of the bolt being drawn on an automatic weapon. I'm sure that was done to convince me just how seriously this man wanted me to put down the camera and go across the street. As he repeated his command, I, being well versed in this procedure by now, put the camera down and went across the street.

A short time passed. Ray, Jay and I were casually talking about how testy these people seemed to be, when I was ordered to recross the street and make the camera work. I didn't argue; I recrossed the street. Another guard emerged from nowhere and looked into the viewfinder of my camera. It was obvious to me that he was making certain there was a picture in the viewfinder. Convinced that this was really a camera and not a weapon or a bomb, he directed me to come and retrieve it. I tried to engage him in conversation to convince him that we were harmless U.S. journalists. Was that stupid! There's no such thing as a harmless U.S. journalist. (Oops, better watch my editorial comments here.) Anyway, the man was not interested in my story about how we were to meet Arlen Specter or our interview at the palace. So I returned to my position across the street with my companions.

Ooh-a-ooh-a-ooh-a! That's my imitation of the siren sound I heard. It was the bomb squad coming to check out a car. Apparently, someone had parked the car on a street near the palace, and no one knew to whom it belonged and it was suspect. That was the state of affairs in Israel in 1982; everyone lived in a state of constant fear and suspicion.

Finally, the senator showed up and we attempted to grab our gear and follow him up to the palace. The senator was stopped, but evidently his name was on a list of expected visitors because he was told to proceed to the front door. We tried to stay close on his heels, but obviously our names weren't on the list. The guard separated us with his gun and told us to return to our position across the street.

We tried to explain . . . well, why go through that again; it didn't work. Senator Specter shouted back that he would try to work things out for us, and he did. Half an hour later, there we were, kibitzing with Menachim Begin. We were able to conduct our interview with the prime minister, and afterwards, we all went out and celebrated before heading back to the United States.

I was sitting at the dinner table with Senator Specter, our crew and several dignitaries from Jerusalem. Because there was nothing especially memorable about the occasion, the exact details of this next encounter are a bit fuzzy. I was about halfway through my meal when a man came up to me on my left. He introduced himself as Jules Grunbaum. He said, "Excuse me, how have you liked Jerusalem?"

Being a little reticent about speaking to strangers after what I had been through the past several days, I responded in some way other than cordial. We had been warned not to talk to strangers. I went back to eating.

The man persisted. He said, "Is there any one thing you would like to have seen that you have not seen?" I responded by saying, "Yeah, Bethlehem. Christmas and all that." He said, "I have a car outside. Come, I will take you there."

Why I left with that man, I don't know. It didn't make sense to go off with a stranger in Jerusalem. But I did indeed go out and get in his car, telling no one I was leaving. We drove for what seemed a short distance to Bethlehem. It may have only seemed short because he was pointing out some of the religious sights along the way. The only remembrances I have of Bethlehem are a cobblestone street of sorts, and a stone wall with a gate. He drove through the gate. Once inside, he stopped the car. Immediately upon leaving the car, I was overwhelmed by a strong emotion. My eyes welled with tears and I began to cry. It was the kind of emotion you feel when you do something good for someone, and get "goose bumps." It was like that, but maybe ten times stronger. I knew there was something very powerful there, but I didn't necessarily connect it with religion or God. I just knew something strange was going on.

The gentleman got out of the car and asked me if everything was all right. I nodded. "Yeah." He said, "Get in and I'll take you back." My brush with Bethlehem was just a few brief moments. I went back to the restaurant in the hotel and found that everyone had finished their meals and left.

I decided to do a little shopping. I wanted to get a Christmas ornament I had seen. It was a little wise man on a camel. I also purchased a ring for my wife and then turned in for the night. The next morning we got up, said our good-byes to Israel, and headed for the airport.

We waited in an endless line to have our baggage weighed and checked in. I was the last of our group in line, and as I placed my bag on the scale the man behind the counter said, "You have to leave." I said, "I know I have to leave. That's what I'm doing, leaving."

"You don't understand, you *have to leave*," he insisted. I was thinking to myself, of course I don't understand, you speak broken English. How can I understand?

The man had a very troubled look on his face, then he blurted out, "A bomb, a bomb!"

A bomb? I looked to my left and then my right, and he and I were the only two people left in the airport! It was like something you'd see in a movie! Then I heard a familiar wail, ooh-a-ooh-a-ooh-a. No one had to tell me twice what that was! As I ran outside, an emergency vehicle pulled up and two men jumped out, dressed like goalies for a hockey team. With a long pole-like object they picked up something that looked like a briefcase or a small suitcase and left with it! Ooh-a-ooh-a-ooh-a, and off they went. I was back in the airport in a shot! Oops, bad choice of words! You can bet I was first in line. I finished checking in, boarded the plane and left for home.

A man on the plane introduced himself and struck up a conversation with me. He explained that he was an Israeli actor who was going to America, hoping to perform. He said, "I have a friend in America, maybe you know him." "Highly unlikely," I replied. "America is a big place."

"He works in television, as you say you do. His name is Al Julius." You could have knocked me over with a feather! Al worked at the same television station that I did. I'd known him for years. What was the probability of that happening?

Upon returning to the States, the trip received much notoriety, as did our story. I was even the subject of a few newspaper articles as a local angle to the mideast war. All of this caused me to reflect on the experience frequently, but the part about Bethlehem never crossed my mind again. It was not a profound religious experience for me at the time. I was not moved to go back to church. I simply went about being me.

I guess I always had some kind of interest in religion though. I wouldn't turn away people that came to my door. If they were Mormons, I would listen to their story. If a Baptist was talking, I would listen. But I never made a personal commitment to anything. That is not to say that there were not religious feelings in my heart at all. I recall my mother asking me what I wanted for my birthday one year. I am sure she was shocked when I replied, "A Living Bible." She got it for me, but with my limited ability to read, it was impossible for me to get through it. My reading problem was compounded by a burning sensation in my eyes when I tried to read anything. The Bible just sat around for a very long time.

I went about my life, for the most part, focusing on making more and more money. Although my KDKA salary was substantial, I was always trying other financial adventures to fulfill a dream of mine. I wanted fast cars, big boats and lots of land . . . all the pleasures of life. My friends and I lived by the motto, "He who dies with the most toys wins," long before the expression ever appeared on a bumper sticker. We couldn't have been more wrong.

I don't know if the Lord was correlating the amount of my material possessions with the amount of physical pain He was sending me. All I know is that the more *toys* I gathered, the worse the pain got. In June of 1983, Dr. Steele, searching for a solution to the increasing pain, prescribed that I join a health club. He hoped this would strengthen my muscles and enable me to carry the heavy camera equipment. This effort not only failed but made matters worse.

In July of 1984, Dr. Steele was convinced we were dealing with more than the inability to carry weight because of weak muscles. He decided to run some tests to see if I was susceptible to arthritis.

Bad news. The tests results were positive. With that consideration, Dr. Steele gave me a drug called Feldene, which relieved much of the pain. He also arranged an appointment for me with a rheumatologist, and the diagnosis was confirmed. The rheumatologist explained to me that he didn't want me to take Feldene. He explained that it would destroy my kidneys in five years. Knowing that, I was willing to accept it. I would take the five good years, and cash it in at the end of the five. Without the Feldene, it was tough to exist. So I kept getting it from Dr. Steele.

Carrying a camera and recorder puts a lot of stress on your back; performing the job requires a lot of bending. Rheumatoid arthritis affects the structure of the joints and causes great pain. Not only do the joints swell, but also the structure around the joints becomes inflamed and very painful. The rheumatologist told me that I would become disabled and the prognosis for my future mobility was bleak. I made a conscious decision to keep on taking Feldene.

Just so you know what my life was like without it, I would need my wife's help to get out of bed in the morning. I felt like an old man, and it would sometimes take me fifteen minutes to straighten up. I couldn't sit at the dinner table for more than five or ten minutes without having to get up and walk around. I couldn't twist the cap off a ketchup bottle, or pop the tab off my beer cans. I'd have to ask my wife to do these simple things for me. It was humiliating.

My doctor then prescribed enrollment in a program at the Falk Pain Clinic to help me to learn to deal with the pain. The news flash I had for everyone involved was that you don't learn to live with this kind of pain, you suffer!

All this was making my life pretty much unbearable. I had given up most of the sports I enjoyed: hunting, golfing, and was now even considering giving up the easiest sport of all, fishing. My joints hurt so badly that I couldn't even perform the needed work around my farm anymore. None of this was helped by the lack of sympathy at work. The only consolation from my employer was payment of the bills through worker's compensation because my condition was aggravated by the heavy equipment I carried. Feldene was the only thing that made it possible for me to work at all. In fairness to KDKA management, I don't think they really understood exactly how much pain I was in and what effort it took just to get to work each day. The only enjoyment I had left was travel. This was the easiest thing for me to do because there was such a variety of non-stressful activity involved.

Fortunately, I got to do an extensive amount of traveling. In September of 1984, KDKA sent me to Los Angeles to do a story on the then popular, prime time soap, "Dallas." Mary made the trip with me and we spent a week vacationing in California after I completed my work. While there, Mary appeared on the game show, "Tic, Tac, Dough." She was the champion for five days! One of the many prizes she won was a trip to Greece. We were finally going to go to Europe together and scheduled the trip for May of

1985. However, it was cancelled because of the hijacking of the TWA airliner in Athens. Due to that incident the United States would not guarantee the safety of its citizens traveling in Greece. The game show tried to get us to take an alternate trip, but we had our hearts set on Greece. We were willing to wait.

In June, KDKA sent a reporter, Bill Flanagan, and me to Wyoming to do a story on an archeological dig. After completing the assignment we took advantage of being out west and spent a week traveling through the Rockies. Finally, in September, travel in the Mediterranean was deemed to be safe again. So off we went to Greece. The package Mary had won included six days of land travel and four days cruising the Greek Isles with a stop at Kusadasi, a port in Turkey. During our brief stop in Turkey, we visited the ruins at Ephesus where the Blessed Mother lived in her later years. This had no significance to me at the time.

In October of 1985, I, along with my Uncle Stanley and a good friend of mine, Dean Fediaczko, decided not to take our annual salmon fishing trip to Oscoda, Michigan. We had heard that the fish were tainted with chemicals and not fit to eat. No sense fishing if you can't eat them, and with my arthritis, it wasn't going to be all that enjoyable anyway. Even though I'd only returned from Greece a few weeks ago, how I longed to go back to Europe again! When I suggested Europe, Stan and Dean thought that was a great idea, if the price was right! It turned out it was.

We packed up and flew to Amsterdam; rented a motor home and filled it up with beer, cheese, and bread; everything three guys would need to have a good time. Our goal was simply to see as many countries as we could drive to in the time allotted, with no particular place in mind. We were having a ball!

Stanley, a Sunday Catholic, mentioned a place called Lourdes, France. He expressed his interest in fitting Lourdes into our trip. Dean asked, "That's some kind of religious place, isn't it?"

"Yes, the Blessed Mother appeared there," Stanley said. I reminded him, "Stanley, this isn't a pilgrimage." We're drinking beer and having a good time and aren't going to do anything religious."

Continuing on our way ... through Holland, Germany, Switzerland, Italy, we were clicking the countries off at one hundred miles per hour! Most of what we saw was through the windows of the motor home.

When we passed through the French Riviera, I decided it was time to head north. As close as we were to Spain, I only wanted to cross the border so I could say I had been in Spain. But we were near Europe Expressway 56, our route north, and to deviate from our schedule seemed impractical to me. Informal as our schedule was, I calculated that we would arrive in Paris, our next destination, right on time.

Dean and I had been having a great time kidding Stanley. He was like our father on the trip. Stanley was a faithful husband, very true to his wife. We kept trying to get him to go over and ask women directions. I wanted to videotape him talking with women and have a little fun with him and his wife upon our return home.

Soon, Dean made his first suggestion about our itinerary and suddenly the entire mood of our trip changed. He said, "You know, you planned this trip out and said where we were going and everything without any input from me. I really don't know much about Europe, but there is one place I would really like to go: Barcelona, Spain."

I shook my head and said, "Dean, I wish you'd have mentioned that sooner. It's kind of out of the question now. Barcelona is southwest of here and we have to start heading north. That's about an eight hour drive out of our way."

He said, "Well, it's really not fair. You guys got to go to all the places you wanted to go, and there's just one place I want to go, and that's Barcelona." I truly believed that it was out of the question. There was no way we could do it.

That was the first night the three of us shared any words that weren't in absolute friendship. We went to sleep in the motorhome that night just a little off pitch. We didn't fight or anything, but there was a tension there that bothered me. So much so, that I got up after Dean and Stan went to sleep, started the motor home and drove straight through the night to Barcelona, Spain.

When we arrived, it was awful. There was an atmospheric inversion. The air pollution was so bad you could hardly see any of the buildings. They dumped all their sewage into the streams and rivers and the smell was held down by the inversion.

I awoke my friends about six-thirty or seven o'clock in the morning and said, "Wake up Dean, take a smell. You're in Barcelona." It was terrible!

Barcelona turned out to be no fun at all. We arrived there during morning rush hour. Backed up in traffic, we decided to take some side streets. The side streets were very narrow and the buildings were so old, they leaned into the center of the street. The motorhome got stuck between two buildings. We knocked on the doors of people who spoke only Spanish. When someone answered, we tried to convince them that they had to move their cars off the street so we could back the motor home up without damaging any more property.

We successfully backed out of there and Dean came up with his second suggestion of the trip, "Let's get out of here." After an eight hour drive and only two hours in Barcelona, we were leaving. This unplanned detour had altered our trip dramatically. Now, rather than travelling Europe 56 all the way to Paris, we had to cross over the Pyrenees Mountains, all on back country roads! There were three tunnels going through the Pyrenees, and two of them were closed. We had to search for the one tunnel that was open.

We drove over the mountains and found the open tunnel that would allow us to cross from Spain into France. The second town we encountered in France was called Lourdes.

I said, "Stan, is this the place you were talking about?" He said, "Yeah, son-of-a-gun! Can we stop?" I reminded him, "We aren't on any religious pilgrimage!" Now Stanley was the unhappy one.

To make Stanley happy we pulled in. We hadn't planned to go there, but there we were, in the little town of Lourdes. The place was really beautiful, especially the church. It was magnificent. There was a place where water came out of the ground. Supposedly the Blessed Mother, to prove she was there, pointed at a rock and a spring broke forth. That water was being pumped from the spring to a battery of faucets on a hillside and people were filling up bottles with the water. Some bottles were even shaped like the Blessed Mother. I thought, "This is really goofy. These people actually think they are going to take this water home with them and it's going to do something." It didn't seem right to me.

There were hundreds of crutches hanging around the grotto, symbols of the cures that supposedly took place there. Not that I didn't believe in the Blessed Mother, I just didn't believe things like miraculous cures really happened. It was much the same feeling as seeing evangelist healings on TV; that it's all for show. At some point in my making light of Lourdes I raised my hands, looked toward heaven and said, "Hey, in case I'm wrong . . . " Something powerful happened then. I was overwhelmed with emotion and tears started rolling down my cheeks. I got the same feeling in my flesh that I got in Bethlehem; like when you do something nice for someone, but ten times stronger. I didn't want Stan or Dean to see me crying so I slipped off somewhere, until I dried my eyes.

I went back to the grotto and lit a candle. Not that I thought the candle was going to do anything for anyone. I did it just because everyone else did. The same was true for kneeling down. I knelt down because everyone else did and tried to say a short prayer in front of the statue of the Blessed Mother. "Ah, hi! How are you? I'm here. You probably don't know me." That was my simple prayer.

We departed Lourdes and continued our trip. Surely what happened to me there made an impression somewhere in the back of my mind, but again it changed nothing immediately.

When we finally arrived in Paris, on what we thought was a Saturday, I found it odd that all the shops were closed. We parked the motorhome and got out near the Eiffel Tower, with the intention of climbing it. I stopped someone and asked why all the shops were closed and we were told that the shops were always closed Sunday. Yipes! We had lost a day somewhere, and we still wanted to go to London and Belgium before leaving Europe!

Back into the motorhome. A glimpse of the Eiffel Tower is all we had time for and only about two hours in Paris altogether. Our whirlwind tour continued; next stop London. In Calais, France, we left the motorhome behind and traveled by hydrofoil to England and then by train to London to spend the entire day. That evening we returned to pick up the motorhome and head for Amsterdam for the flight home. Once home, I forgot the incident in Lourdes. I assure you, it had not been the high point of my trip.

Despite the enjoyment of my recent travels, my arthritis was getting the best of me. My wife realized how few pleasures I had in my life at this point. She knew my frustrations well. If there was anything she could do to make me feel better, she did. Presents always made me feel good. I loved getting presents, but there wasn't much she could buy me in the way of a gift that I didn't already have. In December, 1985, she asked me what I would like for Christmas. Because of my dyslexia, I hadn't read the Bible my mother had given me. And, even though I was still not involved in any religious activity at this point, I continued to have this ongoing urge to read it. I had spotted the Bible on audio cassettes in a store and suggested the idea to Mary. She didn't consider it to be the perfect Christmas present, but she got it for me. When I opened her gift, I was elated. There were fifty-six, hour and a half long tapes! But, how in the world would I ever have enough time to listen to all of them?

The Lord's plan continued. In late 1985, KDKA was in the process of appraising the type of news vehicles to purchase. As chief photographer, I was asked to be involved in the process. I convinced the station to buy Jeep Wagoneers because I owned one myself and knew they would be perfect for the job. I offered my opinions on the option packages and the station agreed. These approved options did not include an audio cassette player. However, on the Jeep I was to drive I paid extra to have a tape player installed. The tape player in the Jeep allowed me to listen to the Bible cassettes. Many days I would have to drive as much as a hundred miles to a story location. Even so, fifty-six tapes would take 84 hours of listening!

In the summer of 1986, I was assigned to one story for approximately twenty-five days. My job was simply to sit in my news wagon and wait while a large section of woods was methodically being overturned in search of murder victims. I sat in the Jeep for twenty-five days and listened to all of the Bible tapes, while the officers did their job.

The tapes were professionally produced and were so enjoyable they were addictive. It wasn't just someone reading the Bible. They were dramatized, with several actors performing the words, and were enhanced by powerful background music. I couldn't stop listening to them. I shared my excitement with only those close to me. Although I wanted to tell everyone, kind of like you feel after seeing a good movie or going on a great vacation, religion was not an accepted topic of conversation in my circle of friends. Again, this experience did not noticeably change my life. Summer soon faded into fall and it was time to take another vacation.

In September, 1986, Dean Fediaczko and I went back overseas, this time accompanied by my wife and my friend from KDKA, Bill Flanagan. We planned to go to Morocco, Spain and the southern portion of Portugal, called the Algarve.

We landed in Lisbon, Portugal, where we connected with a flight to Casablanca, Morocco, in North Africa. Morocco was beautiful and the culture was so intriguing. I guess the best word to describe the time we had in Morocco is enchanting. It was like taking a five hundred year step back in time. We continued on the same crazy schedule I'd become accustomed to in previous years. From Casablanca to Marrakesh, over the Atlas Mountains to Meknes and Fez, and on to the capital, Rabat. It was a shame we only had a week to spend there.

Dean and Bill had two weeks vacation; my wife and I had three, and the time seemed to be going really fast. From Rabat, Morocco, we returned to Lisbon and drove through southern Portugal. Then it was on to Spain. We traveled through Seville, Jerez, Cadiz, took a detour to check out Gibraltar, then Málaga, Córdoba and finally Mérida. There Mary and I said adios to Dean and Bill. They headed back to Lisbon to fly home, and we headed for Madrid.

Mary was a Spanish major in college and she was excited to be spending time in Spain, especially Madrid. It was the foundation of everything she'd studied, the seat of history and art, including one of the world's most famous museums, El Prado. A museum! A huge world class museum! My tolerance for museums is under an hour. Mary, on the other hand can spend days in them. I can look at pictures, no matter how old or famous, for just so long. I knew it was going to be a rocky road ahead.

An hour after arriving in Madrid we were looking at paintings and other museum junk. By the second hour I was totally exhausted. Suffering from rheumatoid arthritis, it didn't take me long to become exhausted, and my wife never really understood that. Immediately my mind started racing, searching for an alternative to this torture. Anything I came up with failed. Mary's reply was always, "I don't know. I'd really like to visit a few more museums."

This was going to be harder than I thought. My gentle nudging turned into agitation; the agitation led to arguing. The arguing led to not speaking at all. Then it hit me! I said, "Wouldn't it be great if we went up to France to the Bordeaux wine country. Maybe we could visit a medieval castle or two." We were both lovers of white wine. She went for the bait, but only after demanding, several times, that I take her home then and there.

We left for France and visited some intriguing chateaus. The climate was decidedly cooler than in Spain and a little rainy, but we spent three days touring old castles, drinking wine, and eating exquisite French food and pastry. This was truly great because we were both enjoying it.

We stayed overnight in a chateau that had its own winery, as most do. I learned one thing though. Always ask the price of the wine! As we were enjoying a wonderful dinner, the maitre d' suggested that we have some wine and presented me with the wine list. "Voila," is about as extensive as my French gets and to save myself embarrassment, I just pointed to one on the list. The waiter replied, "A very good choice, Sir!" To our delight it was! So much so, that Mary and I ordered another bottle. The meal was exquisite. The wine was wonderful! The bill was shocking! And that's why I say, always ask the price of wine! It was seventy-two dollars a bottle! Even as affluent as I thought I was, that was more than I wanted to spend. Our wines in Spain and Portugal had only been around eight or ten dollars a bottle. The total cost of the evening was something like two hundred and fifty dollars! I think it was then, that we decided to leave France.

We started the return drive to Lisbon, visiting little villages along the way. They had the most wonderful pastries in the little pastry shops. We took advantage and stocked our car well!

At the Spanish border, not wanting to backtrack over the same roads we took north and see the same scenery, we decided on another route. Once again, a quirky change in our itinerary altered our trip drastically. Now we were cutting across northern Spain and angling down to hit Portugal somewhere in the center. My aim was to get us back to Lisbon, our point of departure.

As we were crossing over the mountains between Spain and Portugal, we ran into a torrential downpour. Driving in that kind of rain, on mountainous roads, caused such tension that my muscles began to spasm and I experienced great pain. With rheumatoid arthritis, I was no stranger to pain.

Under stress, arthritis really begins to flare up, and is at its worst when it's associated with the low pressure system carrying a rain storm. The stress of crossing the mountains, on treacherous rain drenched roads and the low barometric pressure system that brought the rain, caused the pain to become greater than I had ever experienced. It was excruciating and exhausting! Turning to Mary, I said it was becoming impossible to drive any further. And certainly it was dangerous for her to drive in the downpour, so the decision was made as we were passing through a little village called Batalha. We would get a hotel room so I could lie down. It was about noon. After taking some extra Feldene, I laid down and went to sleep. In two or three hours, I woke up feeling much better.

We decided to take a ride to explore the little village, but not to push on anymore that day. I was still quite tired. As we returned to our hotel, I noticed for the first time that next to it was a magnificent building that looked like a cathedral. It was huge. I took a walk around it, by myself, while Mary went to the room.

I have just discovered from a book about this area that we brought home, but hadn't read until recently, that this building is a great shrine to the Blessed Mother. Its name is, "The Monastery of St. Mary of Victory." It was so named because of a war the Portuguese army believed they won against their adversary, Spain, through the intercession of our Blessed Mother. I was really impressed with this building, not realizing I was brushing up against the historical trail of the Blessed Mother.

Mary met me outside the hotel later and we got in the car and drove around a bit. We came upon an intersection and a sign that pointed left. The sign read, "Fatima 12km." I said to my wife, "Is that the Fatima the church talks about?" She answered, "It must be. Fatima is in Portugal somewhere."

For those of you who are not familiar with Fatima, it is where the Blessed Mother appeared on May 13, 1917, to three children. Her message centered on the conversion of Russia, which would come about when Russia was consecrated to Her Immaculate Heart by the Pope and bishops of the world. If it was not, Russia's errors would be spread throughout the world provoking wars.

I said to Mary, "Do you want to go?" "Not particularly," she answered. I responded, "Then I don't want to go either."

We turned around, went back to the hotel, had our dinner, and turned in for the night. The next morning we got up and headed for the coast of Portugal, to a small fishing village called Nazaré. On the way out of town, we passed that sign again that said, "Fatima 12km."

I said, "It seems a shame to be that close to a famous place and not go there. Maybe we ought to drive through just to see what it looks like." If nothing else, it would be nice to be able to say I've been there; to add it to my list. It was fun to brag about all the places that I had been.

You would have to vacation with me sometime to understand the process. Once I drove three hundred miles out of my way at one hundred miles an hour, just to get to

Liechtenstein. Someone had told me it was the smallest country on earth, and I wanted to get there just so I could tell people I had been there. The last time I was in Europe, I was only fifty miles away from it and didn't know of its existence. When I came home from that trip someone who knew the route we had traveled, asked me if I had stopped in Liechtenstein, and I had to say no. I was not going to make that mistake again. That's the way I felt about seeing Fatima. I wanted to go just so I could say I went to Fatima.

That's why I made that left hand turn that day. We pulled into the village, and I was uneasy with all the little shops that sold all this religious stuff. It was almost as tacky and blatantly commercial as Lourdes. I parked the car and we ran from tree to tree, to keep out of the rain. It was drizzling and cold.

Mary and I became separated, so I found myself alone in a gazebo-type structure that housed a statue of Our Blessed Mother. I can recall walking up to the statue, looking at the Blessed Mother and saying, "Hi, it's me again." Tears started to roll down my face, and I got that feeling in my flesh. I was concerned about my wife finding me crying, so I took a walk until I got myself dried out. I finally caught up with Mary, and we left. We probably spent less than an hour at Fatima. As we drove away, my wife said to me, "Boy, I got choked up there. I even got tears in my eyes." I don't know why I was willing to admit it but I said, "So did I." It was weird.

It didn't shock me at all to see very few people at Fatima. Totally unaware of how many people visited there annually, I didn't even wonder why most of the shops were closed. I wasn't going to buy anything. It wasn't until late in 1989 that I found out millions of people visited there yearly! When Mary and I were there, the season was over. Our Blessed Mother has a season?

We continued our journey. Fatima became a distant memory. It didn't change my life or get me back to church. . . . at least not then.

Next stop, Nazaré. The fishing village on the Atlantic coast at Nazaré was a photographic bonanza. I took many photos of the colorful boats on the beach. And now, in research for this writing, I discovered that Nazaré, as well as Batalha, has a great shrine to our Blessed Mother! I just think it's wonderful the way the Lord was taking me to places dedicated to His Mother, without my knowing it at the time.

We pushed on to Lisbon, Portugal, and the next day we were on a plane headed home.

Chapter 5

Medja What?

At home, I went on about my business, still at KDKA, and life was comfortable for me, except for my arthritis. During the summers I was living at my home less, and on my boat at the yacht club more. Yes, I had a boat big enough to live on. Having a boat is like having a disease. You start off with a small boat, and you're happy for a while. Then you start shopping for a bigger one, and a bigger one. I went through four in about five years!

In 1980, I bought a small aluminum fishing boat. It was fourteen feet long with a ten horsepower motor. That was good enough until I got it on the water and saw a beautiful, fiberglass ski boat with an inboard/outboard motor! My goodness, the engine in that boat was as big as the one in my Oldsmobile and had seats almost as plush! I figured I could fish out of one like that and be a lot more comfortable! I found a good deal on one, and took my wife to see the boat. To my dismay, she didn't find the idea the least bit enchanting. "You buy that boat and you'll have two things, a boat and a divorce!" I bought the boat.

It took Mary only until her first ride to fall in love with the boat. We docked down at Northshore Marina on the Allegheny River in downtown Pittsburgh. For a little over a year, we were happy with that boat.

The following Spring, just seeing boats bigger than mine on the river made me thirst for one. One day, I boarded a boat that had a "For Sale" sign on it, just to look.

It was beautiful! A place to cook, a head, and room to sleep six. I wanted it! I got down off the boat, to take it all in. She was sitting on a trailer, twenty-four feet long, with an eight foot beam. How could a car pull something that big? A man came out, and asked me if he could help me. I said, "No, I'm just dreaming."

He started to walk away. I said, "How much is she?" He said, "$13,000." It seemed like a lot, not for that boat, but just a lot. Not out of the question, however.

I took Mary out to look at the boat. She said, "Honey, I know I was wrong about the other boat, and I really like it, but this is too much! You buy this and I really will leave you." I bought the boat! Again, it took Mary only one ride to fall in love with it. We decided to leave our marina and opted for the one next door, Dave's Marina. Dave's had a boat ramp and with the easy access to a ramp we could trailer the boat more often.

I was right on target in asking myself how a car could pull that big boat . . . a car couldn't. That meant only one thing, I had to buy something that could. I bought a Ford Bronco. On several weekends, I would trailer the boat to Sandusky, Ohio to putter around on Lake Erie. Pulling a boat that size, even with a Ford Bronco, causes a lot of stress. Well, with my arthritis, that didn't last long. I decided not to move the boat around any more. It wasn't worth the pain.

In the spring of 1985, I was out boat shopping again. Brand new, right out of the box, I spotted a beauty! It had a ten-foot beam. If you don't know what that means, that's the width of the boat. We now had the biggest and newest boat in the whole marina! With a boat that nice and a brand new yacht club going in up the river, I began to wonder if I didn't belong up at the yacht club. But the owner of the marina, Dave, was my friend and I didn't want to offend him by leaving. I came up with the perfect solution. I decided to dock at Dave's during the week, allowing Mary and me to live on the boat and go to work from there. Pittsburgh wasn't twenty-five miles away anymore, it was right here, in my own back-water! On the weekends we moored at the Fox Chapel Yacht Club and partied. We met many new friends there. And almost all of them had a bigger boat than we did! Can you see how this works? It just never stops. Bigger, bigger, bigger! Hell must be a big place!

Being on the boat as much as we were, Mary and I didn't see many of our old friends. We were rarely at home, but my Uncle Stanley was fortunate enough to find me there one day in August, 1987. He wanted to have a little talk and show me something. He came in the house and said, "Hey, Tom, remember when we were on vacation in Europe? Do you recall the place that we stopped at called Lourdes?" "Sure, Stan," I replied. "Do you remember what Lourdes was about?" he asked. I replied off-handedly, "The Blessed Mother supposedly appeared to some kids there, right?" "That's right. Now look at this newspaper article," he said, "the same thing is happening in Yugoslavia. The Blessed Mother is appearing to some kids there."

Stanley was showing me a small blue and white newspaper. It was written by a journalist named Wayne Weible. It had a picture of the Blessed Mother on the front. The headline read, "MIRACLE AT MEDJUGORJE." Medja what? It had a sub-paragraph stating: "It is reported that since June, 1981, the Blessed Virgin Mary, the Mother of Jesus, has been appearing daily to a group of young people in a remote mountain village in Yugoslavia." I chuckled and asked, "You don't believe that, do you?" He answered, "I don't know. You ought to read the article."

I said okay, but I don't think my intentions were to read it. One, I thought it a little strange, and two, at this point in my life, I didn't read much! From the time that I left high school to this point in my life, I hadn't gone to church or read a book. But a day or two later I attempted to read this newspaper and I was amazed that it wasn't difficult.

I finished the article, then I thought, "Wow, what a news story!" The Blessed Mother appearing did not strike me as within the realm of possibility, but all the miracles and amazing things they talked about struck me as a great opportunity for a free trip overseas through KDKA. I didn't care if it was true or not, it was my intent to try to convince KDKA to send me over there to do a news story. I solicited the help of my reporter friend, Bill Flanagan. He, too, thought it would make a great story, and we approached our news director, Sue McInerney. Her answer was no. A resounding no! She explained that the Pope was coming to the United States, and that was all the Catholicism KDKA-TV needed for that rating period. Well, it didn't sound like I had much of a chance of going to Yugoslavia to do a religious story.

We have a saying in the news business, "If you can find a newspeg to hang the story on, you have a chance of getting it on the air." A newspeg is an overwhelming reason to do a story.

I went out in search of something or someone to try to convince KDKA to do this story. I found a man named Pat Geinzer, a radiologist at Mercy Hospital. He had gone to Medjugorje and because of what happened to him there, he explained to me, he now had intentions of becoming a priest. "You mean that place affected you so much that you're going to quit your job and become a priest?" I asked him. He said, "Yes, it did."

Then I asked him, "Would you go on TV and tell your story if I can get the air time?" He said, "Yes, but first I want you to watch a video and read a book so you will know a little bit about Medjugorje." I agreed to do that.

I went back to KDKA and explained to the management that I had found a man from Pittsburgh who was going to become a priest because he was so overwhelmed by his experience in Medjugorje. The place changed his entire life. Certainly this was reason enough to send a crew to Medjugorje and investigate. Not to them! Sue McInerney reiterated her position about the Pope coming. I was kind of bent out of shape, but that wasn't the first time I'd been bent out of shape.[1]

I started carrying around the book Pat gave me, "The Queen Of Peace Visits Medjugorje." One day I found myself at the Fox Chapel Yacht Club, just sitting on my boat, alone and bored. I picked up the book and started to read it. Surprisingly, it did not seem difficult for me to read. I found it interesting enough to read all the way to the third chapter. It was in the third chapter that a voice spoke to me and said, *"Thomas, I took you to Bethlehem.*

---

[1]   In September, 1991, I received an invitation from the Passionist Community to attend the "Profession of First Vows" of Patrick J. Geinzer.

I took you to Lourdes. And I took you to Fatima.
Can't you understand that this is real?"

There was no question in my mind what was going
on. This was Jesus Christ speaking to me. The only thing
I could think of to answer was, "Why me? Why would You
come and talk to *me?"*

I couldn't get off my boat fast enough. I was racing
to find a church. I went to a little town called Aspinwall
near the marina. I drove from street to street looking for
church steeples trying to find a Catholic Church. I knew
there was one there somewhere. Finally, there was St.
Scholastica Church. Finding the doors of the church locked,
I circled the entire block looking for an entrance to one of
the buildings and came upon the rectory. That door was
locked also. But I rang the doorbell and eventually a woman answered. I asked her if I could talk to a priest. She responded, "any particular priest?" I told her I didn't know
any of them. She then asked me, "May I tell him what it is
that you want to discuss?" "That is personal," was my
reply.

Leaving the room, the woman remarked she would
check to see who was available. What seemed an endless
period of time passed. I sat in the waiting room, my palms
sweating. A priest walked into the room, and introduced
himself as Father John Silozitotz, the pastor. Father asked
me if there was anything he could do for me. I attempted to
explain to him about my being away from my Catholic faith
for twenty-five years, and that something had just happened to me, making me understand what a mistake that
was. I related to him my immediate need for confession.

Father John invited me into an office and asked me to sit down. We had a brief discussion which led him to ask me if I wanted to make my confession right there inside his office or go inside the church. I didn't quite understand what he was saying to me. My vague remembrance of confession was telling my sins to a priest in a dark, gloomy box with a barrier between us. As a child, confession frightened me.

As this was racing through my mind, I asked Father, "What do you mean, here in the office or in the church?" It was here I was introduced to something I didn't know existed in the Catholic Church, face-to-face confession! I'm sure he realized now that my twenty-five year absence from the church meant there was much I didn't know. So he explained that many things had changed. Now parishioners had an option; the old fashioned way, or face-to-face. I tried to swallow and couldn't. I was as frightened as a child, but I didn't want to delay the process any longer, and said, "Let's do it right here." He said, "Go ahead."

Many of the things in my life that offended God came to mind immediately. Actions that I always justified as a normal part of my life, I was now admitting were wrong. I explained to Father that I wasn't about to sit there and try to conjure up twenty-five years of sin, with all the embarrassing details. What I would do is highlight the most serious. Stealing, not always honoring my mother and father, not loving my neighbor. I tried, but I wasn't real successful.

What probably weighed heaviest on my mind was my position on abortion. It was amazing to me that just a half-hour before I had believed it was a woman's right to choose abortion and now, I knew how wrong it was. God forgive me.

Then there was the matter of my being married in the Catholic church, divorced and remarried outside the Catholic faith. This seemed to be the greatest stumbling block to my new and greatest desire, to return to the Holy Eucharist. I don't think I knew the full significance of the Eucharist then, but I had this tremendous desire to receive Jesus. Father John explained that he needed to call and talk to the Bishop because of my marital status. He seemed compassionate in listening to the circumstances surrounding my first marriage, but said this kind of decision was beyond his authority. He would have to call Bishop Bevilacqua. I left the church that day with the joy of being totally absolved of my sins and with the hope of being able to return to the sacraments as a fully reinstated Catholic.

The Bishop sent back dispensation to allow me to return to the sacraments. The condition of the dispensation was that I immediately file for the annulment of my first marriage. He understood the absurdity of the circumstances surrounding my first marriage and felt there would be no problem obtaining an annulment. That would make it possible to have my present marriage validated in the Catholic church. Now, most certainly, I knew that God's grace was guiding my life.

Only God knew what He had in store for me. Just as you should not be upset with Christ for taking a prostitute and transforming her into a saint, I pray that you won't be upset over what the Church did for me. If you are involved in an annulment process and are running into problems, know that I ran into the same kinds of problems and it took *fifteen years* for the solution to come about. Trust in God and eliminate the anger Satan pushes on you . . . and most of all, be patient. When you finish this book I hope maybe you'll understand why I say this.

Reviewing my life, I became so much more aware of the wrongs I had done. It was all so much clearer to me and I wondered about the entire process that was taking place in my heart and mind. After I left the church and headed home, the Lord spoke again, *"Take a look at your life, Thomas. Look at all of the people you have offended. How do you find all of those people and say you're sorry? You can't. You are fighting with your neighbors. Go take care of that."*

As I told you earlier, I had a violent argument going on with my neighbors over the right-of-way to my land. It involved guns, blockades, a lawsuit, and an immense amount of hatred. The hatred was building day by day. What you have to understand is how the gates affected our daily lives. Imagine this. We were dressed up, going out to dinner and it was raining very hard. I drove to the first gate between our property and the neighbors', got out of the car, walked up to the gate and opened it. I walked back to the car and got in. I drove the car through the opened gate and got back out of the car. I walked back and closed the gate and then got back into the car. I then drove across the right of way through the neighbors' farm, to the second gate. I got out of the car and walked up to the gate and opened it. I walked back to the car and got in. I drove the car through the opened gate and got back out of the car. I walked back to close the gate and then got back into the car. I was then soaking wet and my shoes were muddy! The bad news is . . . I knew I had to do this all over again when I returned home. Not only do we have to go through this process but, everyone who visits has to go through it also.

Remember, my neighbors placed a chain and lock on the gate closest to my house. The anger had been building up every time I had to open and close those gates and the locks just added fuel to the fire. If I expected guests, I had to go and meet them at the gate to unlock it. Unexpected guests would sit at the gate and blow their horn hoping I would hear it. If I wasn't home they would have to back out of the driveway, a very long distance. And what about an emergency, a fire or someone needing an ambulance?

The worst case scenario occurred when my father came to visit the first time after the gate was locked and I wasn't home. He was elderly and had severe diabetes. To get to my house he climbed over the gate. The sides of the gate were fenced to prevent anyone from going around. While he was attempting to climb over the gate, he cut his leg, complicating an already serious situation. Because of the diabetes and the other complications, his leg could not heal. The doctors eventually had to remove it. This caused a tremendous decline in my father's health and, I believe, led to his premature death.

I hated these people with everything in me and they hated me. Mary and I hated them so much that in 1984, we put our farm up for sale. For four years we attempted to sell it, but we couldn't find anyone to buy it. We didn't get one offer in all that time. We felt like prisoners on our land. What began as my dream, was now hell.

So now, the Lord is telling me that in order to be forgiven, this situation should be corrected. I should go and apologize for my part in the hatred.

I said to the Lord, "You don't understand. I am the persecuted party." The Lord's reply to this was, *"No, Thomas, you don't understand. You are to turn your cheek seventy times seven. Go and take care of that problem."* It was as if He was saying to me, "I'm going to give you one shot at this. I've been after you for so long and you keep turning your back and walking away." Just like the original doubting Thomas, I was hard to convince.

The hardest thing I ever did in my whole life was to go to my neighbor's house to apologize. When I got home that day I started up the driveway. I know the Lord had to have gone with me because I could not have done it alone. I walked to the first house on the road and found myself, with my hand raised, knocking on the door. An older woman, matriarch of all the neighboring families, answered the door. I said, "I am here to apologize for berating you and for my participation in all of the problems concerning the driveway." I guaranteed her I would never fight with them again. Some of the family accepted that and some of them didn't. I was sure that the whole situation would change when they saw how I had changed.

When I left my neighbor's house it seemed like half the weight of the world was taken off my shoulders. Going back down the road, I made a covenant with the Lord. I said, "You know better than anyone, Lord, how hard I tried to sell this farm so that I could get away from these people who were destroying my life. In all that time no one ever offered me a cent. But now all that doesn't matter anymore because I'm going to take my house off the market, stay here, and prove to you that I can love my neighbor." On returning to my house, I called up the Realtor and removed the property from the market.

That same week, I got a call from a Multi-List Realtor saying, "Mr. Rutkoski, is your farm for sale or isn't it? It was in the computer the other day and now it's not." I said, "No it's not. I just pulled it off the market. My reasons are personal and I don't really want to get into all that." "Well," she said, "it's been on the market a long time and we have somebody that's interested. They might want to make an offer."

The voice in my head spoke again, "Thomas, you don't own this property yourself. Why would you make a decision like this alone?" True, I hadn't consulted my wife at all. I said to the Realtor, "To tell you the truth, I haven't discussed removing the listing with my wife. In fairness, I'll talk to her about it." I had made up my mind to stay. I was determined to prove to God that I could stay there and make it work.

I told the Realtor, "Have your clients come over on Sunday and take a look at the place and make sure they want to make an offer. If they do want to purchase the property and my wife wants to leave, I won't force her to stay." She said, "Okay, we'll bring them over on Sunday."

Meanwhile, I was still looking for a newspeg to hang Medjugorje on since the Pat Geinzer story did not convince KDKA to succumb to my desire to do a story. I then heard of a woman by the name of Rita Klaus who had experienced a miracle through Medjugorje.

I reached her by telephone and I asked if I could come over and talk to her. She said yes. We made arrangements to meet at her home. I found her to be quite cordial. We sat down and had a long talk over coffee. She unfolded her amazing story before me, and what a story it was! I was almost as swept away by what she told me as I was by what was happening in my own life, although I revealed none of that to her. Rita had been stricken with multiple sclerosis. She taught at a Catholic school from a wheelchair for many years. Through a simple prayer to the Blessed Mother of Medjugorje, she was made perfectly whole.

Rita related to me the prayer she said prior to her cure, in essence "Help me in my unbelief." Gradually, over a day or two the miracle happened. She could walk again! I was ecstatic. I said to myself, "Wow! This is the overwhelming reason for KDKA to do the story on Medjugorje!"

During our conversation, I asked Rita if she would go on TV and tell her story and she said, "No!" She was in semi-seclusion, hiding from all the harassment, the many phone calls and inquiries about her great cure. Many did not accept the fact that the cure was miraculous. People suffering with MS wanted to know what medication she took. Then there were the scandal sheets wanting to exploit her story.

I was sympathetic to a point, but recall saying to Rita, "How can you hide like this? If I had a miracle like that happen to me, I would shout from the rooftop what Jesus Christ did for me!"

We talked a while longer and Rita said, "Somehow I am drawn to trust you. Maybe I will go on TV and tell my story." As we finished our visit I said, "You know Rita, I can't believe I live as close to you as I do and I never met you before today." Rita responded, "What do you mean? How close do you live?"

"If you go out your street and make a right and go to the bottom of the next hill there is a small dirt road that goes back to a farm. I live on that farm." "Oh, my goodness," she said, "I was going to meet you on Sunday." Rita Klaus was the one coming to look at the farm. Coincidence? No. As one person explained to me, not a coincidence but a Christ-incidence. Were they right!

"Christ-incidences" started to happen daily. Another example happened while I was on my boat one day. After finishing the book Pat had given me, I was convinced I had to go to Medjugorje whether or not KDKA sent me to do a story. I was sitting there wondering which travel agent I would use to get to Medjugorje, Yugoslavia, a communist country. It had to take special arrangements to get behind the Iron Curtain. Just then, Bill Harper, the guy who docked his boat next to mine, came over to visit me. He said, "Tom, you go to Europe most every fall, don't you?" "Yes, I do" I responded. "Would you do me a big favor?" I said, "You name it, Bill, you got it."

He said, "My sister, Joycelyn, is in the travel business, and I would appreciate it if you would book your trip overseas through her."

I said, "Absolutely! It doesn't make any difference who I book it through. As long as she can do the job, I'll be more than happy to go and see her."

"Well, there is one catch." he said, "She lives in New Orleans. You'll have to make a long distance phone call." I said, "Give me the number, I'll make the call."

I called his sister and explained that her brother had asked me to contact her. I said I was going over to Europe and he had suggested I book my plans through her.

She chuckled and said, "That Billy! He's always trying to do such nice things for me, but he is a little off base here. You see, I'm not a regular travel agent. I don't book trips throughout the world, I only book trips to a little place in Yugoslavia that more than likely you've never heard of.. . Medjugorje."

I don't think that it was ever easier for a person to get to Medjugorje. Christ-incidence?

Chapter 6

Medjugorje

In the summer of 1987, Uncle Stanley and I decided to go to Medjugorje with the expectation of touring several other countries. After all that had happened to me, Medjugorje was most definitely the reason we were going to Europe, but it wasn't going to be a major portion of the trip. I had set aside two or three days for the pilgrimage. The rest of the time we were going to travel through Romania, Bulgaria, Hungary, Czechoslovakia and Poland. We booked the Medjugorje portion of the trip through Joycelyn. A local travel agent and friend, Ira Horowitz, scheduled our air transportation.

The decision to go to Europe at this particular time did not make everyone happy. My mother was very ill. She suffered from cancer and in September 1987, she took a turn for the worse. Things didn't look good for her recovery. I was going on this pilgrimage and the rest of my family was upset. They felt it irresponsible for me to go off on vacation to Europe when the possibility existed of my mother dying. I didn't look at it as going on a vacation. In my mind, there was absolutely nothing I could do for my mother at home. Over there, there was something I could do about it. I could pray and ask the Lord's intercession. So I was going against the wishes of my family. On September 18, 1987, Stanley and I departed Pittsburgh.

I have a long-time friend, Erika Becse who emigrated from Hungary to the U. S. in 1965, when she was eighteen years old. Her mother and stepfather, Piri and

Matyas Nagy, had just visited America in May. Although they didn't speak English, they conveyed through their daughter, an invitation to visit them if we were ever near Hungary. Stanley and I decided to take Erika's parents up on their offer.

We flew from New York to Budapest expecting them to meet us at the airport, as arranged. We got our luggage and waited awhile, not quite understanding why the Nagys weren't there. Then we had our first encounter with the language barrier. Neither of us could speak Hungarian. We approached person after person before we finally found a man who led us to an information desk. There a woman who spoke some English helped us. She paged Erika's parents.

Unbeknownst to us, there were two sections to the airport in Budapest and the Nagys were waiting at the other section. They heard the page and made their way to where we were. Although the experience was enjoyable, it was most difficult because of that language barrier.

I had reserved a rental car for us to pick up at the Budapest airport. Since only Stanley and I would be using it to travel around Europe, I'd decided against a *very* expensive larger car in favor of a more economical one. What I thought would be a nice, smaller car.

Much to our surprise, the Nagys had taken a bus to the airport intending to ride back home with us. I went to the rental counter and picked up the car. It was called a Zastava, a Soviet car. It was the smallest, most bare bones vehicle I had ever seen in my life. I knew immediately it was not capable of transporting four people and our luggage. But that didn't stop us. We loaded as much luggage as we could into the trunk. What didn't fit we tied on the roof of the car. The Nagys, Stanley and I squeezed into the car and started off. Erika's parents were pointing left or right, guiding us to their home with hand signals. After about an hour, we arrived at the village of Jaszbereny.

The countryside going from Budapest to Jaszbereny was interesting but it really isn't all that different from Pennsylvania. There were rolling hills with people working in the fields. There was obviously less technology at work there than in America, but it most certainly didn't seem like they were particularly oppressed. Their lives were simple, but not depressing, as I had imagined.

We got to the Nagy home where we were to stay. The property was enclosed by a very high, wooden fence that connected to the house at each end on the street side. There was no door at the front, just windows. The only way to gain entry was through a locked gate in the fence. Inside was a lovely, private garden. The house was comfortably large and furnished in typical European style.

Settling in with the Nagys was enjoyable. They offered us a drink, so of course, trying to be cordial guests, we accepted. It was served in a small glass, straight from the bottle. They pronounced the name of the drink, Palinka, but I think we would put it under the classification of "White Lightning." Wow! It was throat-burning, mind altering and more powerful than anything I had ever drunk. It tasted great! Then we had a drink that tasted a little bit like caramel, Unikum. This was delicious. After trying several different drinks, we figured it was best to slow down. We were having a hard enough time trying to communicate with them sober.

After a wonderful meal, they showed us to our room. Actually, it was a one-room guest house that sat in a corner of their beautiful courtyard.

Later that afternoon they took us to the motel next door, where they found someone who could speak some English. We tried to explain that we were only going to stay a couple of days, but it was difficult because the translator's English was very limited.

When we returned to our hosts' home and sat down, the most we could do was smile at each other. Their little dog, Mosi, was on the floor next to me. We understood each other perfectly! I'd pet him and he'd whine contentedly. When I stopped, he woofed to get my attention, so I would pet him some more. That was easy!

The Nagy's hospitality was unbelievable. They were probably the most loving and generous people I have ever known. I wanted them to know where we were headed and share with them what I had read about Medjugorje. I tried, but I just couldn't make it through the language barrier. I wasn't able to tell them much at all.

They took us for a tour around Jaszbereny. Both of them were smiling when they, jokingly, pointed out the Jaszbereny "Mall." It was one building and very limited in what they had for sale. You see, while visiting the United States, they had been totally overwhelmed by the size of our malls and grocery stores and the amount of merchandise for sale. I was glad they could laugh at the difference.

We went shopping at the Jaszbereny "Mall." I bought myself a leather trench coat, which I still have today. It has served me well, probably because it was made in Poland, the land of my heritage.

Their guided tour next took us through the village itself, where we stopped at the local church. I was surprised to see that here, in a communist country, they did have an open church and people were still able to attend. I understood that communism made their lives more difficult; and although they were harassed for it, some did go to church.

We went back to their home, ate a little snack and turned in for the night. The next morning after breakfast, we started putting our things back into the car. I still needed to try to tell them where we were going. So I got out my brand new rosary. It was the first rosary I'd ever owned in my entire life. My wife bought it for me on my birthday, a month before we left. I pointed to the medal that was on the rosary with the picture of the Blessed Mother, then I pointed to a map I had. It didn't show the town of Medjugorje, but it showed the region in which it is located. I pointed to my eye and pointed to Stanley and me, trying to show them that we were going to see the Blessed Mother. We folded our hands to show that we were going there to pray. I had no idea whether they understood that Mary, Our Mother, was appearing in a little town in Yugoslavia. We said our good-byes, got into our rental car and drove off.

As we drove, we began to experience the fun of traveling in a country where we couldn't read road signs and there were no route numbers. In the United States, if you want to go somewhere, you have route and exit numbers for highways. Roads and streets have names. Accurate directions can be given to almost anywhere you want to go. In Hungary, and in most communist countries of Europe, there are no route numbers. There are just signs along the roads indicating the next town. You have to plan your trip from town to town to town, even making turns by town location. Often it was very difficult to decide where the turns should be taken. All we could do was hope that the road we were traveling would eventually take us to Yugoslavia and our next destination, Medjugorje.

We drove as fast as that little car could go. After about six hours, we stopped at one of the few little shops along the road. All they had for sale was some lunch meat, some cheese and a couple bottles of what appeared to be orange drink. We each bought a bottle of the orange drink and a little something to eat. We got back in our car. I told Stanley to open the orange drink so we could quench our great thirst. He opened up one bottle and gave it to me. I lifted it to my mouth and took a great big swig and almost choked. It turned out not to be orange drink but an orange syrup used to *make* orange drink! It was concentrate and it tasted terrible at full strength. So we went back into the store to see if there was something we could mix with it. We bought bottled water, but it was carbonated. It was like a comedy. . . Stanley and I trying to pour this thick syrup into the bottles of bubbly water. When we attempted to shake it up to mix it, the carbonated water would fizz up and run all over the place. We managed to salvage enough to satisfy our thirst and had a good laugh doing it. We learned to deal with the little problems that came up as we traveled. Stanley and I were having a very good time.

Driving from Hungary to Yugoslavia, we experienced our first border crossing. It was very different from the familiar process of driving through North America. Going from the U.S. into Canada or Mexico might take you a couple of minutes. In Yugoslavia, the car was searched and documents were carefully examined. We learned to be patient at that first border crossing. It took an hour or more but, finally, we were in Yugoslavia. We had about six more hours of driving before reaching Medjugorje so we pushed on.

About 9:30 p.m., we were nearing our destination. I could just feel it . . . from miles away! The excitement was building and my heart was pounding. There was no doubt in my mind that the Mother of God was appearing in Medjugorje, and now here I was, only moments away. Even now, thinking about it brings tears to my eyes.

We finally came to that last right hand turn where the sign pointing down the road read "Medjugorje." Then we saw the twin spires of St. James Church. It truly did choke me up when I realized that I was really there. The journey was over, or so I thought. What I was about to discover was that my journey was just beginning.

We parked our car and walked across a courtyard to St. James Church. People were just beginning to file out. We wanted to ask someone how to find the woman with whom we were to stay. Although I knew her name, I didn't know how to pronounce it. I saw a man dressed in a brown habit. I didn't know what to call him; he looked priestly. Approaching him I said, "Excuse me, Father, do you speak English?" In a low-bass tone he said, with a heavy accent, "But of course, I do."

I explained to him that I was looking for a certain woman and asked if he could possibly help me find her. I produced a picture Joycelyn had given me to aid in finding her, just in case I had trouble. Thank goodness she had, because now I needed to use it. I showed the picture to him and asked, "Do you know this woman, Father? I'm supposed to stay at her house and I need to find it. Can you help me?"

"But, of course I can," he said. " Her name is Jelena. That's me standing beside her." Sure enough, there was a man in a brown robe standing beside the woman I now knew to be Jelena. It was another one of those Christ-incidences, I guess. My having this picture and meeting this priest, who, I later found out, was the pastor of St. James Church, was meant to be.

Father called someone over and asked him to take us to Jelena's house. He knew right where to go. We drove a long distance, or at least it seemed that way. Maybe it was just the excitement of being in Medjugorje. The man took us to Jelena's house and he made the introductions. Jelena showed us to the room where we were to sleep. The room was barren; a picture of Jesus, four white walls and two couches. The backs of the couches folded down to provide more width for sleeping, similar to an old-fashioned davenport.

Stanley and I unpacked our car and brought our things in while Jelena made us something to eat. She explained it was well after the dinner hour but she knew we had to be hungry. She was communicating as best she could, as we were. It was a little easier than it was in Hungary, because Jelena had housed many English-speaking pilgrims, and had picked up a few words.

As she cooked, we unpacked our things. I was overwhelmed by a desire to go over to Krizevac Mountain. I don't know if it was my intent to climb that mountain right then, or just go over to be near it. Without saying a word to anyone, I got back into our car and headed for Krizevac. The young man that took us to Jelena's house had pointed it out as we passed it. I returned to the spot to which he had pointed, parked the car and got out. It seemed a little cool so I slipped into the leather jacket I carried. I tried to see the mountain, but it was too dark to see anything. Suddenly, the idea of climbing to the top came to me. As I stood there it became a certainty. I didn't know how high the mountain was nor did I know how long it was going to take me to get to the top. What if it was such a long climb that I couldn't make it back down that night? I had a sleeping bag in the trunk for emergencies. I pulled out the sleeping bag and lifted it over my shoulder and started up the mountain at a rapid pace.

I rounded the first bend, came upon a cross and thought it was nice that someone put a cross there to mark the start of the journey. I continued on past the cross, full steam ahead. I started to get warm and unzipped my jacket and pushed on a little farther. It got warmer. Soon I was sweating so much that having my jacket on wasn't such a good idea. I took it off, and carried it and my sleeping bag under my arm.

I could sense that the path was pretty rocky, but my attention was drawn away from where my feet were going to what I was hearing. It was a howling sound that was bone-chilling and it was unlike anything I'd ever heard before. I live on a farm and from my house you can barely see a light in the distance. My closest neighbors are a half mile away. I do a lot of walking on my farm, sometimes alone at night, and I've never felt any fear. I am certainly not afraid of the dark. But this sound had me concerned, because I couldn't identify it, and it seemed to be getting closer, coming at me from all directions.

I became more and more frightened and I started to pray. What did I know about praying? I couldn't remember any prayers. Although I was trying to learn a couple, I still didn't know any by heart.

I started thinking back to my childhood and any religious words I might have learned. I came up with the words, "*Yea, though I walk through the valley of the shadow of death, I will fear no evil.*" (Psalm 23). I couldn't remember anything else. Then I started saying, "Jesus, I'm scared, and I know from the little bit I've read about you that if I trust in you, I will always be okay. But I'm frightened here and I don't know what that sound is and it's coming closer. Help me, *please*."

Then I came upon a second cross. This time I didn't pass by the cross so cavalierly. This time I fell on my knees at the base of the cross, embraced it and kissed it. The strange sound started to dissipate and then vanished completely. I still don't know what the sound was; I just know that it frightened me and brought me to my knees, embracing the cross.

I continued my journey and came upon cross after cross. Each cross I came to I embraced and kissed. I poured out my heart to Jesus. I told Him I was confused and that I was trying hard to understand what was going on. Suddenly, the climb and my progress seemed to be impeded by thorny brush and I turned around not knowing which way to go. I wondered to myself if I were lost. Then I heard that voice in my head, *"Yes, Thomas, you are."* Somehow I was turned around and guided back to the path.

Back on the path, I climbed higher and higher. While embracing one of the crosses, I thought to myself, "This must be the twelve Stations of the Cross." Oh, I know now that there are fourteen, but I didn't know it then.

Just ahead in the moonlight, I could see the huge white cross gleaming majestically above the scrubby trees. It was the cross that was pictured in the book, "The Queen of Peace Visits Medjugorje." I rushed forward. I wanted to kneel down in front of the cross and pour my heart out to Jesus.

When I approached the front of the cross, there were four or five people sitting at the base and one man off in the distance. What I wanted to do, I didn't want anyone around to see or hear. Drifting off to the right of the cross, I waited. I asked the Lord if I could be alone with Him. In a few minutes, the people had gone.

There I was, all alone with this huge cross. It must have been thirty or forty feet high. I knelt down at the base of the cross and started to talk to Jesus about my sins.

I can recall the tremendous emotion I felt, kneeling there. For the first time I experienced true contrition for my sins. I started to list them to the Lord, one at a time. I begged His forgiveness for all the things I had done in my life that offended Him. I never knew a human being could cry that hard.

I must have been kneeling there for an hour or more when I heard this beautiful music coming up the mountain. It sounded like angels singing. In five or ten minutes a group of pilgrims arrived at the top; it was they who were singing. They approached the cross and formed a semi-circle around me, trapping me against the cross. If I had wanted to leave, I would have had to excuse myself and break their ranks to pass through. They had already begun to pray and I didn't want to interrupt, so I just remained kneeling. At first I tried to ignore what they were saying and concentrate on my own prayers. Before this, I'd been speaking aloud to the Lord. Now I was silently praying within my heart. Although I was trying to concentrate on Jesus Christ, it became impossible not to listen to the people gathered around me.

I realized it was a group from Ireland by their accents and talk of their troubled homeland. I found that they were there for the same reason as I. They wanted to lay the problems of their lives at the foot of the cross. Maybe that's what Medjugorje is all about . . . a place to come to dump your sins, lighten your load, hand it all over to Jesus, and start over.

They talked about the war in Ireland, personal problems and family problems. The Irish pilgrims finished their stay at the cross by singing another song. It was the first time I can remember having heard "Amazing Grace."

It was like Jesus Christ had sent them there to deliver a message to me! To instruct me on exactly what was going on in my life. The words were, "I once was lost and now am found, was blind and now I see." This was truly what was happening to me. I had been blind and the blindness was being lifted. I was lost in a world of materialism, a life of serving myself and those close to me. Jesus was never part of it and now He was showing me how wrong that was. The effect that song had on me was tremendous. I thought I was crying hard before, but as the Irish pilgrims departed singing, they left me lying on the ground a slobbering mass of nothing.

I don't know how long it took me to regain some semblance of control, but eventually I got up from the cross and walked around to the other side. I had now been at the foot of the cross for about an hour and a half on my knees. With rheumatoid arthritis, that's virtually impossible. Obviously there was tremendous grace at work there.

It was becoming quite cold forcing me to put on my coat and zip it up. I thought about lying down in my sleeping bag and going to sleep. The whole mountaintop is very rocky. Although I couldn't see much in the dark, I could feel the sharp rocks with my feet. I searched around for a smooth place on the ground to lay my sleeping bag. The little blue foam pad I brought to help protect me from the ground, did not prevent the rocks from protruding right through it. There were no smooth spots. I moved again and again. It seemed impossible to find anything that even came close to being comfortable. So I just accepted my plight and tried to fall asleep on the rocks in the shadow and splendor of this wonderful cross.

Its silhouette against the sky made the cross look pure black. I looked up at the stars and there were millions of them. I don't think I have ever seen the sky filled with so many stars. I recall seeing three shooting stars as I gazed upwards. They represented, to me, the Father, the Son and the Holy Spirit.

At this point in my conversion, I was starting to find something special in everything, realizing that nothing ever happens without a reason. People tell me I read too much into things. I think that people just don't read *enough* into what happens to them. This world is one big miracle after another and we are too blind to see them.

It was difficult to fall asleep. It was late September and although it didn't seem that cold down at the base of the mountain, it got extremely cold at the top. Though I was tucked deep in my down sleeping bag, the bitterness of the cold was biting. I don't know how long it took me to fall asleep but I did eventually. While speaking to Jesus, I just faded off into a sleep that would find me awakening in the morning, a brand new human being.

The sky was never bluer. The air never smelled sweeter. Everything seemed so crisp and clean. There is a phrase in religious circles that I've always disliked . . . "a born again Christian." Boy, did I feel born again! I felt like a brand new little child. I went off that mountain with bells on my feet and feeling truly forgiven!

I got about halfway down the mountain and was amazed how rocky it was! I had no recollection of the huge boulders that I would have had to climb over to get to the top. I recall the climb being somewhat difficult, but looking at what I saw on the ground before me, the massive boulders, the treacherous terrain; most certainly the Lord was guiding me up that mountain the previous evening.

I was amazed to run into Stanley coming up the mountain. My uncle was not a happy camper. He was upset with me for having taken off without saying anything to him the night before. He suspected that I had headed for the mountain because I had talked a lot about the cross at its summit, and how I wanted to go there. We ironed out our differences and arranged to meet later in the afternoon and do some of that 'Medjugorje stuff'. What does one do in Medjugorje? Well, you pray. And in your spare time, you pray. And when there is nothing else to do, you pray.

My first few days in Medjugorje I evaluated what I thought was going on there. I came to believe that the power of Medjugorje lay in the feeling that someone was listening to my prayers there. In Medjugorje I learned to pray with my heart. Praying with your heart brings you to say prayers that I feel God would *want* to listen to. Sincere prayers, prayed through tears, expressing words of deep contrition, sorrow for sins and love for God, bring results. I feel certain that the prayers I prayed in Medjugorje were heard, because I was learning to pray with my *heart*.

When I prayed seriously and attended all the services, every door that could possibly be opened in Medjugorje, was opened for me. Most pilgrims are enthralled at the possibility of standing with a crowd in front of a visionary's home and getting a glimpse of one of them. I got that chance along with everybody else and together we stood in front of Vicka's home listening to her speak about her experiences through an interpreter.

The desire in my heart was to sit down with a couple of the visionaries and talk to them one on one. I was particularly drawn to Marija and Vicka. I had brought a home camcorder with me. I wanted to ask questions on tape so I could present the information to KDKA in hopes of stimulating their interest in this subject. I made a request to meet with the children through an interpreter. As a result, I was invited first into Marija's home and then Vicka's.

This was how the process went. Uncle Stanley, an interpreter and I entered Marija's home and were introduced. We sat down, I got out my Bible and asked if we could pray before we started the interview. I think that made Marija very happy, because she smiled and said, "yes". Maybe that is what moved her to spend so much time with us.

After praying together, we started the interview. As I began to ask questions, I realized what a complete lack of knowledge I had about my faith. The questions I asked seemed so frivolous and became embarrassing to me, but we went on for about a half hour.[1]

Q: What would you say to the management of a large television station to convince them that they ought to invest the time to come here and do a story on Medjugorje?

***Marija*:**   **The message of Our Lady stresses the importance of changing our lives. Everyone is involved in this conversion and so it should touch everyone. Our Lady has said that her message is one of conversion, prayer, fasting, confession, and Holy Mass and this concerns everyone, this returning to God, and she has given this message for everyone and everyone should be concerned.**

Q: I'm having much difficulty convincing them (KDKA) to do a story about Medjugorje. Is there a reason this station should do it?

---

[1]   The interview has been edited to eliminate the translator's portion.

Marija: The most important thing is to pray and to give good example and if we give good example, then we can give others the message.

Q: Has the Madonna said anything particular to Americans because of their affluent lifestyles?

Marija: She isn't saying anything special to any particular country. What she's saying is really for everyone. The whole world.

Q: Then I guess that the Madonna is pleased when she sees a lot of Americans coming.

Marija: Our Lady is really happy whenever she sees anyone come to Medjugorje and practice her messages.

Q: Does the Blessed Mother want people to go back to their home countries to be what Father Jozo said we should be, "apostles?"

Marija: Our Lady is always happy when people go back and give witness with their lives, not with their words. Because when we give witness with our lives, then we can change others.

Q: I don't know if it's true for the rest of the world but in America there are many skeptics. What does it take to convince people that need miracles, or proof given to them, to change their lifestyles and stop ignoring God?

Marija: She says that the best way to help these people to change is through prayer. Prayer and fasting. Because with fasting we remove the obstacles that keep us from believing and so with prayer and fasting we will keep coming to the will of the Father.

Q: But if I am a believer, if I pray and fast, will that be enough of an example to convince someone that doesn't really believe at all?

Marija: **Yes, it is.**

Q: They say that miracles happen here, that the sun spins; that the cross spins on the hill. Do these things really happen?

Marija: **Yes, Our Lady says that these things happen so that we can have greater faith.**

Q: It is known that good Catholics believe in the Madonna, but there are many religions in the United States that believe in God and practice their faith and go to church but they believe the Madonna was just the Mother of God; she was just the Mother of Jesus Christ, and they can't believe she could be in Medjugorje because that would make her equal to Jesus Christ.

Marija: **Our Lady has come only to help us go back to Jesus and that Jesus should be the center of our lives, so this shouldn't be a threat.**

Q: But some don't believe at all that She can even be alive and be in Heaven, that She was just a human being who died like anyone else. They can't believe in Her because it's against their teaching.

Marija: That's why Our Lady took us as witnesses and showed us Heaven, Purgatory, and Hell, so that we can be encouraged by that and know that they exist.

Q: She has shown the six children these things but the non-believers haven't seen them, so they say that she should be in the grave just like anybody else waiting for the Final Judgement Day.

Marija: It is very important for us to pray for their conversion because Jesus said, "He that knocks, the door will be opened to them." So we should pray for them so that their conversion can happen.

Q: Would it be the same for the Jewish population that believes that the Savior hasn't come yet and that Jesus was just a prophet?

Marija: It's just as important to pray for their conversion.

Q: I've heard that the children have been given ten secrets. From what I understand, the first seven have been of personal nature and the last three are chastisements. Could you explain the ten secrets?

Marija: At the present time, two of the children have ten, Ivanka and Mirijana, and the rest have received nine secrets.

Q: Can you not say even that there are chastisements?

Marija: Our Lady has nothing further to say to the world about the secrets.

Q: So what we hear, that the first seven are for the children and that the last three are the chastisements . . . we should not believe then. That is just rumor?

Marija: Mirjana has been told concerning the secrets and maybe she has said something concerning the secrets. But I don't know because I haven't spoken to Mirjana about them. She says that the only one she can speak about is the seventh secret. Because of prayer, it has been completely eliminated. There is no longer a seventh secret.

Q: Is it possible that other secrets could be eliminated through prayer?

Marija: Our Lady hasn't spoken about the others in that way.

Q: People are always asking questions. Are they possibly asking the wrong questions? Are there questions they should be asking instead?

Marija: We pray for their conversion during the apparition. We take their intentions and this particular intention to Our Lady every night.

Q: In many of the messages I've read where the Blessed Mother scolds you and the other children because you're not doing what her messages tell you. Do you feel like you're being scolded?

Marija: **If we do something that isn't right, she corrects us, but she does not scold us every day.**

Q: Not everyday, just sometimes.

Marija: **Just the times when we need it.**

Q: The pressure from having a changed life like this, from living a quiet simple life in a Yugoslavian village to having people around your house all the time would change anyone from a nice person. How do you tend to handle the stress that this situation creates?

Marija: **It is very difficult to have your life changed with so many people around always, but it brings also so many of God's blessings on what we do and makes it easy.**

Q: Are there times when you wish there weren't so many people, that you wished for a quiet moment?

Marija: **When I need to, I go to a quiet place. You find time for everything, what you need to do.**

Q: I had my medals blessed by the priest in church. I wore my medals in church, when the Blessed Mother was speaking to you. Were they blessed by Our Lady also?

Marija: Yes, everyday I ask Our Blessed Lady to bless everyone and everything in the church, and Our Lady does, every day.

Q: This is indeed a special grace to the people that are present!

Marija: The blessing that Our Lady gives the blessed items we get are a protection, and they are to help us. We should wear for our protection the things that God has given.

Q: A lot of Catholics and priests, are waiting until the Pope says that this is really happening. Are Catholics not to be concerned with this until the church makes a decision? What does our Lady have to say about that?

Marija: Jesus has said you know a tree by its fruits and Medjugorje has been given fruits. It will be years before the church will be able to recognize what has happened.

Q: Is there an immediacy to the message and in the church taking a long time in a decision, could this be damaging and possibly cause a loss of souls?

Marija: Our Lady has said that this is a time for prayer and we should take this time and pray and then the fruits will be given.

Q: If I would listen to my priest who says do not go because it is not of the church, and I feel I must come, am I wrong in doing that or is it alright?

Marija: The truth is that Our Lady is appearing here and she's appearing here continually and the church can't give official approval until the apparitions are over. Then the church can give official approval, but then it will be too late. It's not in ten years, it's today that man must change. Conversion must take place now.

Q: Are you telling the people who may watch this video tape to change their lives and reconcile themselves to God right away no matter what anyone is saying to them?

Marija: To the people who are watching, now is the time for them to convert as Our Lady has said it's not in ten years she needs your conversion, because we don't even know that we'll be alive in ten years. *Today* she's asking us for our conversion, *today* she's asking us to pray and fast and live the messages and return to our God.

Q: Is the church accurate in moving so slowly? Maybe they should have acted upon this a lot more quickly.

Marija: The church always moves slowly on these matters and that is good because they are asking for proof. They need to find out what's happening. We need to live in the practice (messages) so that the church can go on with approval and it is through us living in the practice that the church will find the proof it needs for official approval. Our Lady has given us all these messages and all are already given in Holy Scriptures and she has come to help us put into practice what already has been given.

Q: How would blessing with holy water affect a Satanic vision?

Marija: **Our Lady has said that Satan runs away from anything that has been blessed that is put in his presence.**

Q: Do you think that a TV station that has the ability to talk to millions of people has a responsibility to let people know about Medjugorje.

Marija: **Every person is free to respond to what God is asking them to do.**

Q: Are there other apparitions going on? There are reports of apparitions in Russia, and in Italy to a priest. Are there other apparitions going on?

Marija: **Our Lady has not said anything specific about any other apparitions.**

Q: Do you have a loving, caring relationship with Our Lady? As though she were your best friend?

Marija: **Even deeper and more loving than that.**

I wanted to express my thanks to Marija, and as she extended her hand to shake my hand, I bent down to kiss her hand. I was so embarrassed when she withdrew her hand rapidly and left me there kissing air. That little incident stayed with me a long time and I often wondered why she did that. All I had wanted to do was express my gratitude and I felt truly offended by her reaction. Later I will explain how the tables were turned to make me understand what had happened.

Marija has a very serious personality and only occasionally would she smile. She's very meek, mild and humble. When we visited with Vicka we found her smiling and happy. She enthusiastically expressed her affection for the Blessed Mother and the Lord. When she explained something, she just seemed to explode with joy. She was outgoing and so effervescent, yet humble and meek.

I talked with Vicka for about a half hour as well and this time I tried to make my questions more meaningful. The interview was a little more coherent than the first one, but still I was not pleased with the questions.[2]

Q: Is there an immediacy about the messages that the Madonna is giving to the children and does this conflict with the church opinion of wait until we prove that this is right?

Vicka: **They are messages of peace, love, prayer, fasting, reconciliation and penance, and are given to us so that we can understand and live them. If we**

---

[2] I would like to enter this note of caution. When asking the same question of several visionaries I have received conflicting answers. This is not necessarily contradictory, because each child has been given varying degrees of information and answers with the knowledge they have been given to that point in time

live them, eventually, we will understand what they mean. There is no such immediacy.

Q: Does it bother the Madonna or does she wish that the Catholic Church would respond sooner?

Vicka: **Our Blessed Mother says nothing about that**.

Q: Many rumors come out of Medjugorje about things that are going to happen. Rumors about impending disaster before the year is out. Do you know anything about this?

Vicka: **I know nothing of this. Maybe some people made up those things.**

Q: The young people are in the process of receiving ten messages. Is it true that the seventh one has been eliminated?

Vicka: **Those secrets that Our Lady gives; she gives ten of them to Mirijana and Ivanka, and nine to myself and the other three. The seventh secret is not totally eliminated; it's just reduced.**

Q: Your sickness seems to be unexplainable, do you think it is a test of your faith and is it endurable?

Vicka: **I don't like to talk about it.**

Q: We have read that you would like to be a nun someday. Is that true?

Vicka: **Yes, that is true.**

Q: Did you ever have the idea of being a nun before the apparitions?

Vicka: **No! Of course not. (Laughter)**

Q: It is said, and I don't mean to offend you, that if you have an illness, you cannot be a nun. If this is your desire, could this possibly stop you from doing that?

Vicka: **I am ready to go where God calls me. Let God's will be done. I don't think of it as some kind of sickness.**

Q: All of the words that the Madonna speaks of: peace, prayer, fasting; there may be people who don't believe at all. This means nothing to them. Is there anything you can say to people who don't believe enough to get involved in these things, to help change their minds?

Vicka: **We can pray for those people.**

Q: The station that I work for has the ability to reach millions of people. Is there anything personal that you would say to them?

Vicka: **There isn't anything special I would say to all those people. Even though they are so far away, the prayer group and the visionaries keep them in mind and recommend them to our Lady, even though they cannot come here. We will keep them in our prayers. There is one thing I would like to tell them. The only real way to live is through**

Jesus Christ and I think everybody should try to go that way.

Q: Do you have any special feelings when you're with the Blessed Mother, any difference in intensity of feelings than when you're with your friend or somebody you care a lot about?

***Vicka*: I cannot express my feelings when I am in the presence of Our Lady.**

My interviews with the visionaries placed in my heart an overwhelming desire to be present with them during an apparition. The Blessed Mother was appearing to Marija and Jakov in the choir loft of St. James Church everyday. Fr. Slavko Barbaric was always present. I walked up to him one day and said, "Father, I would like to be in the apparition room with the children when our Blessed Mother appears. I work for a television station and I would like to shoot some video tape." In the back of my mind I thought this would enhance my case to convince KDKA to do a story on this subject.

He said, "Absolutely not, that's out of the question," and he strolled off. I said, "But, Father," . . . he kept going, not listening to me.

I saw him the next day and I asked him again. "No, I told you yesterday, and the answer is still no," he said, without stopping.

The third day I stopped him again. "Excuse me, Father. I know I've already asked if I could go up to the choir loft and be with the children during the apparition. Before you say no again, let me say this: if I can go back home and relate my feelings, my experience, to one other human being, and it brings them back to Jesus Christ; if it causes one conversion, you tell me that's not worth it, and I'll leave you alone. I won't ask again."

He looked at me with eyes that seem to stare right through me and he said, "You be here at six o'clock, right by that door, and tell no one . . . no one! Stand by that door and if I nod to you, get in the door as quickly as you can."

Oh, I was there at six o'clock alright. Marija went in, then Jakov, and Father was right behind them. He nodded his head and I followed them. We went up the staircase of the bell tower to the second or third landing leading to the choir loft. The pilgrims were filling up the church and starting to pray. I started to walk across the choir loft floor and Father instructed me, "No, don't let anyone see you. Get down low." I crawled on my hands and knees across the floor to the other side. There, kneeling in front of a statue of the Blessed Virgin Mother, were Jakov and Marija.

Positioning myself a little off to the side, I started to ask myself what I was doing there. I had no right to be there and shouldn't have intruded. I didn't even know what to do.

Soon Father escorted two other men into the loft. They had a professional television camera much like the one I used at KDKA. They started to set up behind me in order to catch the apparition on video tape. I felt like a rank amateur with my home VHS system next to those guys with that big professional unit, but I was prepared to do the best I could with what I had. I thought I should be praying, so I took out my rosary and started to pray. The other two men began to chit-chat, talk shop. That was up-setting me to no end. I turned to them and I said, "Don't you realize where you are?" They immediately stopped their conversation. The Mother of God was going to be ap-pearing right next to us in a few moments, and I couldn't understand how they could even open their mouths except to pray.

I returned to praying, falling into a depth of prayer that was then, and still is now, beyond my comprehension. I just slipped away, bent over, with my rosary in my hand, and slid into semi-consciousness. I was unaware of what was going on beside me for the next seven minutes; the vi-sion had begun without my realizing it.

The other crew was busy videotaping, getting shots of the visionaries in their ecstasy as the Blessed Mother spoke to them. There I was, oblivious to it all. Next I felt someone shaking me and I heard this voice, "The vision, the vision." It was Fr. Slavko, bringing me back to reality. The vision, I believe, lasted a total of eleven minutes that day, and seven or eight minutes had already gone by.

I came to and looked beside me, and the children were no longer staring at the statue of the Blessed Mother, but much higher in the air. I could see them nodding their heads, with their eyes transfixed. Their lips moved in uni-son as though they were reciting poetry, but there was no sound. Sometimes they would smile. I immediately reached for my video camera and started to tape.

I got wide shots, shots of their faces and close-ups of their eyes. It was so frustrating using a home camcorder for this task, because I had to shoot toward a window. That is one thing that can't be done with a home camcorder because the iris is automatic. The iris is the part of the camera that controls the amount of light that enters the lens, which determines the exposure of the video tape. When the light from the window hits the lens, the whole picture darkens up. The frustration continued as I tried to shoot what I was seeing and experiencing. I did not have the technology with me to get the images I wanted.

The vision ended. Marija instantly got up and went over to a small bench, got a little pad, and began to write what I can only assume was the message just delivered by Our Lady. When she was finished, Father Slavko read what Marija had written and she nodded her head as though confirming the meaning of what he saw on the paper.

I watched this process while I knelt there. I tried to return to prayer, but my mind was so overwhelmed with a feeling of euphoria that it was difficult. What a wonderful experience! So much that I didn't understand seemed to be happening at one time.

Suddenly, I felt that this was not the place for me to be, and I decided to get out of there. So no one would see me, I started to crawl across the floor of the choir loft. I got over to the door on the other side of the room, and there was Father, standing there. He pointed for me stay exactly where I was . . . I wasn't leaving. He wasn't going to allow anyone to see me emerge from this place. He did not want to hear the complaints if anyone discovered that I'd been in the choir loft with the visionaries. Left with no other choice, I found a little kneeler and I started to listen to the Mass going on downstairs.

I became absorbed in the Mass. It was the most wonderful Mass I had ever experienced. I wanted so badly to see the part of the Mass where the Eucharist is elevated, the consecration. I wanted to see Jesus, because I truly believed then, as I do now, that the consecrated host *is* the Body and Blood of Christ. I peeked up over the balcony and saw all the people in St. James Church. It was almost frightening to look down at them, questioning again what I was doing up there.

Then it dawned on me. I was trapped in the balcony! I had become so accustomed to receiving Jesus Christ everyday. I couldn't see how I was going to be able go to communion, and it hurt so badly, I started to cry. I didn't want anyone to hear me crying and tried to contain it inside and that made it worse. The tears were rolling down my face. I got my handkerchief out. Then I felt a tap on my shoulder. It was the visionary, Marija. She motioned for me to come with her and pointed at her tongue. Suddenly there was a big smile on my face as I realized she was leading me to where we could receive the Holy Eucharist.

I followed her down the stairwell of the bell tower and she motioned for me to stand in front of a door. We stood there for a few minutes. Suddenly, the door opened, and there were a thousand people standing out there to get a glimpse of Marija and Jakov, and there I was. Again, I thought, "What in the world am I doing here?"

The priest came over and gave Jakov his Jesus, Marija her Jesus, and then me, my Jesus. Then he closed the door, and we went back upstairs until Mass was over. I used the word 'euphoric' before; but it's the only way to describe the state I was in.

I recall nothing else until I found myself outside the church, where I met up with Stanley. He said, "Where have you been? I've been looking all over the place for you." I answered, "Gee, Stan, I was up in the choir loft with the visionaries." He was wide-eyed. "How was it?" "I can't even explain it," I replied softly. "I'm three feet off the ground and if I'm a little incoherent, you'll have to excuse me. That truly was the most powerful experience of my entire life!"

The miracles in Medjugorje continued for me. One day outside St. James Church, the sky caught my attention. I looked up and there were two suns. Both of them were gyrating violently. Then they came together as one. A big, dark disk moved in front of the sun, and I was able to stand there and look at it for a very long time. This amazed me as I watched different colors spewing out of the top of the sun. I saw images being created from this red color that poured from it.

Being able to stare at the sun for any period of time certainly defies conventional wisdom. I remember very little about my high school education, but I do remember my favorite class, physics. We were taught that to view an eclipse of the sun it was absolutely necessary to look through several layers of smoked glass to protect your eyes. Otherwise, it would permanently damage your retinas and could cause blindness. There I was, looking directly at the late afternoon sun for a prolonged period, and it didn't bother me in the least.

On the third day, I changed my normal practice of going inside the church. It seemed every time I would sit inside the church for Mass, I'd surrender my seat to a little old Croatian lady in a babushka. I would then be standing in the aisle with many others. Being as tall as I am, I would surrender my position closer to the front to someone else, so as not to block anyone's view. After a time, I would find myself outside the Church anyway. So on this particular day, I thought, why even go inside? The rosary and Mass were broadcast on the loudspeakers outside so that everybody could participate. There were thousands of people that could not fit into the church.

I had heard that Jakov would sometimes go out through the back of the church to sit down to say his rosary. I figured, if it was good enough for him, it was good enough for me. I went around to the back of the church. I sat on the ground, with my back to the church and looked up at the beautiful cross on the top of Krizevac, reliving my experience the night I arrived. I took my rosary in hand and I started to pray. This week was the first time in my life that I had ever said the rosary, and I found it difficult. Now I was attempting to pray it in English along with the rosary being broadcast in Croatian. Imagine how difficult *that* was for me!

I tried to go along with the prayers. I had a pamphlet that helped me do that. It explained how to say the rosary and contained all the prayers I needed to know. At this point, I'd been a practicing Catholic for just over a month. I didn't know any prayers. I didn't know how to say the "Our Father" or the "Hail Mary" from memory, so I would use the rosary pamphlet. As I looked at the pictures of the mysteries and read the stories of what Jesus Christ did for me, I would look up at that cross on the mountain in awe. At one point when I looked up, a silhouette of the Blessed Mother enveloped the entire cross!

It resembled a large cloud in the shape of Mary. It lasted about eight seconds and then it disappeared. I pulled a pen from my pocket and started to draw what I saw, using the rosary pamphlet to draw on. When I finished, I thought, "Could that have really been the Blessed Mother?" It was like a battle starting in my head. One side of my mind said, "Why would the Blessed Mother appear to you?" The other side said, "But look at this, you drew it!" The response, "Yeah, but you draw a lot of things." I said to myself, "No, that's what I do for a living." I go somewhere with a camera and document what is happening at a particular scene for the entire community to see. I couldn't do that here, so I did the best I could with a pen and the rosary booklet I had. I convinced myself that it had to be the Blessed Mother I'd seen. I said to myself, "Why did it only appear for eight seconds? Maybe that's how strong my faith is, eight seconds worth."

As soon as that thought ended, the image returned. This time it lasted only *one* second. Then it went away and that voice in my head said, *"No, Thomas, this is how strong your faith is."* That reduced me to tears. There I was, sitting on the ground, crying again.

Medjugorje, as a village, was a new experience. Even the place we stayed was an important part of the pilgrimage: the environment in the homes, the meals prepared by the host families. It was like going to Grandma's: the pork chops, the mashed potatoes, the homemade soup and bread everyday, and the desserts.

All the pilgrims fell in love with the families with whom they stayed, and so did I. I felt like the Sivrics were my own family. On an afternoon walk, I got a warm feeling waving at Grandma, or Baka as they called her, tending the sheep. Or maybe we'd pass Jakov working the farm and he'd smile at us as though he knew us. Everyone in the family had his or her own work to do, all contributing to the care and feeding of the pilgrims. The families didn't have much time to sit around and watch TV. They had televisions; they had radios; they had cars just as we do. They drove small European cars that fit through the narrow dirt alleys between the houses. Their lives weren't so different from ours in some respects, except they were a lot less complicated. I found it all so intriguing because my world was so complex and that started to bother me.

Maybe that is why the Blessed Mother takes us to a place like Medjugorje; to show us how complicated our lives have become and how simple they should be.

The miracles continued. Each day the Blessed Mother had something new in store for me. Late in the evening of the fourth day, after all the services were over, I met my uncle outside the church. He said, "Tom, are you going back inside? They are going to have a healing service." I shook my head, and smiled. "No, Stan, I don't much believe in that kind of thing. Oh, I believe what happened to Rita Klaus happened. But that's one in a million. I don't know why the Lord cures some people and not others, but I don't believe just anyone can go inside a church and say, "I have this wrong with me, or that wrong with me, or I'm dying of cancer, or a bad heart, help me; and help comes. I just don't believe that. I've seen evangelists on TV, and they begin praying over people and these people supposedly walk away healed. I don't think that's really true."

Stanley said, "Go ahead. Leave me alone again." He looked awfully sad. So I said, "No, Stan, I won't leave you again. Let's go back inside." And we went back into the church.

I can remember specifically where I was in the church that evening. We sat on the left side, about halfway down toward the altar, in the center of the pew. The church was packed. There was a priest standing up in front saying, "Take what you have wrong with you, your hurts, your pains, take your heartaches and offer them up to Jesus and ask Him to help you." I thought, how silly this is. The priest went on to say, "I want this entire church linked up. Take your left hand and put it on the shoulder of the person next to you. Let's everyone be touching each other in this church as we offer our prayers to the Lord."

I put my hand on the person's shoulder to the left of me and the man to the right of me placed his hand on my shoulder. It was truly agonizing. I had stopped taking my Feldene the very first day we arrived in Medjugorje. I don't know why I stopped, I just stopped.

Feldene was an amazing drug for me. It somehow compounds in your system; the first day you take it, it takes away a little bit of the pain; the second day it takes away a little more; the third day, a little more, and each day you feel a little better. Well, that is exactly the way it works when you stop taking it also, only in reverse. In Medjugorje, when I stopped taking it, the pain got a little worse each day, and by Thursday, I found out how far advanced my arthritis was. I was truly in agony with this man's hand on my shoulder. I couldn't take it much longer, and the priest was saying, " I can feel people holding back, offer it up to Jesus."

I hung my head, and I said, "Lord, I'm sorry, I just can't buy into this. Can I just bow my head here and say a few prayers?" I bowed my head and attempted to pray, but suddenly the pain in my body jumped a considerable degree. Three times I denied the ability of Jesus to help me, and three times that pain jumped to a higher intensity. The third time it got so bad, it brought me to say these words, "Jesus, if it were possible for you to take this pain away, who am I to ask? There are people in this church in wheelchairs; why don't you take what you might give me and give it to them." And the pain jumped to a threshold that I couldn't understand. There were tears rolling down my face from the agony. Finally, I said these words to the Lord, "*Jesus, if you can take this away, please take it away.*" In the flash of a second, the pain was *gone!* I have never again had to take Feldene for rheumatoid arthritis. My own miracle cure in Medjugorje.

What started out to be a planned stay of two or three days in Medjugorje turned into an entire week. All the things that were happening to me made it impossible to leave. We had planned on going to many other places so eventually we had to pack everything back in our car and drive on. I'm sure Stanley was feeling the same as I, heartbroken at having to leave this place of grace and miracles, this place of love; the place where I learned to pray from the heart.

We sadly left Medjugorje behind and began our trip across the mountains of Yugoslavia. Our route took us through Bulgaria, Romania, Czechoslovakia, back through Hungary and into Poland.

So many things had happened on this trip, so many extraordinary experiences. It was hard to understand what they all meant as they were happening. There were also tremendous lessons in patience and love, although we didn't always react to them correctly. They were, nonetheless, experiences that inspired us.

The border crossing between Bulgaria and Romania took five or six hours, and we were searched many times. Two guards took turns going through our things. One spoke a little English and was more pleasant than the one who could not. The soldier who could not speak English went into the back seat of the rental car and found my Bible laying on top of my other belongings. He pulled it out and started to thumb through the Bible in a belligerent way, taking the pages and forcing his fingers across them to snap to the next page. I feared he was going to tear the pages, so I snatched the Bible from his hands. He got very upset at that and started arguing with me, trying to get the Bible back.

The English-speaking guard, hearing us arguing, walked over and split us up. He took possession of the Bible. He said to me, "Do you believe what's in here?" I said, "Yes, I do, every word." He said, "When is the end of the world?" I said, "Only God knows that." He closed the book and gently handed it back to me. I hoped that this little brush with the Bible was perhaps the start of his conversion.

Midway across Romania, we saw a woman standing on the road with several children. She flagged us down. We stopped to see what she wanted. Of course she spoke no English. She indicated what she wanted by tugging on my jacket. It was apparent to me that she wanted my clothes! I gestured to her that it was out of the question I pulled twenty dollars out of my wallet and gave it to her. She was tugging on my jacket, pointing to her kids. I figured surely she could *buy* some clothes with that twenty dollars!

We got back in our car and drove away. We hadn't gone very far, when it dawned on me what a foolish thing I had done. What was that woman going to do with twenty U. S. dollars in the middle of Romania, a communist country? If it wasn't useless to her, it was most certainly a dangerous thing to have in her possession. I could just hear the questions. Where did you get American money? Who gave it to you? The simplest thing I could have done was to give her what she'd wanted - my jacket. I could have easily stopped to buy other clothes in the next town. Little did I know how long that memory would haunt me.

Soon, we arrived in Poland. Stanley and I are both of Polish descent so we were excited to be there and planned to stay a week. We stopped first in Krakow, looking for a hotel that was rumored to be the best in town. We found it with little trouble.

Like our friends' home in Hungary, the hotel was furnished in a style straight out of the twenties, clean but sterile. There was nothing hanging on the walls, but the sheets were crisp, clean and inviting. Stanley and I turned in for the night.

To me, a morning without a shower is almost impossible to face. I enjoy showers and I was annoyed to find there was only a bathtub. I resigned myself to the discomfort of sitting in a bathtub and turned the water on. I held my finger on the stream of water coming out of the faucet so I could tell when it got warm, and I waited and I waited, and it wasn't getting warm.

Getting tired of kneeling there, I figured I would get my shaving equipment out while the water was getting warm. It might have taken me five minutes and when I got back the water was still cold.

I got on the phone, called room service and asked for someone who could understand English. A man who spoke a little English got on the phone. I said, "There's no hot water" and he said to me, "Maybe in two years." Two years? It was his hope that in two years their hotel might get hot water. We managed to wash in cold water.

We went out in to the streets to walk around and possibly visit with some of the local people. Stanley spoke Polish and he had a chance to use it to converse with a few people on the street, some of whom even spoke a little English. Some, when they found out we were Americans and heard about the kind of life we lived, began to cry.

The city was dusty, dirty, and the buildings were all in bad shape. It was all very sad; the demeanor of the people and the condition of the city. Stanley and I just couldn't take it. We planned to stay a week in Poland, but only stayed a day. Still today, the memories of Poland often serve as a reminder of how fortunate we are as Americans, of how much we have.

We opted for driving through Austria reliving a previous and most pleasant visit. We then headed toward Hungary to make our exit to the good old USA. We stopped back in Jaszbereny to say good-bye to the Nagys. We stayed with them overnight. The next day, they took us to Budapest to visit Erika's sister, Edith. She could speak a few words of English but not enough to have a conversation.

One word she spoke shocked us! Medjugorje! Apparently, Stan and I actually did get through to the Nagys with our attempt to tell them where we were going. They spoke to their daughter, Edith, about our journey, and she was moved to go in search of written material about Medjugorje. Edith came up with a book, written in Hungarian, about Medjugorje. "You will speak your words in foreign lands and all will understand." (From the hymn "Be Not Afraid"). I thought to myself, with all that is happening to me, I just may "see the face of God and live." We finished our trip and headed back home. I was a totally changed individual.

I'd been out of contact with my family for over two weeks and although I prayed for my mother while I was gone, I did not know if she was still alive. I was very happy to find her not only alive, but much improved. My prayers just may have done some good.

Chapter 7

The Silence Ends

I came back home with a burning desire in my heart to tell the world about Medjugorje, to tell the world about my miracle cure.

But fear of how my story would be received silenced me more than I imagined it could. What was I going to do, go around telling people that God was talking to me? That while on my boat He spoke to me and changed my life? That I suffered from arthritis and after I visited this place called Medjugorje, it was gone? I worked for KDKA-TV, a place with a supposedly great reputation for truth and honesty. Wouldn't I damage it with that kind of talk?

I could just envision my telling people that Jesus spoke to me! That would be laughable to almost everyone I knew. I imagined conversations buzzing about a crazy man at KDKA, who hears God talking to him. No, I wasn't about to tell anyone. I kept this all down deep inside my heart.

In my day-to-day life, I tried to live the Blessed Mother's messages. She was teaching us from Medjugorje that she wants us to go to Mass everyday, say fifteen decades of the rosary every day, fast on bread and water on Wednesdays and Fridays, go to confession once a month and have conversion of the heart everyday.

I started going to Mass once a week, twice a week, and then three times a week. Finding it more convenient to go close to my job, I joined St. Mary's parish in downtown Pittsburgh, often going before work. For the times that I might miss morning Mass, I looked for a place closer to home to attend in the evening. What had seemed impossible, was becoming a regular part of my life. If it looked like circumstances were building that could interfere with my getting to Mass, I would panic. I can remember talking to a priest about it, and he thought it was odd that I felt that way. Most people didn't go to Mass everyday, he explained. His explanation did not help me. The feeling I had about going everyday didn't go away.

I started to assess belonging to St. Mary's parish. Only going to Mass there, I hadn't developed relationships with any of the parishioners. I didn't take part in any of the social events and felt I was missing something by not doing so. I couldn't take part in much because of the distance from our home, so I finally found a church near my home.

It was a plain little cement block building with an austere interior, St. Ferdinand. I thought it strange that it was so plain. All the Catholic churches I recalled from my childhood were overwhelming, with magnificent architecture and statues and paintings. They *seemed* like a place where God would live. It didn't take me long to realize that no matter how magnificent or humble a church might be, *God can live there.* I went to Mass at St. Ferdinand Church on several Sundays and fell in love with the place.

On my way home from work, late one evening, I stopped at St. Ferdinand Church to visit the Lord. I went in, knelt down, and started to pray in the darkness. There wasn't another person around and somehow that pleased me. I was praying intently when a young priest, a large burly man with a beard, startled me. He looked at me quizzically and said, "Can I help you?"

"No, I'm just praying," I answered. "I'm not very good at it, but I'm learning." He was obviously puzzled about something. What I didn't realize was, he was concerned because I had parked my company vehicle just outside the door of the church. The vehicle had the station's logo, KDKA-TV, painted on the side panels and he wondered why someone from a television station was in the church.

My explanation to him was that I had recently been to a place called Medjugorje and felt moved to spend more time in church. He didn't seem to be interested in hearing about Medjugorje, even though as I found out later, he had already been there. We talked a short time and he left. I continued my praying. Little did I know then, I would end up joining St. Ferdinand Church.

Oh, how I loved kneeling in front of a crucifix all by myself, just talking to Jesus. So, the first request the Blessed Mother made, to go to Mass every day, became something very easy for me to do, something that became my desire. But the other requests were not so easy. I tried fasting, but I would get terrible headaches. Fifteen decades of the rosary every day? Well, who had the time? But amazingly, I found the time.

I found the best place for me to say the rosary was in my car, because there were no intrusions. I soon discovered that it was totally unnecessary to use the radio because my travel time, a forty-five minute commute to and from work, became my prayer time.

On the way to work, I found myself consumed with the first five decades of the rosary, The Joyful Mysteries. The way home consumed the second five decades, The Sorrowful Mysteries. Sometime during the course of the day, I would try to squeeze in the Glorious Mysteries. At times I was successful, at other times, not so successful. I know that I took a long time to say each rosary, but the Blessed Mother had influenced me to slow down by teaching me to pray with my heart.

My conversion of the heart seemed to be happening all by itself, but most certainly, Jesus was always there tugging at me. I was changing rapidly and developed an insatiable thirst for religious material. Two booklets were given to me by new friends. One booklet was on the devotion to The Divine Mercy and the other, the Pieta Prayer Book.

I was deeply intrigued by the Pieta Prayer Book. In it, I read about a series of prayers which, when said every day for a year, brought grace and indulgences beyond my comprehension. This devotion could actually enable me to leave Purgatory and join Jesus and Mary in Heaven within the first week after my death! That astounded me. For someone who was, until just recently, going straight to Hell, I could be given the opportunity to eliminate a lengthy stay in Purgatory and enter Heaven! I said the prayers every day, along with the rosaries and developed a new attitude as I prayed to Jesus: tell me what I have to do and I'll do it.

I probably have the world's worst memory, but somehow, in about six months, I memorized the fifteen prayers in the Pieta. Each day driving to work, I would read the Pieta Prayer book. Remember the book, "God Is

My Co-pilot?" He had to have been mine, because I don't know how I got to work safely, driving and reading at the same time. My prayer life continued to grow. I found so much happiness, a happiness I had never known.

My former concerns, my search for success, always trying to make extra money here or there so that I could buy those finer things of life, didn't seem as important anymore. I used to think material things made me happy. A new car, a boat, a bigger boat, always bigger and better. Now I know that making the pursuit of material possessions the most important thing in my life, and believing they could make me happy were lies that Satan taught me to live.

Not all of my past fell by the wayside. It was the first winter after my cure, and with no arthritis, I felt like hunting again. November, 1987, found me in the woods at our old campsite, teamed up with my old buddies. Strangely enough, the place where we hunted was called New Bethlehem!

It was just like the old days . . . or was it? We left on the Friday before the first day of buck season, which started the following Monday. One thing that had changed was that I found the usual drinking to excess and profanity to be intolerable. The anticipated feeling of excitement for this hunting trip soon faded away. Another thing that changed was I now wanted to go to Mass Sunday morning. It bothered me to miss Mass on the previous two days and I wasn't about to miss on Sunday. I asked if anyone wanted to go with me and was shocked to find Dan Depuydt and Bernie Gamble willing to go.

Late Sunday afternoon, I went to a friend's house to take a much needed shower. It was a relief to get away for a few hours. I just couldn't take much more of the old hunting camp life. I got my shower and started back to camp.

On the way, I got out my spotlight and hit a few fields in search of deer. My light landed on a large buck, whose rack was so big that it looked like he had a Christmas tree on his head! How my heart pounded! What I wouldn't have given to have a buck like that in my sights the next morning, opening day! The thought ran through my mind to go back to camp, get my gun and return immediately to bag him, but that would have been illegal! Satan tempting me again!

I returned to camp and told my buddies about the buck. I don't think they all believed me. But Dan Depuydt did. He said, "Let's go get him." I told him we couldn't do that. We could be arrested. Dan didn't care; he wanted a trophy buck. "Let's go," he urged again.

I somehow talked him out of wanting to shoot the buck, but that didn't stop him from wanting to go see him. I pondered over going. It would be exciting to see him again, I thought. Then again, maybe I shouldn't go. What were the chances of the deer still being there? If he wasn't, would Dan think I was a liar? Dan badgered me until I caved in. As it turned out, God was at work again.

In the car, on our way to the location where I had seen the buck, conversation led Dan to ask me what was wrong. He said I didn't seem the same. I told him that the continual drinking and swearing bothered me. Dan explained he didn't care much for it either.

Dan then asked me about having gone to church earlier that day. "I didn't know you were Catholic and went to church," he said. I explained that something had changed my life and I had just started going. "What was that?" he asked. The hook was now set! "Medjugorje," I said. Dan asked me what a Medjugorje was.

I started to relate the experiences about Medjugorje that altered my life, something I had never done. Before I finished, we both were crying. There we were, two big, brave, hunters driving down the road crying our eyes out. That night changed Dan's life. Now *he* wanted to go to Medjugorje. We saw the big buck, but it didn't seem as important anymore.

In the midst of all my newfound joy in talking about Medjugorje and the Lord, I also found much sadness. I started becoming depressed because of the fear of failing the Lord after all His Divine Mercy had done for me. What could I ever do for Him? And seeing so many people, the way I used to be, stuck in their unbelief, truly frightened me. What if I slipped back to the way I had been?

Driving to St. Ferdinand Church one Saturday morning, about a half mile from the church, I started talking to the Lord. I said, "Jesus, I feel so deeply that you have forgiven me for what I've done, but I'm frightened of failing you. While I still feel like I have a chance to get into Heaven, why don't you pull me out of here, and take me home?"

Again, that voice started inside me, very softly at first, *"Thomas, just try, just try."* Then it got louder and louder. The closer I got to the church, the louder it got, until it was booming in my head. *"Thomas, just try."*

So I try. Every day I start over. I evaluate the day before and apply what I learned to each new day, always trying to correct the mistakes I've made. I am not always successful! Even with all the grace that is being poured on me, I still make many mistakes. But it is in recognizing the mistakes and attempting to correct them that I grow. And the Lord is there, constantly guiding me.

Then Jesus started leading me to Scripture and helping me to understand it. Reading the Bible fascinated me. When I had a question, that voice in my head answered me. Confirmation would generally come the next morning from the readings at Mass. I would then return home to dig further into Scripture to understand it all more fully. Not that I spent a lot of time reading the Bible. Mostly I was just checking to confirm that what I heard was really in the book. I was getting more involved with my religion.

I developed a little habit. Each time, in my going to Mass, I would ask Jesus for permission to go to communion. Please understand why I did that. If you recall, I told you that when I went to St. Scholastica to make my first confession in twenty years, the priest had to call Bishop Bevilacqua to discuss my situation with him.

I had been married in the Catholic Church, divorced and married my present wife outside the Church. The Bishop gave me dispensation, enabling me to go to the sacraments, while I was in the process of getting an annulment of my first marriage. As I've explained, the circumstances surrounding my first marriage were absurd.

When I was told to apply for an annulment, the Diocesan authorities said it shouldn't take very long and they were right. Filing the papers was what took a long time. With dyslexia and the lack of writing ability, it was taking me forever to fill out the forms; they are extensive!

I was beginning to understand how much effort the Lord was putting into changing my life. I was especially thankful for the grace that allowed me to go to the sacraments while the annulment procedure unraveled. I never wanted to approach Jesus Christ unworthily, not even one time. So I would ask the Lord before each communion, " Jesus may I come and have communion with you?" Inevitably every time I asked that question, I heard inside my head, *"Yes, Thomas, you may."* Sometimes, I would just *think* about asking and the answer would come, *"Yes, Thomas, you may."* I am not recommending that the whole world start asking "Jesus, may I come and have communion with you?" I don't know if that's right for you or not; I only know it was right for me then.

That is exactly how the process went every time, except once. It happened when I started getting rather busy. Trying to fit in all the prayers I wanted to say and still get things done around the farm, plus working at KDKA and my other activities, I ran out of time. I got so backed up that I decided to put a couple of things on the back burner to free up some time. I was getting to Mass and saying fifteen decades of the rosary every day, fasting fairly well and going to confession once a month. It seemed to me, as active as I was becoming in my church and prayer life, it wouldn't hurt to set aside the rosary for a little while, just until I caught up with some of my work. So I stopped saying the rosary for a short time.

That was on a Tuesday or Wednesday, and each time I went to Mass that week I continued to ask permission. "Jesus, may I come and have communion with you?" And He said, *"Yes, Thomas, you may."* But that Sunday at Mass, when it came time to celebrate the Eucharist, I asked, "Jesus, may I go?" And the voice responded, *"No, Thomas."* I panicked.

I started to beg. "Why, Jesus, what did I do? What did I do wrong? Just tell me what I did and I'll change it." In my begging, like a father giving in to a son, that voice inside me said, *"Come, Thomas, come to communion."*

The words He spoke to me this time didn't feel right. Before this, when I would receive communion, it was so powerful. I could just feel Jesus through my whole body. My eyes filled with tears when I went to the altar to receive Him. But this time, there was nothing. I didn't feel anything and it hurt.

After Mass, I got back into my car and started driving home. I began begging the Lord, "Why, Jesus, what did I do? Just tell me what I did and I'll correct it."

Again, very clearly, His voice spoke to me. *"Thomas, you have been neglecting my Mother. If it wasn't for my Mother, I wouldn't be speaking to you now."*

Suddenly it became clear to me exactly what the Lord meant and how much the rosary was to be part of all of our lives. It was given to us by the Blessed Mother as a gift, to encourage us. It was our weapon to use against Satan. The rosary helps us to recall the birth, life, death, and resurrection of our Savior. By eliminating the rosary, I was saying "No" to the intercession of the Blessed Mother. I was saying that I didn't need to relive the life of Christ each day and more than likely, I was leaving the door open for Satan. Without the rosary, where was I? The words He had just spoken to me, *"If it wasn't for My Mother, I wouldn't be speaking to you now,"* haunted me. If Mary hadn't said "yes" to God, we wouldn't have our Jesus; we wouldn't have a Savior and Redeemer, and where would we be? I made the rosary a part of my life again, immediately.

Although I had shared very little of my conversion experience with others at this point, when I did it seemed to have an effect. When I talked about Jesus, people listened intently, but I was really keeping the story of what Jesus did for me buried deep down in my heart. I still wasn't willing to tell anybody that God was speaking to me.

Wanting to do *something* to show the Lord how much I appreciated what He had done for me, I made a commitment to the Lord. I told Him I would take a hundred people to Medjugorje just to say thank you. In late June of 1988 I made the big decision and called travel agencies that might be able to do the job. A local agency that had taken pilgrims to Medjugorje quoted a price, much higher than I had anticipated, but I reserved space on a June 1989 pilgrimage anyway. I actually reserved a hundred seats! Immediately, I began collecting pilgrims, made up some flyers and put them in a couple of churches. At my church, St. Ferdinand, I spread the word about my return trip to Medjugorje and my intent, this time, to take some people with me. Hopefully, taking people to Medjugorje would in some way make up for my unwillingness to tell people that Jesus was speaking to me or to share all the miracles that were happening in my life. This commitment seemed like the perfect solution.

Also in June of 1988 I had to make another big decision. I got a call from my sister, Betts, asking me to come to Florida. In the Spring my mother got sick again and now she was worse than ever. She had been placed in a hospice program for the terminally ill because there was nothing further they could do for her. She had been given so much radiation, she couldn't tolerate any more and the children of the family all agreed that having her at home would be the best thing for her. Unfortunately for me, Betts' home was in Florida and I couldn't get down to see her very often.

Now, Betts was saying, it didn't look like our mother was going to make it through the week. I wanted to make sure it wasn't a false alarm, but my sister reassured me it was not. Mother hadn't been out of bed for months and she was gradually getting worse, and now it looked as if she had days to live. I needed to get down there immediately.

There was something that compounded the problem of my going down. I was subpoenaed for a court trial as a juror in Erie, Pa. It was an unusual situation. They were moving a jury from Butler to Erie. It's called a change of venier[4]. I called up the court to explain that I wouldn't be able to come because I had to go to Florida to be with my mother, who was terminally ill. Judge Fisher got on the phone with me and told me that my story wasn't going to work. I had to be at that trial and if I wasn't, he would find me in contempt of court and jail me. If this was the case, and my sister's assessment of my mother's condition

---

[4]   A change of venire: to import a jury from one judicial district to another. Not to be confused with a change of venu, the change in location of the trial.

was accurate, this could be the last time I would have to spend with my mother.

I wasn't too interested in the judge's threats. I was going to go to Florida no matter what, but I was going to do all I could to iron this out before I left. I contacted an attorney and asked him to call the judge. I explained that my story was not an excuse to try to get out of jury duty, but that my mother was truly terminally ill. He got in touch with the judge and tried to explain. Judge Fisher told my attorney that if I made any other attempts to get in touch with him regarding this subject, that he would find me in contempt of court and jail me.

Well, I did make one more attempt. I called the hospice program in Tampa, Florida and asked them to air express a letter confirming that my mother was terminally ill and that I was urgently needed. I purchased a ticket and planned to leave straight from work the day of my flight. It didn't matter to me what the judge said, I was going. It must have been minutes before I left that the judge called KDKA to say that he had received the letter from the hospice and I could go.

I went to the airport and got on the plane. On the way down to Florida I was speaking to the Lord and I said, "Jesus, all I want is one good week with my mother and then You can have her. She's been so ill for so long and I haven't had the opportunity to spend much time with her. Please, could I have just one good week with her?"

I arrived in Tampa in the evening and went straight to my sister's house. My sister, Betts, immediately guided me into my mother's room. Betts was concerned that mother wouldn't even make it through the night. I walked into the room, and not wanting to look gloomy or down, I put a big smile on my face. I wanted my mother to feel some kind of excitement when she saw me. I started kidding with my mother to hide my concern. I said, "Come on, Mom, get up and have a glass of wine with me and we'll talk about what we're going to do the rest of the week. We're going to go out shopping and we're going to do all kinds of things." She looked up and tried to muster a smile, obviously happy to see me. Finding it difficult to talk, in a very weak, faint voice, she said, "Okay, I'll try."

We chatted a little bit. It was more one-sided with me doing most of the talking, trying to keep my spirits up. Feeling that all my talking may be wearing her down, I said with a smile, "You get your rest now, Mom, so you'll be strong for the morning, and then we'll go and do some of the things we talked about. Okay?"

I went out to the living room and chatted with my sister awhile. As we were talking, my sister got a look of shock on her face. I said, "What's the matter, Betts?" She said, "Your mother's up!" I turned around, and there was my mother standing there. She said, "I think I'll have that wine now."

We sat down and had a glass of wine and talked a little bit. My mother's voice was amazingly stronger and my sister was awestruck. She didn't understand how this could be happening. We all talked a short while, then my mother said, "If we're going to be going places tomorrow, I better go and get my rest." She went back to bed all by herself.

My sister said, "I don't know how this is possible. She's been in that bed for months!" I told my sister that I had prayed for a good week with Mom, and I expected to get a good week. Without a tremendous faith in prayer, people might find it impossible to believe that this could have happened. I'm sure my sister had a hard time believing what I had asked for could come true. We talked a while longer and retired for the night.

In the morning, about 7:30 I got up, showered, dressed and walked into the living room. To my amazement, there was my mother, sitting on the couch, dressed and ready to go. She said, "What took you so long? I thought you told me we were going out shopping today. You said you were going to take me to all kinds of places." "Yeah, Mom, that's exactly what I said. Wait till I get a couple of things and we'll go." I'm the one who believed so much in the prayer I had said, but still I was shocked. I asked the Lord for this favor fully knowing that He had the ability to give me that week with my mom, but I didn't expect there to be a complete turn-around!

We went out shopping that day, and went out to dinner, and my mother drove her own car! She did things she hadn't done in a year or more and by all appearances, there was absolutely nothing wrong with her. She looked as vibrant as she ever did and as healthy as she ever was. There was not even a question of her having enough energy to do all of the running around we did. She had more than enough energy. When we were walking in the mall, she laughed just like a little girl, and said, "Look at these people in walkers. I don't need anything like that to help me get around. I feel so good."

The whole week went that way. The nurse from the hospice program that took care of my mother, was to come to my sister's house to bathe my mother on Tuesday as she always did. She called prior to coming to let Betts know what time she would be there. My sister said, "Don't bother." The nurse said softly, "Oh, did she die?" My sister responded, "No, she's out shopping at the mall with my brother." "What?! That's impossible!" Betts said, "No, my brother thinks he's some kind of faith healer or something."

The hospice people were equally as shocked as Betts and couldn't understand what was going on. I don't think any of us could. It was just one more piece being placed in the mosaic of my life. God was showing me His absolute power, demonstrating that if you pray to Him with your heart, and back up what you pray for with fasting, prayer works. Maybe having this time with my mother was a reward the Lord wanted to give me for taking these hundred people to Medjugorje. Who knows why these things happen, but believe me, it happened! The Lord wants us to understand that these things do happen.

At the end of the week, my sister, in her amazement, listened to a conversation my mother and I had. My mother expressed a desire to come back home with me. "Of course you can," I said. "We don't have an airline ticket for you on this flight, but we'll get you on the next available flight, and you can come back home."

We made the arrangements for her to follow on a flight that was leaving a couple of days later. As I was leaving her house to go home, my sister said to me "I can't believe all this has happened." I said to my sister, "Know this, Betts. Your mother's coming home to die." I told her this, knowing what my agreement was with the Lord.

We came home and my mother was okay for a day or two, then she gradually started slipping. She became more and more ill, and soon got to the point where she couldn't be left alone. I didn't have any more vacation time left to be off work and stay with her. It broke my heart to put her in a nursing home, but I moved her into a beautiful little place just down the road from me, in a little town called Harmony. We got her a nice room and furnished it well, with beautiful white wicker furniture and pictures on the walls. We made my mother as comfortable as possible. I went to visit her every free moment I had.

I was deeply involved at that time in doing the fifteen prayers in my Pieta prayer book. I happened to read on pages twenty and twenty-one about the Three Beautiful Prayers; subtitled, "which are very useful for a dying person and should be said often and offered as an act of Mercy." It explained the grace that could be obtained for a dying person by saying these prayers. I wanted my mother to have these prayers said for her if she was in danger of dying. What if I wasn't with her to do that? I instructed the nursing staff that if she took a turn for the worse, and I wasn't there, to read these prayers as my mother was dying. I felt great consolation in knowing that this would be done for my mother.

On July 21, 1988, around eight o'clock in the evening, my mother passed away. I had just read those beautiful prayers to her, a half an hour before. The feelings I experienced during the death of my mother were in direct contrast to what I had felt when my father died. When my father passed away, prior to the starting of my conversion, I was so angry at God. Why did He take him away, just when I was beginning to fall in love with him? My dad and I had many problems dealing with each other over the years. I always felt as if I had failed him somewhere along the line. And then, just when we were getting along, he was taken from me, and I was angry. But, with the death of my mother, it was so different. I believed with all my heart, that God was listening to and answering my prayers. I knew exactly where she was going and that she would be taken care of. I thank God for all the gifts he has given me, but I especially thank Him for the week with my mother and the gift of understanding her death, and being able to say those prayers for her while she was dying.

Through all of this my faith was continually growing, but I had one problem. I felt torn between my loyalty to Jesus and my devotion to the Blessed Mother. It seemed that each time I tried to cultivate my relationship with Mary, I felt as though I was taking something away from Jesus. I spoke to the Blessed Mother once saying, "Dear Mother, it is not my intent to offend you, but each time that I turn to you, I feel like I'm taking time away from my Lord."

That's the only time that I ever heard a response that seemed like it was from the Blessed Mother. She didn't identify herself and it wasn't a male or a female voice - it was that same voice in my head that I always heard, but this time, because of the response, it had to be Her. *"It's alright, Thomas. My Son is taking personal care of you."* I took great relief in those words!

I continued to grow, unfortunately in two directions, closer to the Lord and away from Mary, my wife. Several times, as in many marriages today, we had discussed divorce. But now, with Jesus Christ in my life, I thought everything would be perfect.

My temper became somewhat subdued, but there was distance growing between Mary and me. Mary just did not believe what was happening to me. Oh, she knew very well that I went to Medjugorje with rheumatoid arthritis and came back home without it, and she could see that it was changing my life tremendously. But she complained that I was changing all the rules, and these weren't the rules we agreed upon when we got married or lived by during the past fifteen years. I tried harder and harder to get her to feel what I felt. The harder I tried, the worse it got. Soon we started to argue again, more intensely than before.

I can remember one specific incident where I got so frustrated, so fired up, that I had to unleash my anger somehow. What could have led me to striking out at my wife was averted by slamming my bare foot into the corner of our sofa and breaking my big toe in three places. I was in such agonizing pain that I ended up going to the doctor the next day. He confirmed what I already knew, multiple fractures. I hobbled around for several long months.

I discovered that Jesus allows you to experience before He instructs, and He allowed me to feel all this frustration to the point that it was explosive. Then He started to instruct me on this very problem.

"Remember how patient I was with you Thomas? I took you to Bethlehem and I waited. I took you to Lourdes and I waited. I took you to Fatima and I waited. Why are you pushing your wife, Mary?"

Again, the instruction was so simple, so complete, that I knew I had to work on patience and understanding. I started to back off evangelizing Mary. I tried to absorb more, to be less sensitive to the things I thought offensive and to offend others less. It seems we still have difficulty seeing things from each other's side. Time, I pray, will fix that also.

One pleasing event was a call from my hunting buddy, Dan Depuydt. He was calling to sign up for the Medjugorje trip in June and was going to witness first hand what was changing my life. After our talk in the woods he started going to church more often and started saying the rosary. Amazing Grace!

Dan was one of the first ten, of the promised one hundred, to sign up for the trip and that was exciting. However, the plan didn't seem to be working very well. After seven months of trying, only about thirteen people had signed on. It was now January, 1989 and the travel agent was getting concerned about the hundred seats she had reserved in my name because I wasn't able to come up with a passenger list. I told her, "Don't worry. I'll have the people." In reality, I was as concerned as she was.

On January 18, 1989, while working at the computer entering information on the few pilgrims that had signed up, I had a thought about my difficulty in filling the hundred seats. I spoke to the Lord saying, "Jesus, I think I made a mistake. I *told* you I was going to take a hundred people to Medjugorje to thank you for what you have done for me, but I never *asked* you for your help. I know from Her messages and the books I read, that the Blessed Mother is crying in Medjugorje because so few people have responded to Her call. I don't want Her to cry. I want to lead this pilgrimage to make Her feel better. So now, instead of telling you what I am going to do, I'm asking you to please help me gather these hundred people."

Almost instantly the phone rang. It was a man by the name of George Voelker. He was one of the people that had signed up for the pilgrimage, whom I had not met. He was calling to invite me to Holy Trinity Church in Ambridge, a little town about twenty-five miles from where I live. The church had a Medjugorje prayer group that met on Fridays. George assumed I had a devotion to the Blessed Mother and felt I might enjoy coming for the Mass and fifteen decades of the rosary. I told George that my schedule was so demanding that it couldn't be worked in. He encouraged me several times to meet him there and several times I rejected the idea. He didn't seem angry when he hung up, but he did seem disappointed. I realized how insensitive I had been and wondered if George was concerned about sending me money. He had promised to send me a large check for the trip to Medjugorje, and he didn't even know me. I should at least go to meet him . . . I owed him that much. Without returning his phone call, I decided to go.

That Friday I went to Holy Trinity and participated in the Mass and the fifteen decades of the rosary. It truly was beautiful. Afterward, they had a social in the church basement. Father Vince, the pastor, was there. I walked over to him, introduced myself and asked him if he knew a man by the name of George Voelker. I explained that I didn't know what he looked like, and wanted to find him.

"Yes," he said, "I know George." He said he hadn't seen him around that evening, but if he did, he would point him out to me.

As I was talking to Father, Helen Furman, an acquaintance from St. Ferdinand Church, walked up to us. She was one of the few people that I ever allowed to hear even the smallest part about my religious experiences. She walked up and said, "Oh, Father, let me tell you about Tom." I felt a bit of panic about what she might disclose to the priest, and I turned and headed for my seat. Father replied that he didn't have the time then and saved the day for me. However, the next thing I knew, Father Vince was up in front of the group saying, "Could I have your attention? I have some disappointing news. We were supposed to have a speaker here tonight, but unfortunately we don't have one. I have a youth group meeting upstairs that will take about an hour. If you want to wait, I'll come back and speak to you then."

Father started out the door, stopped and came back in. Pointing in my direction he said, "Hey, you, come here." It looked like he was pointing at me, but he couldn't be; he had just met me. So I looked over my shoulder to see who he was pointing to. He said again, "Come here." And I pointed at myself, "Who, me?" "Yes, you. Come here," he repeated.

I walked over and said, "What do you want, Father?" He said loud enough for everyone to hear, "How about standing here and talking to these people for an hour. I'll be back," and he started to walk away.

I said, "Are you kidding me? What am I going to talk to them about?" As he was going out the door, I could hear the people saying, "Who is he?" Father stopped and turned around and said, "I have no idea," and went out the door leaving me standing there in front of all those people! Suddenly a strong feeling came over me and I was filled with emotion. I said aloud, "Well, do I have a story in my heart? Yes, I guess I do."

I began to relate what had happened to me since the time the Lord started working in my life. Oh, did I cry that evening, telling that story through my tears! I could barely make out the people's faces, but I could tell that many were crying with me.

When I finished, a man walked up to me and said, "I can't believe I'm going to Medjugorje with you." It was George Voelker. Other people came up and said, "Can I touch you?" I backed away from them saying, "Why do you want to touch me? I can't do anything for you. Let *Jesus* touch you."

After I told them about the trip, many people in that room wanted to go to Medjugorje with me. Several of them gave me checks that very evening. More joined the trip through phone calls the next few days. What a whirlwind of excitement that talk generated! Here were many of the people I needed to fill the trip!

I spent the weekend trying to figure out exactly what had happened. What I tried to hide in my heart for so long, the Lord Jesus drew from me in that one hour. All those people now knew my story. What would the ramifications be?

That Monday, back at work, I continued my efforts to persuade KDKA to send a news crew over to Medjugorje, but they kept refusing. But more and more, I heard the word "Medjugorje" in Pittsburgh. It was ironic that I couldn't convince TV news to do the story. But one morning, Pittsburgh Today, a one hour talk show on KDKA TV, sent a producer to talk with me. "Tom, I understand you've been to Medjugorje. On Wednesday we're doing a program about Medjugorje. Would you be willing to go on the show and talk about your experiences?"

"Oh, no, not me." I said. "Something just happened last week and a whole bunch of people know a whole lot of personal things about me and I'm not about to go on television and tell a half million people about my life." He responded, "A friend of yours is going to be on the show. I think she is a neighbor of yours, Rita Klaus."

I've already related my first encounter with Rita Klaus. She told me about her miraculous cure; I asked her to go on television; and she told me "No." I had said to her that if something like that had happened to me, I would stand on my rooftop and shout about what Jesus did for me. Now here I was, rejecting the idea of going on television, and the Lord said to me, *"You told Rita you would stand on the roof and shout what?"* Recalling the scenario with Rita, I responded to the producer, "Wait a second. I'll be on your show."

The day of the show, January 25, 1989, I went to work as usual. But this time one thing was different, I wore a suit. Many times I was behind the camera doing my job; now I was going to be in front of it. Everything about my work in television had always been so matter-of-fact for me.

I was often in the presence of dignitaries, presidents and kings and to me they were just people. I was never nervous in any kind of TV situation, but here I was, sitting in *front* of the cameras realizing I was going to announce to the world that Christ speaks to me. Maybe that's what made me nervous . . . very nervous, indeed.

Jan and Ed Connell were the first to be interviewed. They were both attorneys from Pittsburgh and their lives had been changed by Medjugorje. They explained their reasons for going there and told of their visits to the tiny Yugoslavian village. Rita Klaus was second to be introduced and she told the story of her miracle cure that she attributes to Medjugorje.

Then it was time for me. Knowing the television business, I realized there were about seven or eight minutes left in this segment. That's all the time I had to tell the world about all that Jesus Christ had done for me in the past few years. It was mind boggling to me how I was going to accomplish that in seven minutes, but the words just started to come.

I explained how Jesus took me to Bethlehem, Lourdes and Fatima and how He spoke to me while I was reading the book, "The Queen Of Peace Visits Medjugorje." When I said the words God spoke to me, *"Thomas, I took you to Bethlehem, I took you to Lourdes and I took you to Fatima. Can't you understand that this is real?"*, it brought tears to my eyes again. The story was out. Everybody at the station would now know what Tom Rutkoski was about, and so would the whole city. It frightened me.

During the program it was customary to take questions from the audience and, by phone, from viewers. Some questions were sincere, others, skeptical. One woman called in, and the question she asked was more of a statement. She said, "Satan can come as a messenger from God . . . I would be very leery. This is either Satan himself or some demonic apparition."

Jon Burnett, the co-host, asked me to respond to the caller. I had no idea what I was going to say, but the words just starting pouring out of my mouth. "The Bible says you can tell a tree by its fruit. Why Satan would want me inside a church every day of my life, when I couldn't have cared less before Medjugorje, is beyond my comprehension. The Blessed Mother doesn't contradict anything that Christ says, She leads everyone *to* Christ. If we go to a store and we find something we like and buy it, it's valuable to us, so we protect and prize that. Why does everybody want to discard the container that Christ was delivered in? What could be more precious than the Mother of God?"

The hosts had done some research. Jon Burnett had found an article that he thought refuted what we, the guests had presented. It explained that Bishop Zanic of Mostar, had formed a commission to investigate what was happening in Medjugorje because it was in his diocese. The commission of ten theologians and two psychiatrists had unanimously determined that the apparitions were not real. Jan Connell responded. She told the viewers that the commission, about which that article had been written, was disbanded by order of the Holy Father and he had established a new commission to study Medjugorje. Although Bishop Zanic does not believe the apparitions to be true, he can't stop individuals from going there.[5]

At the end of the show, Patrice King Brown, the other co-host, mentioned that I had a pilgrimage scheduled for June and the Connells had one scheduled for August. She

---

[5]   The Vatican removed all authority to investigate Medjugorje from Bishop Zanic, and Pope John Paul II has stated, " If going to Medjugorje brings you closer to God, then go to Medjugorje. The church is studying it." The Church has been studying the apparitions for almost eleven years and has found no basis to discredit them.

advised viewers who wanted more information on Medjugorje or about the pilgrimages, to contact Pittsburgh Today and they would get them in touch with the guests on the show.

The program was over. Jon Burnett, came over to me and said, "I never really believed in much of this, but you make it sound so convincing." I left feeling really good about being on the show that day.

I got home and looked in amazement at my telephone answering machine. It displays the number of messages received. Generally, the number would be three or four, at times as high as six. This time, it read **forty-six**! People had called KDKA-TV wanting to know how to get in touch with me and the station was giving out my number. There were messages from forty-six people who were interested in Medjugorje! Priests were calling, asking if I would come to their church and tell my story!

From the time I prayed and asked for His help, only a few days had lapsed. What I couldn't do in seven months of trying, Jesus Christ accomplished in no time at all. He gathered the pilgrims that I needed to make the hundred, and was blessing me with the *privilege* of taking them to Medjugorje!

The travel agent that booked the pilgrimage was amazed that I gathered one hundred people so quickly. Little did she know, I didn't. God did.

The time I would have had to spend gathering pilgrims for the trip, was released for me to do something else. That, I guess, is what the Lord had in mind. There was a secondary reaction to my appearance on television. I accepted the invitations I received from the priests to speak at their churches.

To get me to tell my story the first time, the Lord had to orchestrate the circumstances that found me standing in the front of the church in Ambridge that day and He had to draw the words from my mouth. The same was true for my appearance on KDKA. But the other times I spoke, I freely decided to go and I was anxious to tell my story. I went out evangelizing, saying "Yes" to Jesus. I always felt nervous and I would always wonder what I was going to say. My legs would shake and my brow would get sweaty. I had never done any public speaking before Ambridge.

When I arrived to speak at St. Peter's Church there were about twenty people in the pews when I arrived. I wondered, oh my goodness, is this all that's coming? I knelt down, and prayed, asking for strength for what I was about to do for the Lord. I don't know exactly how long I knelt there, but when I turned around you could have knocked me over with a feather. The entire church was filled. There must have been six hundred people there!

The priest went to the podium and introduced me. From the moment I stepped forward, for the next hour and a half, the words just came. The story unfolded for the third time. You could have heard a pin drop in that church.

I could see in their faces that they were feeling what I was feeling. I had tears in my eyes and they had tears in theirs. It became apparent to me that Tom Rutkoski wasn't at work here; I can't create that kind of emotion. Jesus Christ was working *through* me, using me that night, once again.

After the talk, people came up to meet me. I was amazed by their stories and touched by their words; how deeply the talk had affected them; how it made them think. One family was off to one side and it was obvious to me they were patiently waiting for me to finish. Everyone who wanted to come up and talk to me got that opportunity. I kept glancing over and seeing that family with tears streaming down their face. They waited until everyone left and then came over to me.

The man spoke, "Mr. Rutkoski, we have been away from the Catholic faith for over twenty years. I don't understand how we ended up in this church tonight, but we saw a little article in the newspaper that you were going to tell a story tonight about a place called Medjugorje. We had never heard of it before. Why we made the decision to come here tonight, we don't know, but your story has changed our lives."

At that point I was crying just as hard as they were and I was rejoicing with them. They continued, "We just came from the priest's office where we went to confession for the first time in twenty years, and we just wanted to say thank you." "Don't thank me," I said. "There's nothing to thank me for. I didn't bring you back to your faith, Jesus brought you back." I pointed to the tabernacle and said, "Go thank Jesus."

I left that church in awe of what was happening after my talk and how it was affecting the people who had heard it. I was joyful in one sense, confused in another. "Why me? Why did You pick me to do this job? Why wouldn't You go after someone who practiced his faith all his life, someone who's worthy? You came to me, who couldn't have cared less about You all those years. Why?" I just couldn't understand what was happening.

I continued to grow, read scripture, and talk to Jesus. More calls came asking me to speak at other churches. I had received several requests from people asking if I could send them a videotape of my talk. That was out of the question because, at the time, I didn't have one.

The next place I was to speak was the Consolata Mission House in Point Breeze, a small suburb of Pittsburgh. Being a photojournalist, the problem of needing a video tape of my talk was not difficult to solve. I asked my nephew, who worked with me at KDKA-TV, if he would come to the Consolata Mission House and videotape the talk for me. He agreed to help me out. I was always well equipped with what KDKA made available to me. I could show up at a church with a wireless microphone system, plug it in and walk around unencumbered.

The building where I was to speak was a beautiful, old, Victorian house that had been turned into a chapel, and the PA system was an antique. My wireless microphone system wasn't compatible, so I had to hold the microphone in my hand and I felt restricted. I wasn't able to walk around a lot, but I guess that made it easier for my nephew to video-tape my talk.

As it turned out, I was so sick with the flu, I can't even believe I went to speak that night. But how could I cancel? My nephew was on his way and so were all the people that expected to hear me. The talk was very hard to do but I managed to get through it somehow. Generally, I have the sniffles during a presentation because of the tears, but this was ridiculous. Between the tears and the flu teaming up against me, the evening was a disaster, at least to me.

After the presentation, people came up to thank me. I was grateful for the encouraging things they said. They gave me the strength go on. One woman came up to me after the talk, and said, "Mr. Rutkoski, while you were there speaking, there was this large, golden glow around your head." As she started to relate to me what it looked like, I spoke to the Lord in silence. "Jesus, if you want me to continue this, please, keep the kooks away from me.

I had a hard enough time taking the first step forward to tell folks that you speak to me. I'm afraid that if people start coming around with craziness like this and word spreads, it could hurt Your mission for me." The thought of this incident puzzled me on the way home but I turned to other thoughts of that evening. When I got home, there were messages on my answering system from people who had been at the talk, inviting me to speak at other churches.

The talk at the next church went as well as the others, but again after the talk two women came up to me and said, "While you were speaking, there was a large golden glow around your head." Again I said in the silence of my heart, "Jesus, what's our deal here? Keep these kinds of people away from me, would you please?" All the time I was smiling and thanking these women who I felt were weirdos.

The whole idea of the golden glow concerned me deeply and caused me to wonder whether I was really dealing with the Lord. Although I had been hearing a voice in my head, I never really questioned who it was. I just assumed it was Jesus Christ. The voice started to come so frequently and there were so many changes in my life in such a short period of time, that it moved me to ask, "Who are you?" With the love of a mother and the firmness of a father, I heard very clearly, *"I am Jesus Christ, your Savior and Redeemer."*

You would think, just to hear those words, "I am your Savior and Redeemer" that I would be left speechless. Maybe it was the journalist in me that made me respond, "How do I know that? How do I know you are not Satan and maybe you are just leading me down some path of deception, making me think all of this is holy. What if it's your plan to trip me up and make me worse than I was?"

Just as quickly as I snapped my question, the answer came back, gently, *"You can tell by your fruits, Thomas. Look at your fruits."* Now, He had confirmed that it was He, and Jesus was telling me to look at my fruits. This caused me to reflect on how many people had told me that their lives were changed after hearing the story of my conversion.

The church where I spoke the following week had a little gathering in the social hall following my talk. It had become obvious to me that people enjoyed sitting and talking after the presentations, so I went to the hall to greet everyone. I had just stood in front of these people for over an hour and a half and they still wanted to hear more. After chatting awhile, and being a little tired, I looked for a place to sit and found only one open seat at one of the cafeteria tables. I went over and sat in the free chair. The woman across the table, whose name I later found out was Marie

Jenkins, said to me, "Okay, I'll tell you." I said, "Excuse me?"

She said, "While I was watching your presentation, there was a large, golden glow around the back of your head. I said to the Lord, 'If I tell that man there was a golden glow behind his head the whole time he was speaking, he'll think I'm crazy. If You want me to tell him, bring him over and put him in this chair and I'll tell him.' So I'm telling you."

"Thank you for telling me," I said to Marie as I pondered it all in my mind. After this confirmation, I felt remorse about the thoughts I had of the other women who had told me about the glow.

I still didn't understand the golden glow, all I knew was that I loved Jesus very, very much and wanted to do His will. I was learning how little I knew about the mysteries surrounding the saving grace of God.

The golden glow continued to puzzle me. Why had people seen it? What did it mean? Glows around heads were always associated with Saints and I certainly wasn't in that category. Especially in remembering what my past was like. I sought counsel and one priest told me, "I don't know anything about a golden glow, Tom, but you don't have to be concerned about your past. Your past has nothing to do with your future. Mary Magdalene is the best example for that."

I asked another priest about it and he explained to me, "Tom, that golden glow is a phenomena of the Holy Spirit. When a person is speaking in the Spirit and someone is listening in the Spirit, that phenomenon can occur."

I felt a little better after both explanations. The miracles in my life and the golden glow continued to happen. My confused mind kept asking, "Why me, Lord? Why did you pick me?"

Chapter 8

101 Pilgrims

In May of 1989, I heard of a Marian conference to be held at the University of Notre Dame, May 11-13. Gail McDowell, a woman I had met through one of my speaking engagements, called and asked if I would like to speak at the conference. She had a possible connection and might be able to work it out. I was willing to go anywhere, anytime the Lord called. I told her yes, even though this would add more stress to an already heavy schedule. Preparing for the trip and speaking elsewhere was tough, but I filled her request for a tape to be sent to Notre Dame for their approval. All appeared to be going smoothly until a lay person from Pittsburgh intervened and prevented my speaking.

Maybe it wasn't what the Lord had in mind at the time or it might have been Satan at work. Gail and I were both disappointed, but whatever was God's plan, was okay with me. It was difficult for me to understand how there could be jealousy between factions claiming to be working for the Blessed Mother. Realizing this was a test, I was not going to get upset and fail the Lord as I had in the first half of my life. He was teaching me to love everyone and pray for all. Although several other situations arose where people said things about me that weren't true or were distortions of facts and caused immeasurable harm, I simply pray for them, completely opposite of the way I would have reacted before.

My buddy, John Rabick, heard about the conference at Notre Dame and called trying to convince me to go. It would have been easy to let pride stop me from going, because of my not speaking there, but going might be exactly what I needed. Even with the many miracles that were happening in my life, my exhausting workload put me in need of spiritual uplifting. He finally convinced me that maybe the Marian conference was just the right place to go, to hear all the stories of the other people who had their lives changed. Surely, that would lift me. So on May 11, John and I left for Notre Dame.

I was probably alone in my feelings. Everyone else who went there seemed spiritually uplifted by the speakers, but for me, it seemed like homily after homily. I don't mean to criticize or hurt anyone's feelings, but that's the way it was for me. It just didn't pick me up. Oh, there were a few stories I enjoyed. A bishop from New Orleans, whose story really made me laugh, showed me that there was a human side to this, and that it wasn't all so serious. The bishop talked about when he helped a woman up Krizevac mountain. The woman was rather large, so it took a great deal of effort on the bishop's part because he is a small man. When he got her to the top she knelt down and was saying loudly, "Thank you, Jesus, thank you Jesus." The bishop was miffed. "This woman could have never made it up here without me," he said. I found that humorous and one of the few bright spots for me at the conference.

For John and me, the second day of the conference was to begin with Mass at the chapel at Notre Dame. Waiting for my friend outside the hotel, I thought about the conference. I didn't know why it depressed me so much, but it did. I wanted and needed to be moved greatly. I'm sure all the stories of conversions and miracles tremendously moved the others that were there, but because I had experienced so much personally, maybe it took a lot more to move me. The way I felt was my own fault more than anything else, but there I was, leaning against the fender of the car, feeling sorry for myself. I looked up and saw the miracle of the sun with the dark disk in front of it, blocking out its intensity, dancing around and spinning. The same miracle I saw in Medjugorje. The same miracle I experienced many times at home. It was as if the Lord was saying, "Look, Thomas, I'm still here."

Just to show you that I'm not a real bright individual, I actually said to the Lord, "Even that doesn't lift me up anymore, Lord, I see that all the time." Suddenly, a big, red crucifix was placed across the sun! Tears streamed down my face when I realized what I had said, and what the Lord was trying to do for me. He wanted to keep me encouraged so that I would go on, so that I wouldn't fall backward. He knew what it was like to fall with His cross, with no one there to help him, or pick Him up, just soldiers to kick Him when He was down. He was sparing me that experience, not that my cross was like His. He was there to pick me up and was giving me the encouragement I needed. I felt sad that God had to go to this length to keep me on track.

The second day of the conference went much better for me. Maybe I had a better attitude. Perhaps it was a lesson in persevering in trial, to know that He's always there whether you're in the desert of emptiness or basking in the spiritual glory of His light.

The adrenalin was flowing. It seemed like only days since we left the conference and already it was June 8,

1989. The big day had arrived. I was leaving for my second visit to Medjugorje, only this time I was taking the promised one hundred pilgrims. Well, actually one hundred and one because I'd acquired an extra seat for Sister Mary Catherine, a nun from Brazil.

The experiences getting there weren't all pleasant. When we got to the airport in New York, the travel agent gave me a pile of boarding passes and said, "Pass these out to everybody." At first glance it seemed a simple enough job; I could do that. But midway through connecting people with their seats, I realized the travel agent had been pretty clever. This wasn't as easy as it looked. People started to bicker about with whom they were going to sit and where they were seated on the airplane. This created a lot of confusion. I thought to myself, there has to be a better way to handle this. In the midst of all the chaos, a man came up to me and handed me a small card, saying, "Excuse me, my name is John Kaldos. I'm the sales rep for JAT, Yugoslav Airlines. Here's my business card. When you bring your next tour, give me a call and I'll help you with it."

I smiled at him. "I'm sorry, sir, I'm not the travel agent, that woman over there is. Take your card and give it to her." He insisted, "No, I want *you* to have it." I took it and stuck it in my pocket.

Our group boarded the plane. What a long flight that was from New York . . . about eight and a half hours. My seat was aginst the wall and smaller than the rest, with little room between my knees and the back of the seat in front of me. I could not stretch my legs at all without standing up. Being six feet, two inches tall, sitting in one place for eight and a half hours with my knees crunched up near my chin, was agonizing. My back hurt, my knees hurt, and I was miserable. By the time we landed in Dubrovnik, Yugoslavia, I was exhausted. Before my arthritis was cured, that trip would have been impossible for me.

Again, there was great confusion at the airport when we landed: where to go first, how to get on the buses, handling the luggage and once again, I found myself thinking there had to be a better way. We finally went through customs, boarded the buses and headed to Medjugorje.

There were two buses to transport all the pilgrims. It is a three and a half hour ride from Dubrovnik to Medjugorje. The good part was being able to pray with everyone on the buses. For half the trip, I stayed with the one group and we sang songs, prayed the rosary for an hour and a half and I related to them a few experiences of my conversion. When we made a rest stop in the little resort town of Slano, I changed buses and went the rest of the way with the other half of the people. Again we prayed, said the rosary and sang songs.

Eventually, I recognized the main street leading into Medjugorje toward St. James Church. My heart started to beat faster and emotions swelled inside me. It was like going home. When my eyes saw the twin spires of St. James Church, for the second time in my life, the voice in my head said, *"Rejoice, Thomas, the Blessed Mother loves you."*

It was one of the most emotional moments in my life! I couldn't hold back the tears; they come even now, just thinking about it. But everywhere the Blessed Mother goes, so goes her adversary, Satan, and when we got off the buses, there he was. We tried to unload the buses and get the people settled quickly, but the process of moving the luggage from the storage compartments under the bus, and getting them to the right people in the right houses, ended up being a two-hour process. People were exhausted from the long trip and now tempers were flaring. I looked at this part of the trip and saw it as a disaster also. For the third time I thought, there must be a better way!

The pilgrimage week in Medjugorje was glorious on one hand and agonizing on the other. Taking care of the hundred and one people in my group was not an easy job. We encountered problem after problem as far as the logistics of the trip were concerned. But the hard work was well-rewarded by the warm feeling I got from hearing the people exclaim what a wonderful experience they were having. There are no words to express how I felt watching everyone going through their spiritual renewal or, in many cases, conversion. This was probably one of the greater gifts of the trip, seeing person after person, in tears, full of emotion, surrendering to the Lord. The process was well known to me, having recently been through it myself. The pilgrims were opening their hearts to Jesus and it was truly beautiful. After only the first or second day, people began relating their experiences to me.

In the course of the week, I was walking down the sidewalk on the main street in Medjugorje, past one of the tourist agencies, when a woman inside motioned for me to come in. I went in and spoke to her. She spoke English, and invited me to sit down. I was really shocked and delighted to see an old friend sitting there. It was Jelena, the woman I stayed with on my first trip to Medjugorje! The English-speaking woman said to me, "When you bring trips in the future, we would like to help you take care of all the housing arrangements."

I said, "I don't think I'll be bringing anybody back, I'm just here with this one group and that's it. I'm not a travel agent." She said, "Oh, we know who you are. Here, please take these wholesale price lists, and some literature on how to do this. You can get in touch with us if you decide to bring another pilgrimage on your own. Just give us a call." It all gave me cause to wonder.

There were two women on the trip, Maria Brown and Carmen Cruz, who related a chilling story. They told of climbing Apparition Hill very late one night with the intent of staying there overnight. After an hour or so, an ominous-looking man in a black cape came by with a long staff in his hand. As he walked by them, they were very frightened by him. They saw him wander into the brush and return without the cloak. With no explanation, he walked over to the candles that were burning at the foot of the original cross placed on Apparition Hill to mark the exact spot where the Blessed Mother appeared. This darkly-clothed creature threw something down and a large flame burst forth. This really frightened the two women. The man turned and started walking toward them, the sound of his staff was making a horrifying sound when it hit the ground . . . thunk, thunk, thunk. They were terrified and ran away.

The next night they returned there and the same scenario occurred. The ominous-looking man with his cape and long staff appeared again. The thunk, thunk, thunk of his staff got louder and louder as he drew closer. Driven off by fear the second time, they went to Father Philip to tell him what they had seen. Later, they related to me that Father Philip informed them that what they had seen was dubbed the "cloaking man". The locals believe it was Satan himself, but no one knew for sure. They did know however, that everywhere the Blessed Mother went to try to save souls, Satan followed. When they revealed this experience to me, in all honesty, I took it with a grain of salt. Another pilgrim, Joycelyn, who had arranged my first trip to Medjugorje, had related a satanic experience to me. And my first time up Krizevac mountain, I had some kind of evil experience of my own, but it's always easier to believe your own eyes and ears than to believe others. I didn't know if Joycelyn's story was real. I didn't know if Maria's and Carmen's story was true. So I listened with caution and kept these stories away in the back of my head.

The trip was bittersweet. The process of seeing everybody being bathed in the grace of reconciliation and love from the Blessed Mother was inspiring, but the situation with the travel agent was worsening. On the fourth day I found out that our flight departure time was moved up from noon to six a.m., so we were going to have to leave Medjugorje at midnight to get to the airport at Dubrovnik on time. Knowing how difficult the trip had been from New York to Yugoslavia, I was quite concerned. Considering the age of some of the people on the trip, I didn't see how they could get any rest on the bus ride before taking that long plane flight back home. I rebelled at the thought of leaving Medjugorje at midnight! It would be more prudent to get our passengers to a hotel in Dubrovnik that night and get up early in the morning, rested for the flight home. An argument ensued with the travel agent over who was going to pay for the hotel. I didn't much care who was going to pay; I was more concerned about the elderly in our care becoming exhausted.

So I invited everyone in our group to meet outside in front of the Blessed Mother's statue at St. James Church and put it to a vote. I inquired, "Would you rather leave at midnight and drive through the night or would you rather leave earlier and stay in Dubrovnik overnight?" The vote was unanimous to stay in the hotel overnight in Dubrovnik. The travel agent was furious with me, but it didn't matter. That's what our group decided to do so I proceeded to make the arrangements for the hotel. I made the offer to the people who couldn't pay for their hotel room, that I would pay for it myself. Most people were more than willing to pitch in the additional twenty dollars.

On our departure day we boarded the buses, and I asked the bus driver to drive down to St. James Church for our last good-bye. We pulled up in front of the church and I had everybody gather around the statute of the Blessed Mother and hold hands. We said an "Our Father", "A Hail Mary" and a "Glory Be" and thanked the Mother of God for all the graces that She had bestowed upon us, and thanked Jesus for allowing us this wonderful experience.

The people started to file back onto the buses. I turned around and ran toward the church and knelt down in the foyer looking up at the Tabernacle. Bowing my head, I spoke to Jesus. "Lord, if there's any grace in my bringing these people to Medjugorje, don't give it to me, give it to the people on the bus that it might help them change. Let them go home and be witnesses to your Blessed Mother and what She is doing here." Suddenly, there was a strong scent of roses, almost intoxicating me. Even after I went outside, it didn't go away. It was so overwhelming, that tears rolled down my face. The same way I arrived in Medjugorje, I was leaving, in tears. Warm clay in my Mother's hands!

The flight arrangements for our group departing Dubrovnik were messed up. Instead of all of us going to

Dubrovnik and flying to the States, we had to split up in Medjugorje. There was a mix-up on the tickets and somehow, part of the group had to go to Mostar and get on a plane to Zagreb. About fifteen people volunteered to do that; the rest of us got on a bus to Dubrovnik to stay overnight. The hotel accommodations were okay; not what I would have wished, but okay. The rooms were far down the hall, but we managed to find them. After settling in, we took a tour of the walled city. Everyone was impressed with its beauty. As I am writing this book, the war in Yugoslavia rages. The destruction of the historic walled city and its churches are now a sad fact.

We returned to the hotel after our tour, got cleaned up and about seven o'clock we all met at the hotel restaurant for dinner. There were eighty-four of us. I made an announcement that if anyone would like to come to my room to pray and do some sharing, feel free. Rick Bach was going to come with his guitar and we would sing and take what the Lord had to give us that night. As I was leaving the restaurant, Carmen Cruz said she wanted to talk to me. She wanted to explain to me some problems in her life. That seemed to be a pattern on this trip. People apparently felt comfortable talking to me about their problems. In my discussion with Carmen, I encouraged her to share with us that evening the experience she had on the mountain with the cloaked man. I felt she should share that with people because the story she told me about her family history and what brought her to Medjugorje, was quite unusual. It had, for me, made the experience on the mountain all that more believable.

The group gathered in my hotel room in Dubrovnik and we sang songs. Carmen gave her witness. She told of being taken by her parents to occult meetings in her childhood. In Medjugorje, when she had told Father Philip about her past, he performed an exorcism on her. However, Father Philip realized that she needed more spiritual healing and sent her to Father Jozo. He knew that the group would be going to Father Jozo's church to attend Mass. The following account was witnessed by some of the group.

Father Jozo celebrated mass, talked to the crowd and blessed each person individually after his talk. His way of praying over people was astounding. That a man could touch someone and make them fall over backwards boggled my mind. My thought was, it must be the power of his prayer. Wanting to help in some way, I went up to stand behind people to catch them as they seemingly went unconscious and lay them on the floor. I wasn't such a good catcher. Paying more attention to my praying than catching the people, I soon had to quit.

It was necessary for me to go outside to the bus and because of this I missed seeing everyone getting their blessing. Some of the people from our group told me later that when Father Jozo touched Carmen's head, his hand bounced off her and he said the word "Santeria!" Santeria is an occult group originating in Puerto Rico in which Carmen's parents were involved. Father Jozo called her by her middle name, Yulin. No one there knew her middle name, especially Father Jozo. He started intently praying over her. She fell to the floor in convulsions and remained there for a long time. Later on the bus, Carmen was noticeably a different person. She moved through the bus asking people, "What's your sign?" They would say Pisces or whatever, and she would say, "No!! It's the Sign of the Cross!" Whatever happened to her in Father Jozo's church had affected her tremendously.

Carmen continued sharing her experiences with the group at the hotel room. They were mesmerized listening to her bare her soul about the frightening Satan story. Generally the stories people told were of blessings from the Blessed Mother or gifts from Jesus that were given to them in Medjugorje such as the miracle of the sun, or rosaries turning gold. Understandably, her story frightened some people. Hopefully, it also opened the eyes of some.

The room cleared and it was time to turn in. My roommate, John Rabick, was already asleep. I turned out the lights and knelt down beside my bed to say my prayers. When I started to pray, I felt a kick in my buttocks that physically lifted me a foot off the ground! I fell back down to the floor and was stunned. I couldn't imagine what had just happened to me. I attributed it to a muscle spasm. Regaining my composure, and once again on my knees, I continued my prayer. It happened again! The same pressure was lifting me off the floor by a kick to my other side. Again, I was about a foot off the floor and then collapsed to the floor again. I was panic stricken. The thoughts of Satan being in the room with us were racing through my mind and I jumped up and yelled to my friend, "John, get up! He's in here!" I heard a loud crash in the corner of the room. I switched on the light but there was only John and I in the room. John must have thought I was nuts. Who else but Satan could have lifted me off the ground like that? How I ever fell asleep that night, I don't know. But I did fall asleep, praying.

In the morning, as we all started to gather in the lobby with our luggage, Rick Bach and his wife Barbara, rushed up to me and said, "Boy, when we were leaving your room last night, some strange things happened. There was this big black cat in the hall and he went screaming, running down the hall." There were other incidents people were buzzing about. I had never experienced anything like this in my life. I didn't understand it, nor did I want to.

After breakfast, we boarded our buses to the airport, got on the plane and flew to Zagreb, to meet the other group. We got there about an hour before their planned arrival. Sitting in a cafeteria-like area, I was relating my sinister experiences of the previous night to some of our group. Carmen walked up to me and said, "Tom, what a terrible night I had last night!" She proceeded to tell me about being raised off the ground about a foot from a kick in the buttocks. It was the exact same story I was just relating. People were mystified to think it happened to two people in the same night.

The other group's plane landed and they joined up with us. One of the people from that group came over to the table. It was a girl that I knew from my church, Mary Fleig. She was excited. "Oh Tom," she said, "what a terrible night I had last night! All night long in the hall in front of my door, all I could hear was this loud horrifying sound . . . thunk, thunk, thunk." Now all our mouths dropped open. All the experiences seemed to have some connecting thread running through them. Carmen's and Maria's experience on top of the mountain, hearing that sound from the staff hitting the ground; our experiences at the hotel; then, Mary, telling us about the "thunk" in front of her door last night.

I didn't know what it all meant and I don't know everything that Satan expected to accomplish by it. I only know that it made me all that much more determined to work harder against him, against all that he stands for and what he's trying to do. Obviously, he wanted to scare us away so that we wouldn't want to come back to Medjugorje, or be too frightened to talk about it with others back home.

Thinking of going home made us all sad. It was time to start the transatlantic flight. Earlier, on the bus ride from Medjugorje to Dubrovnik, I had explained to the people on the buses that Satan was going to start attacking us. He was going to try to make us start fighting and arguing with each other; we had to be on guard and defend ourselves with prayer. Well, that very process began when we got to the airport in New York. We found out that our plane from New York to Pittsburgh had already departed and now we had to wait seven hours for the next plane! We were all exhausted from the long flight over at this point, but people seemed to take it okay at first. But as the third and fourth hour passed, the group got more uncomfortable, more on edge. Some demanded to know if there wasn't something we could do? Why don't you do this, why don't you do that? The tempers flared and the arguments started. Finally, the time came to board the plane for Pittsburgh.

The trip had exposed us to so much inconvenience and discomfort that I was more determined than ever to find a better way to go to Medjugorje. I reiterated once again to the Lord that if He was looking for someone to take people to Medjugorje out of love, I might continue to do that.

Chapter 9

Answering the Call

Even though I had been having profound experiences, I was very slow in answering the call. The Lord in His infinite patience, was always willing to wait for me and He had many more experiences lying ahead.

My relationship with the Lord, my speaking to Him and His speaking to me, was enhanced enormously by joining a men's prayer group at St. Ferdinand Church. From Medjugorje, the Blessed Mother has said we all should belong to a prayer group. Joining this one was my attempt to live Her messages. Gathering in front of the tabernacle, nearly every Saturday at 7:00 a.m., three to ten men, along with our pastor Father Ken Oldenski, would submit our lives to Jesus.

When I first joined the group it was in our old church; since then we have a new building. The Tabernacle in the old church was in the center of the sanctuary, behind the altar. In the new church the Tabernacle is off to the right of the altar, behind glass, and that somehow makes me sad. But not as sad as I would be in other parishes that have moved it completely out of sight, behind a wall or down the hall. It isn't that I'm in total disagreement with the Church's decision, because the concept of having a quiet area to pray before the Tabernacle appeals to me. My feeling is that the solution could have been less drastic.

Since our Church is centered on Christ, I believe Christ should always be in the center. A possible solution could be to design the sanctuary so that the Tabernacle is still in the center, but with a room directly behind it to be used for adoration. The Tabernacle could be on a turntable to allow it to be visible to both areas. The subject may be more complicated than I realize, but I'm editorializing again. Back to the subject at hand, the prayer group.

Lining up in front of the Tabernacle, with Rick Bach and his guitar accompanying us, the group would sing songs of praise to Jesus. Between the songs we speak to the Lord, telling Him how much we love Him; recognizing all the things He's done for us that are explained in the Bible; and all the things He was doing for us in our lives.

The meeting starts with great, joyful songs and praising the Lord with great energy. Then the songs become softer and our praising becomes more peaceful and personal. In the end, we surrender ourselves on our knees, calling on the Holy Spirit to come and fill us, to touch our lives, to teach us. At times we include prayers of thanksgiving to our Mother Mary. The morning ends with us lying prostrate on the floor, in front of the tabernacle, being perfectly still and silent, just listening in prayerful hope that the Lord will speak to our hearts and guide us. I'll be the first to admit that the first time I went to this prayer group, it was difficult for me to participate.

All of this was foreign to me at first. I never really sang out loud to Jesus in front of the Tabernacle in my life, and it was very difficult for me to do as the others did. As time passed, however, my visitations to the Blessed Sacrament grew in number and I became more comfortable. The other men expressed how the Lord gave them passages to look for in the Bible. The Lord was already speaking to me before this, but it just *happened*. I didn't have to lie down on the floor.

At first, listening to everyone's experiences, I was astonished. Here was a group of men experiencing the same things I was! It seemed that some missing pieces of the puzzle of my conversion were here in this prayer group. The pieces were fitting together slowly and methodically, in God's own time.

Bible passages were given to me also, as I lay on the floor, and they fit with the passages given to the other men. After fifteen or twenty minutes, we would get up from the floor, and go to another room in the church to discuss what happened to each of us. It was amazing how all the verses of the Bible came together to form a lesson for that day. The theme one Saturday might be peace, and the next week it could contain a unanimous message about praying more or the association between prayer and work. At times the group would get messages and write them down and read them aloud. I, too, would get messages, write them down and share them.

Another day, during the prayer meeting, God spoke to me of His power. Lying prostrate on the floor in front of the Tabernacle, I could hear the roar of the ocean. A voice in my head, quite different from the one I ordinarily heard, said to me, "I am a God of power. A God more powerful than the oceans. Tell the people of My power. Tell them I'm a God to fear, but also a God of great love and mercy. Get up, Thomas, and write this down because you forget so easily."

That part about forgetting was no revelation to me. My memory isn't the greatest and I lose many of the gifts the Lord has given me, because I forget the details. Following His instructions, I got up and wrote it down. There was no pen or pencil, only a yellow magic marker and a booklet in my pocket. Trembling, with tears streaming down my face, I wrote the message. This was definitely one of the most memorable moments of my life! I started to get cold, trembling and shaking. So the other men wouldn't see me, I got up and moved over to a corner of the church to be alone.

My whole body became ice-cold, and that voice in my head said, *"Find your warmth in Jesus, Thomas."* Suddenly, a warmth enveloped me and I started to perspire. A feeling, best described as electricity, started at the tips of my fingers. There was no pain as it passed back and forth, working its way up both my hands at the same time, at exactly the same level. The electricity worked its way just above my wrists and quit. I sat there in total awe of what had just happened. Unknown to me at the time, this was going to be connected to a future event in Louisville, Kentucky.

The prayer group moved into the meeting room. One by one, they explained what had just happened to them. The passages they were given that day were intertwined with the message of the great power of God; a God to fear, but one who was merciful as well. Listening in stunned silence, I realized my experience had exactly the same message as these men just discussed. As I spoke, I began to experience once more what had happened just moments ago. Telling about being ice-cold, I *was* ice-cold. While speaking about the voice telling me to find my warmth in Jesus, I started to get warm again. I was trembling so hard, with my hands on the table, that the entire table shook. Then the electricity started up my hands again; there were tears rolling down my face. One man put his hand on my shoulder to comfort me. Back at home after the prayer meeting, I received a phone call from one of the men who had some reassuring words, "Don't be frightened, Tom, don't let it upset you."

It wasn't frightening. It's hard to explain what it was. Awe-struck is probably the best way to describe the feeling. I've used that word many times, but when these things happen, it's the only word that seems to fit. Why these things are happening to me, I don't know, but I keep being drawn closer and closer to Jesus. I'm also developing a greater and greater thirst for His truth.

The Saturday mornings at St. Ferdinand Church are truly powerful. There was another moving experience after our prayer group met in the new church. While lying in front of the Tabernacle one day, Jesus appeared to me. He was robed in brilliant white. His face was so bright, I couldn't see it clearly and His eyes were like two glowing diamonds, so bright that I could hardly look at them. In a thundering voice He said to me, *"Look into my eyes, Thomas,"* and I looked up.

I was squinting from the brightness. It was almost impossible to look at Him. He spoke again. *"Now I bless you with a blessing only Jesus Christ can give."* Tremendous waves of emotion rolled through my body time and time again, over and over. It was such a glorious feeling, there are no words to describe what went through me. I felt no fear, just, once again, awe. I didn't know then what the purpose of this overwhelming experience was and what the blessing meant; but later it would become perfectly clear to me.

On another occasion, Rick Bach's wife, Barbara, came to me after men's prayer and said, "You know how you told me there's a voice that talks to you? Sometimes I think I hear a voice, though I'm not certain. Last night I spoke to that voice, because of your advice. You said, 'If you think you hear a voice, talk to it. Ask who it is. Pray for discernment.' Well, last night I talked to that voice and I asked, 'Jesus, if this is You, have the men's prayer group talk about John: 10 tomorrow.' My question is, Tom," Barbara continued, "what did you talk about at men's prayer group this morning?"

"If I told you what we talked about, already knowing what you want to hear, what kind of proof would that be for you?" So I suggested, "Why not ask one of the other men at the prayer meeting without any prior explanation?"

She walked over and asked one of the group, "What did you speak about this morning?" Knowing what his reply would be, I remained silent. "John: 10," he said. Barbara looked at me and smiled. This was her confirmation.

One of the most profound conversions came to a man as a result of my appearance on a television program. "Getting Together" is a show on Channel 40, a religious station in Pittsburgh, predominantly Protestant in content. The hosts of the show, Russ and Norma Bixler, met with me at the TV studio before the broadcast to review some things they were going to discuss on the show. They sat down and opened their Bibles to get their passages ready, and suddenly it became apparent to me what they might try to do. Would they come at me with a Protestant point of view, to try to discredit my Catholic beliefs? I said to them, "I hope you're not going to attack me, because you need to know that I work for Jesus Christ. If it is your plan to attack me with scripture, let me tell you I know very little scripture. I did read in the Bible, however, that Jesus said, *'When they try to put you on trial, don't worry about what to say, I will give you the words.'* So know that if it is an attack you have in mind, you're going to be attacking Jesus Christ, not me." That seemed to diffuse the situation greatly, and I appeared on the show with Ron Hembree, a CTV staff member.

As I told my conversion story, they listened with interest. Ron commented that miracles occur outside Christianity; that the *fruits* of a miracle tell the real story. He was more impressed by the 180 degree change in my life than by the miracles of Medjugorje. Our discussion before going on the air possibly made them more compassionate than they originally intended. My conversion was very recent at this point and I wasn't a very experienced speaker. What I was learning didn't come from a book. My knowledge comes from this voice in my head and Jesus continues to teach me every day. There is so much to learn.

The show took an uncomfortable direction for me when they began talking about things I didn't fully understand. Russ Bixler talked about how Catholics believe in Purgatory and how that confused non-catholics. Then he went to the blackboard and drew seven lines, one higher than the other, with a throne above the top. He called it the 'seven levels of Heaven'. I had no idea what he was talking about but I recalled hearing an expression about being in 'seventh Heaven'. The host explained that the Jews wrote in the Bible about the 'seven levels of Heaven'. They believed that God presided over us on His throne above the highest level, the 'seventh Heaven'. All the lines below were levels of happiness achieved in Heaven. "The lowest three levels," Russ explained, "were given a name,

Purgatory, by the Catholic Church around the year 400 AD." For Russ this clarified the existence of Purgatory. He did, however, reject the idea that we could pray for souls in Purgatory.

I told them about Medjugorje, of my healing and everything that happened to me there. Russ Bixler conceded that those kinds of things happen in Christianity. He said he couldn't deny it, "However, we're going to hold out saying what we actually believe for another time . . . but it sounds awful 'new age' to me."

This was the first time I'd ever heard the term. Russ explained that, to him, it seemed that many of the messages from the Blessed Mother in Medjugorje mimic "new age" doctrine. "Most of Her messages talk about peace. The 'newagers' are heavy into peace." (We know now that the peace the Blessed Mother was talking about had nothing to do with 'new age.' She was prophetically telling us of the tens of thousands of deaths that were coming to Yugoslavia if people did not live Her message. The Blessed Mother's messages were always peace, fasting, conversion of the heart, praying and going to Mass and confession. She said wars could be stopped by praying the rosary and living Her messages. Now we know!)

I told them I didn't know anything about 'new age' but Jesus tells us to believe like a child and that's what I'm doing. Believing and living the messages. "You believe that there is no one in Heaven," I said, "that everyone is in the ground waiting for judgement day, and you're incorrect. Jesus said to the thief next to him, *'This day you shall be with Me in paradise.'* That means there *is* someone there already. And know this, if Jesus took a thief to Heaven, you can bet He took His Mother there. If the Lord uses signs and wonders to help teach us, to draw us near, believe me, He can use His Mother to work those miracles."

Wow! I was as startled as they were by the words that came out of my mouth. I had never really heard it expressed that way before and it just came so easily from my heart. At this point I felt used, in a positive way; that the Lord had used me exactly as He said He would. *"Don't worry when they put you on trial, I will give you the words."* What I had just said certainly weren't *my* words. The show ended with the hosts and Ron Hembree reserving judgement about Medjugorje. Ron felt that, "If the fruits of Medjugorje bring people to respect and give dignity to all other people regardless of their faith," he'd have to respect that.

That wasn't the first time the words came as I needed them, although these words concerned things about which I had no previous knowledge. To this day, often while I'm giving a talk, I learn so much from the words given to me by Christ as I speak.

After the show there was a telephone call. A man said, "Mr. Rutkoski, I have to speak to you. Can we meet somewhere?" I asked him if he could meet me that afternoon. He said he couldn't. He seemed to be really upset, so I said, "If you're bothered about something just tell me about it, now, on the phone." He said, "It's too sensitive to talk about over the phone. The show's going to be on again tonight at nine o'clock. Why don't I watch the show again and call you back afterward?"

That was fine with me. I left the TV station feeling good about what had transpired, and a bit confused about the 'seventh Heaven' and this 'new age' stuff. I asked a few people, and found out that there are new beliefs coming into the Church that are not in agreement with the Magisterium and the Pope. They certainly weren't beliefs that I had; that God existed everywhere, in everything. That He wasn't confined to one place like the Tabernacle; that He was in a tree and the grass and nature. God *IS* everywhere, and we witness His power and beauty in these things of nature that He has created, but these are *things*. We cannot worship Him in these things.

That evening the gentleman that had called me at the studio, called me at home, and introduced himself as Glenwood Davis. He was pastor at both a Presbyterian Church and a Baptist Church in Greene County, PA. The area was remote and not well populated. There was a need there in both faiths, so he taught the Baptist beliefs and the Presbyterian beliefs. He said he'd always had this strong attraction to Mary. In one of his churches, there is a stained glass window with a picture of the Mother of God, and every time he talked to his flock, he would be looking at that window. Now, hearing my discussion about Mary on TV and the great love She is offering to all, trying with all Her strength to bring people back to Her Son, had moved him. He was moved even more deeply to hear that there was someone in Heaven already. It made sense to Glenwood that if Jesus had taken a thief, surely He took His Mother. He said all this had affected him so profoundly, that he wanted to become a Catholic. Could I help him become a Catholic?

I told him I would be at St. Ferdinand Church at 7:00 a.m. on Saturday, and asked him to come there so we could discuss it. He agreed. We had a short discussion before the prayer group met, and then we went together in front of the Tabernacle to pray. He expressed some concerns about what would happen to his family and what his occupation would be since preaching was his only source of income. Although preaching didn't provide much and he was having financial troubles, it was providing some income. He had no idea what he would do without it.

During the time we were praying quietly, he suddenly started sobbing deeply as he lay prostrate on the floor. We could hear him talking to someone. I was on his right and Father Ken was on his left. We laid our hands on his back trying to comfort him.

He got up from the floor, overwhelmed and overcome with tears and said, "I just saw the Blessed Mother standing in front of me! I could see my family there with me. She wrapped Her mantle of love around all of us and said, *'Glenwood, everything will be alright'*." Then She invited him back home, back to his Catholic family.

Afterward, we had a chance to sit down and talk. Glenwood explained how he happened to see me on Channel 40 that day. He was scheduled to go on a job interview and came home to get his resume` and some other material. Just before leaving for the interview, he laid his car keys on the kitchen table, went to gather what he needed, came back to the kitchen and his car keys weren't there. He searched and searched. He hunted for those keys so long that it was now past the time for his job interview. He felt his prospective employer would never want to talk to him now. He would be judged irresponsible for not showing up on time.

In his frustration he went outside, trying to vent his anger by cutting the grass, but the mower wouldn't start. His frustration grew. He came back inside the house to sit and cool off for a minute, turned on the TV, and there I was. He watched intently until the show was over, then rushed to call me after being so moved by what he heard. Then he went back to the kitchen to get something to drink and there were his car keys, lying on the table!

Glenwood had a difficult time in the transition from Protestant minister to being a Catholic, but the Mother of God was true to Her word. He persisted through the rough times and became a Catholic. What a glorious day it must have been for Glenwood when he was accepted as a full member in the Church. The grace of God was surely upon him, because his financial concerns were great, but he soon found gainful employment. He is currently writing a book about his experiences. He knows that just seeing me on TV wasn't the only thing that drew him to the Catholic faith. There had been many previous visits from the Holy Spirit to Glenwood that coaxed him into his final decision. My talk on Channel 40 was just the thread that pulled it together for him. It was experiences like these that encouraged me to take additional trips to Medjugorje.

On the June pilgrimage I must have met a half dozen "prophets". As mentioned earlier, many people during that trip offered assistance for future trips, as if they knew I would be coming back. After returning home it didn't take long before I realized that I had to go back. There were many phone calls and requests for another trip, so I blocked airspace on Yugoslav Airlines through a trip wholesaler, for September, 1989. That's right, *I* blocked the space.

On the June 15th trip our guide was Carmel Petrovic. I was very impressed with Carmel and the concern she had for all the pilgrims. Seeing the frustrations I was experiencing, Carmel gave me the name of a woman in the

States that could help me if I decided to return to Medjugorje with more pilgrims. I stuffed Carmel's paper in with all the other information given to me and brought it all back home.

After a week at home, I encountered a tremendous demand for another trip to Medjugorje. I reached into the file of would-be 'prophets' and pulled out the paper Carmel had given me. On the paper was written the name and phone number of Edita Krunic, the owner of Select International, a wholesale travel company. I called Select and talked to Edita. She was more than happy to help me.

Details of the travel arrangements for the September trip kept me so busy that I forgot to tell Edita who had given me her name and number. It wasn't until our second or third conversation, when the subject came up about the guide that would meet us at the airport in Yugoslavia, that Carmel's name came to mind. I told Edita that there was only one guide that I wanted for the September trip, Carmel Petrovic. Edita explained that she couldn't fill that request because she just recently had to fire Carmel.

I couldn't believe my ears. "Why in the world was she fired?" I asked. Edita related that the group leader was very upset with Carmel's performance. Consequently, the agent filed a major complaint against Carmel. "So I had to let her go," said Edita. I exclaimed, "That's not true. *I* was the group leader on that trip!" I related my problems with the agent in question and knew she was angry with me. But since she had no way of getting to me, she tried to blame Carmel for my taking the pilgrims to the hotel in Dubrovnik, to stay overnight. This upset Edita.

There was no way to be sure how much money Carmel had lost by being unemployed because of that letter, but I told Edita I thought Carmel should be reimbursed somehow for her lost wages. I ended up paying Carmel myself because I felt partly responsible.

The subject of money came up again, soon. A man called me and asked how much it cost to go to Medjugorje. I explained the cost was around a thousand dollars. He responded by saying, "Your Blessed Mother only loves rich people, huh?" "NO" I remarked, "that's not true!" He said, "Well then, how does someone that doesn't have the money get there?" "I don't know" I replied. I was at a loss for an explanation, but I knew that the Blessed Mother came for everyone. Sensing that the man felt this was all a fraud, caused me to ponder his question. Opening up to the Lord again, I said, "If You want someone to help the poor people, who can't afford to pay, to get to Medjugorje, I would be willing to try."

For the upcoming September trip I made an effort to help the less fortunate. The tour operator and airline provided one free passenger for every twenty paid trips. On the last trip I had used the free seats for religious and wanted to continue to take nuns and priests at no cost. By adding one hundred dollars to the wholesale cost of each trip, with sixty paying passengers on the upcoming trip, the extra hundred dollars per person would provide six thousand dollars 'profit'. After expenses, there would be enough left for six free trips. Cartwheel time! The Blessed Mother had poor people going! How I wished I had taken the phone number of that man who called me asking about the poor. What a gift Our Lady was giving me! If someone called now and said he or she knew a person who wanted to go to

Medjugorje but couldn't afford it, I was able to call that friend and say, "You're going to Medjugorje! **Free!**"

In no time, the trip was sold out. I had fifty-six paying pilgrims, four going free from the profit and three going free from the one-free-in-twenty deal with the airline. We left Pittsburgh Friday, September 22, and guess who was going to be my guide! Carmel.

Uncle Stanley was going back with me along with my new friend, John Rabick. It was comforting to have companions along. It's a strange feeling, caring for a large group of people on such a long journey. The responsibility is awesome. Having a few friends around kept me at ease.

At the airport I took John a little by surprise. John, Stanley, and I had intended to take a one week vacation after the pilgrimage. We would see the group back to the airport in Dubrovnik and send them home. I felt comfortable doing that since the plane was going directly into Pittsburgh, and the return flight wouldn't be difficult for them.

When Stan and I discussed all the places we wanted to visit, we realized it would require two additional weeks of travel. We didn't, however, discuss that with John. He was retired, so we figured he would just go along with it.

At the airport, I introduced John to the idea of staying an additional week. He looked at his wife in a startled manner, but after he'd had a chance to think about it, he said, "What the heck, okay. I'll stay a third week." He was concerned about how much clothing he had with him. I tried to calm his anxiety a little, telling him it wouldn't be a problem. We would find a place to wash our clothes. So off we went to Medjugorje. It would be my third time back, and Stanley's and John's second.

There was a set pattern while traveling to Medjugorje; getting to the airport in Dubrovnik, boarding the buses, driving up to Medjugorje, singing and praying on the way. This time was different. Because of the vacation afterwards, we decided to rent a car at the airport and drive to Medjugorje. The car would be available in Medjugorje for our own use. So John, Stan and I got in the rental car and followed the buses.

That was the first time John had ever ridden with me in a car and he soon discovered that I'm an aggressive driver. From all my years in the news business, chasing stories, I drive in a hurry. Having previously raced sports cars a little, I anticipate dangerous situations and always have my exit planned in case something goes wrong. I doubt if many people drive that way, but that's my style. Well, John, not knowing me well, didn't understand my ability to drive. He felt much apprehension in a car traveling at a high rate of speed. Frightened as John was of my driving, he never said a word. By the time we arrived in Medjugorje, he was having second thoughts about going on with us for the other two weeks.

Once in Medjugorje the wonderful process began, just like on the trips before. Approaching St. James Church for the third time felt just as powerful as the first and second times.

Everyone unloaded from the buses and went into their host homes. This was the start of our deeply emotional week of heart-changing, eye-opening experience and learning to love the way that Jesus and Mary love. The trip up Podbrdo, (Apparition Hill) and Krizevac (Cross Mountain); the side trips to Father Jozo's church, were all exactly as before, and just as wonderful. What a beautiful privilege it is to watch a pilgrim's conversion, and to be there to lend a hand when anyone had a question or just needed a shoulder to cry on.

We finished our week in Medjugorje and returned to the airport in Dubrovnik. John mentioned that maybe he wouldn't be going on the next two weeks' trip with us It was an awful long time to be away and maybe he should just go home. I said, "John, we planned all this out and you seemed so excited." He replied, "No, I think I'll just go home."

I asked him, "Is it my driving?" He looked at me and said, "Well . . . to tell you the truth, yes. It does frighten me a bit." I said, "John, I'm not going to promise you that I'll slow down because that's the way I drive all the time. My only reassurance to you is that I know how to handle a car and we're going to be okay. I enjoy your company and I think you'll enjoy the trip. Please come along." So John changed his mind again and came with us.

After the pilgrims departed by plane, we began our trip down the Adriatic coast. We cut across the mountains of Yugoslavia and found ourselves on a long, winding mountain road. It was barely two lanes wide. At such a high altitude, we were driving up through the clouds with no guard rails. I was having a good time just winding through the curves. Looking into the rear view mirror I could see John in the back seat, praying. I never saw a man pray the rosary so hard and so fast in all my life. I said, "John, you're really smoking those rosaries!" John said, "My goodness, Tom, the Blessed Mother just jumped out of the car,

She was so frightened!" Realizing it gave him such anxiety, I tried to slow down.

Although we had many wonderful times on this excursion, it was racked with enough problems to make us wonder why we ever left Medjugorje. We traveled through Greece and there we wrecked our rental car. In our travels through Turkey, I ran over a dog. In Bulgaria, I got a terrible eye infection, and on our return trip to Yugoslavia, I finally got stopped for speeding. (The fine was seventy-five cents!)

We finally arrived home, at least it seemed like home. Medjugorje! I consider this trip number four. Why? It was a totally new experience. We were introduced to a new area of Medjugorje. I didn't want to stay in the hotel, as we had with the group, because we were looking for more of a home atmosphere as I had experienced on my very first trip to Medjugorje. I checked around and found another location in an area called Sivric Street. A family there welcomed us into their home. The next couple of days were so wonderful. These people were just like relatives. They were so hospitable to us. We met Vesa and her son, Zdenko Sivric. The street was named after their family. Later we were introduced to grandpa, DiDu. He didn't look ninety years old, but he was and still got around pretty good.

Exploring the street further, I thought, "If I ever get back to Medjugorje again, I would like to stay here." It was quiet, away from the commercialism, but still only a short walking distance to St. James Church. Gathering the names of the other owners of the houses on Sivric Street that took in pilgrims, I found out how many people would fit into each house and the number of bathrooms in each house. I wanted to know everything there was to know about Sivric Street. Each trip I learned a little more. Eliminating housing problems would help prevent needless distractions from the real reason the pilgrims came to Medjugorje. What is not needed on a pilgrimage are problems that can be avoided by simple planning. Satan will create enough; I didn't want to add to them.

We finished our stay, returned to the airport and flew back home. John, I think, was happy that he had stuck it out. He'd had enough experiences to last a lifetime. I hoped he might come back with me again, if that was in God's plan. Stanley is the type who is always ready and willing to go anyplace, anytime. A perfect traveling companion.

One thing I was neglecting at home, because I was so busy, was my boat. It was moored at the Fox Chapel Yacht Club. While there, much of my time was spent evangelizing. It was no longer a place of rest for me. In fact, feeling guilty about owning the big boat, I found it difficult to go there at all. When I asked the Lord if I should leave the yacht club, the response was, *"Who will evangelize these people then?"* I stayed. Frankly, I wasn't happy about it, but I stayed the entire summer. People at the club were getting a bit tired of me talking about God all the time and made jokes. It didn't bother me in the least. I just prayed my evangelizing would draw people closer to God rather than drive them farther away.

At the end of summer I asked the Lord again if I could leave the yacht club and this time He said, *"Yes."* At last I could get rid of one more albatross that was hanging around my neck. Oops! I forgot one thing, I'd better check with my wife, Mary. Was Mary going to want to get rid of the boat? She really loved going there. I prayed before approaching Mary and wondered how to bring up the subject. It wasn't necessary; it just happened. One day on the boat I must have looked a little down and Mary asked, "What's wrong, Tom?" I looked at her and confided, "I don't like it here very much anymore." Mary said, "I'm tired of it myself. Too much hassle. Let's try to sell it." I couldn't believe it was that easy! Prayer works. Thank you, Lord.

We put the boat up for sale. It was autumn and not a good time to sell a boat, but I was confident the Lord would take care of that also. I wasn't going to worry about it. There were plenty of other things to occupy my mind.

It seems the Lord was filling my calendar with speaking engagements and there were a dozen requests for yet another pilgrimage. My life was busy! Was I going to say 'yes' to yet another trip this year? If I were going to answer His call, I would. After what the Lord had done for me, how could I not have another pilgrimage?

Departure date with thirteen pilgrims: November 3, 1989. With a group this small, we all became close. Three people, in particular, stand out in my mind. Robert and Dorothy Kocur and Jeff Bailey. Bob and Dorothy impressed me because they seemed like the perfect married couple. You could just feel the love they had for each other. We had several opportunities to sit and talk, and they both expressed a desire to help me in this rapidly growing ministry. Bob explained that he had some computer experience and when we got back home he would get in touch with me. He also expressed a desire to lead a pilgrimage if ever there was a need.

Jeff Bailey was a non-catholic, wandering through life oblivious to religion, just as I had been all those years. I probably spent more time with Jeff on that trip than I did with any other person. Jeff experienced many supernatural things while he was there. He was being drawn to understand what the Catholic faith is all about.

One night, we were inside St. James Church. Father Philip was leading people in the Divine Mercy devotion. After the prayers were finished, the Lord spoke to me and said, "*Tell Jeff to convert to Catholicism.*" When we walked outside, Jeff said, "Tom, could I talk to you for a minute?" I said, "Sure. I need to talk to you anyhow."

Jeff said, "You go first. What did you want to tell me?" I related what happened inside the church. "The Lord gave me a message for you, Jeff. He wants you to become a Catholic." Emotion overwhelmed Jeff. A big smile appeared on his face. "That's fantastic!" He exclaimed. "That's just what I wanted to talk to you about! I wondered if my prayer to Jesus was okay and I wanted to ask you about it. My prayer was, 'Jesus, if you want me to become a Catholic, send me a message'." So much for long waits.

That trip was especially spiritual for me because I had the time to slow down a little bit, and experience more of Medjugorje. Fortunately for all of us, Carmel Petrovic was our guide again. It amazed me how solicitous she was, trying to make everything run smoothly for everyone. She asked if I would be coming back the following year, and offered her assistance. We went from house to house on Sivric Street with the list of owners that I had previously compiled. Carmel introduced me to the owners and rechecked the number of beds and bathrooms in each house. Carmel said, "Now, just in case you do come back, you can figure out in advance which group will stay where." This proved to be a tremendous help for future trips.

Too soon it was time to go. It was becoming more difficult to leave Medjugorje each time. It had begun to feel like my second home.

Returning from the third and final trip of the year, I resumed speaking two and three nights a week, most weeks, through the Winter of 1989 and into the Spring of 1990. I went wherever, whenever, I was asked. Somehow I managed, but not without a great toll. Driving to work at KDKA, it was hard to keep my eyes open and I spent very little time with my wife. The prospect of improving either of these situations appeared bleak. The obvious solution, cutting back on the amount of speaking engagements, was out of the question. As time passed I was becoming burnt out and I needed help.

Computers became part of the answer. That first trip, I had recorded all the information regarding the pilgrims on a little laptop computer that was very slow. Then I bought a 286 IBM compatible, which doubled the speed of the laptop. It was like adding half a person to my staff of one. My job at KDKA made it possible for me to buy new computer software, and the constant updating kept my hands full. But this gave me the great opportunity to dispense the Blessed Mother's messages twenty four hours a day.

Chapter 10

Gospa Missions

All of the speaking engagements, through the Winter of 1989 and Spring of 1990, generated so much Medjugorje activity in Pittsburgh that what seemed busy before became almost an impossible situation. So many people called and wanted to go on pilgrimage at all times of the year. We had plans for trips to Medjugorje in May, June, July, two in September, two in October, two more in November and one in December! Whew! The number that reserved seats this year totaled around five hundred.

The work to organize the trips, to make it all come together smoothly, took many, many hours of sitting at the computer. It was like I was changing professions. I typed in names, deposits, recorded checks, tracked funds, made arrangements for the aircraft, for the buses, for the lodging. The combination of that and speaking at churches made me work more hours than you could imagine. Something had to give. I didn't have more hours to give. Either office help was needed or . . . one other thing, I could quit my job, but how would that be possible?

With all that was going on in my life, you would think that the Lord would not have to prove to this "doubting Thomas" again, that all of this was really from Him and that He could do anything. Even so, I was still wondering about things I heard in my mind. Because now more than ever I was hearing, *"Take more people to Medjugorje."*

"Is this really you, Lord?" I asked again. I was looking at my picture of Divine Mercy and said, "If this is really you and you want me to take all these people to Medjugorje, give me a sign."

In the process of opening my mail, I opened a letter from John Rabick. A small news clipping fell out. Reading it, I couldn't believe my eyes! The clipping read, "Yugoslav Airlines to fly here." JAT, Yugoslav Airlines, had opened an office in Pittsburgh. The number to call was 538-4596.

Obviously there was some mistake there, because 538 was not a Pittsburgh exchange, it was for Evans City, a little farm community twenty five miles north of Pittsburgh. I called the number and a woman with an English accent answered, "Belinda Held, Yugoslav Airlines, Pittsburgh. May I help you?"

I said to her, "You say Pittsburgh, but how can your telephone number be a 538 exchange?" She responded, "Well, we're not actually in Pittsburgh, we just say that because no one would recognize our location." She continued, "We're in a tiny little farm community about twenty five miles north of Pittsburgh called . . ." I cut her off at that point, finishing her line, saying, "Evans City."

She said, "How did you know that?" I answered, "I know where Evans City is; I live here! Why in the world would Yugoslav Airlines open an office in Evans City?" She said, "That's a long story." My thought was, it's a lot longer story than you'll ever know! I had said to the Lord, "If you want me to take more people to Medjugorje, give me a sign." Well, what a sign! The Lord knew what I needed even before I asked.

Try to comprehend this miracle. Yugoslav Airlines had offices in New York, San Francisco, Cleveland, Chicago, and now, our little Evans City! With this my confidence grew and I felt that I was doing exactly what Jesus and Mary wanted. There was so much flack from travel agents in Pittsburgh who claimed I was stealing their business. I had cut the price to Medjugorje to the bone and they were upset. This confirmed that I should continue. It was for God, not for money. I said, "Jesus, if this is what you want me to do, I'll quit my job for you. That's the only way we'll get all of this done."

How does one ever get the courage to make the decision to walk away from a lucrative profession, and give one's life to Jesus? Had I come to that point? Just then, there was a knock at the door. I answered and there was a man from St. Ferdinand Church standing there. He introduced himself as Charley Gaffney. He said, "Tom, Rick Bach and I were down at the church praying and I felt led to come and talk to you about something we experienced. The Lord spoke to us in our prayer." I didn't find that hard to believe.

He said, "The Lord said to me that you're very busy and you need help. I'm an accountant for a firm in Butler. I don't know how much help I can be, but I'm happy to offer you my services."

Boy, did I need help! I was buried in numbers, and with dyslexia, numbers are no friends. Charley was truly a gift from God. "Oh, Charley," I said, "if you only knew what a blessing this is and what a blessing you are. The workload is becoming so heavy. There aren't enough hours in the day to do it all. I was just upstairs praying and asking the Lord if He wanted me to quit my job."

"No!" Charley said, "That's what He laid on Rick's heart, that you were thinking about quitting your job and you aren't supposed to do that yet! Your credibility, right now, comes from your job at KDKA and the Lord wants you to stay there. Help will come."

Well, Charley became a tremendous friend and valuable helper. His prophecy was accurate; help did come. I was using the 286 computer and it was being overworked. I ran into a conflict between the answering system and the need to use the computer for desk-top publishing. There had to be something out there that could do the job more efficiently. Back into my life came Nick Marchuk, an old acquaintance. Nick and I had dabbled in computer games a few years prior and now he helped me run the answering system. Nick had graduated into building computers and became our hardware expert. Next came Don Gaus, a desk-top publishing expert from IBM. Help would come? It certainly came with Don. With Don's help, the crude little flyer I was making to advertise pilgrimages blossomed into a beautiful brochure. The little Blessed Mother computer operation, run out of the back room of my house, started to grow. A short time later, just to make sure the books were always balanced, the Lord sent Jim Brueckner, a banker.

For the first year I called my ministry, Tom Rutkoski Travel. From scripture and from what the Lord had been teaching me, there was a need for me to become smaller so that He could grow larger in my life. My name should be removed from as much of the operation as possible. I definitely didn't want to continue calling it Tom Rutkoski Travel. Charley was over one day when I was putting together the flyer with Don Gaus. After mentioning my need to come up with a name for my ministry, Charley said, "Why don't you name it after the Blessed Mother?" I said, "Well, I would Charley, but I just can't come up with a name." Charley said, "In Medjugorje they called her the Gospa." I said, "Yeah, I'm familiar with that." He said, "How about Gospa Missions? Our Lady's Missions?"

What a beautiful idea! And it looked great on the flyer, too. I analyzed the idea of Charley naming the operation. Here again, that helped me to grow smaller because it was not my idea, but someone else's. The fact that I was open to something like that made me feel good and I pray that it made Charley feel good also. I hope the name, 'Gospa Missions', makes the Blessed Mother happy. The name, 'Gospa Missions', started to spread in the Pittsburgh area and in the four or five counties surrounding Pittsburgh.

The flyer for the trips, designed by Don, to advertise Gospa Missions, was an inspiration to me. All my advertisement before that had been on one simple sheet, typed on one side, and run off on the Xerox machine. Don Gaus, who I feel was a gift from the Lord, made the flyer blossom into a four-fold, tremendously well-produced product that would have been a prize at any advertising agency. He was so good at what he did. I wanted this to be just right and pleasing to the Blessed Mother. When I took it to the printer, he gave me a price on seventy pound yellowish paper, and I said, "No, it's got to be better than that." Then he showed me other types of paper including a fine textured silk paper. I said, "That's what we'll use." It was rather expensive, but nothing was too good for the Blessed Mother. So the flyers were printed on that silk paper.

After the order was placed and they started to print, I realized my error. Although my intentions were honorable, to please the Blessed Mother, it wasn't Gospa Missions' intent to spend unwisely the funds that were raised. I felt remorse about my decision. We work strictly on donations and all the helpers who work at Gospa Missions do so for no fee. Whatever way we raise funds, whether from trips to Medjugorje or some of the other projects, everyone works so hard for the funds.

These funds are to keep Gospa Missions alive and to give free pilgrimages to those people who can't afford to go to Medjugorje. Instead of sending poor people, free of charge, to Medjugorje, I was using the money on silk paper. I spoke to the Blessed Mother and said, "I'm really sorry, Blessed Mother. My intent was to please you. I should have bought a more reasonably-priced paper for the flyer rather than such an expensive one."

When I went to pick up the flyers I asked the owner what the total bill was. (For a gift like this I need to tell you, it was Huckstein's Printing in Zelienople Pa.) Mr. Huckstein said to me, "There's no charge, Tom, this one's on me." Wow! I couldn't believe my ears. What a gift! I'm sure the Blessed Mother arranged this, just to say, "It's okay, Thomas, you'll make mistakes, but know that I love you." Oh, the flyers were so beautiful! At each talk I would distribute them to encourage each person to go to Medjugorje. This flyer also had the telephone number to call for the Blessed Mother's message from the Gospa Missions' office in my home.

How many people started calling that special number . . . 538-5700 in the 412 calling area. The 5700 inspired me because of the seven being an important number in the realm of God. (I made sure there weren't any sixes in it.) I don't know how much legitimacy there is to those kinds of things but I still hold fast to Pope Urban VIII's statement that "it's better to believe than not to believe." I kept trying to improve the message system at Gospa Missions so that we could dispense the message each month from Medjugorje and tell about upcoming speaking engagements, whether mine or someone else's, and about other activities in the faith community.

One of the messages from Medjugorje, pertains to the chastisements that are supposed to be on the way. Several days before it begins, the world would be informed. I wondered *how* they would be informed. Maybe through computers like ours! Wouldn't it be great to have a network of computers like this in a lot of places? I don't know whether God's going high tech or not, but we couldn't invent all these things without Him. Unknown to me at the time, this very technology was going to play a big part in the spreading of my ministry.

Speaking of technology, the videotape that my nephew Greg made of my talk at the Consolata Mission House went into a drawer along with the two tapes of the visionaries in Medjugorje. These tapes were not to be seen by anyone, because although the quality of these three tapes was technically up to standard, I was personally displeased with the roles I played in all of them. Someone badgered me until I was willing to surrender one copy of my Consolata witness tape. He said he had a friend who couldn't make it to my talk but wanted to view it on tape. So I made a VHS dub of the tape and gave it to this man, not feeling comfortable about giving it to him. Less than six months later I got a call from a man called Chuck Cleaveland. Chuck asked if he could order some copies of my videotape.

I told him that I didn't have a videotape. He said, "Of course you do, why would you say that?"

I said, "Well, I don't know how you know about *that* tape, but I don't distribute it." He was getting upset. "What do you mean you don't distribute it? I've got a copy of it! Well, actually, it's a copy of a copy and the quality is so bad, I can't even see your face." He went on, "This story of yours is bringing people back to Jesus Christ. Who do you think you are, keeping this from people?"

"It was never my intent to keep it from anybody," I replied. "The quality isn't up to par so I'll make another tape some day."

Chuck was a little upset with me. He was so insistent that I finally made some tapes for him. He made me aware that I was making decisions about *how* people were going to receive Jesus. If you find Jesus in something, what does it matter how it's presented or in what medium it's presented; or what the quality of that medium is . . . if it brings you to Jesus. He said, "I want a hundred copies, how much will it cost?" I told him I had no idea but I would check for him.

At work the next day I tried to find my friend, Jimmy Artzberger, who I knew had two videotape machines and could possibly make me some copies. What a strain to put on a friendship! My intention was to ask him to make a hundred copies of an hour-long videotape. I didn't consider how long it would take. But I couldn't find Jimmy and I was a little upset because Chuck wanted those tapes immediately.

Another friend at the station, Ron Bruno, came walking by and said, "What's the matter, Tom, you look kinda sad?" I told him of my need to get videotapes reproduced. "What kind of tapes?" He asked. I said, "VHS dubs of a story I tell in churches."

He said, "I can make ten dubs at a time." "You can do what?" I exclaimed. He answered, "I have a little production unit at my house with ten tape machines. Bring it out and I'll make them for you for just the cost of the tapes." Boy, what a gift! I took the ten-inch version of my witness out to his home and three days later Ron brought me a hundred copies for $2.50 apiece! You can hardly buy blank tapes alone for that amount and they would be cheap tapes at that! But he put it on Sony professional videotape that would last a long time.

I called Chuck Cleaveland and told him the tapes were ready. He was surprised how inexpensive they were. We arranged to meet about halfway between his house and mine. I presented the two cases of tapes to him. He took four out. "Now," he said, "that's all I want. You take the rest and pass them out." "You're kidding!" I was stunned. He repeated, "Pass them out!"

There was another Marian conference coming up, this time in Pittsburgh. I had talked to the folks who were putting it together, particularly, Maryann O'Keefe. I put information about the conference on the Blessed Mother's message machine to let callers know that the conference was going to be in Pittsburgh. I also mentioned it during my talks to help build up attendance.

KDKA radio's Mike Pintek got in touch with me to see if I could get Maryann to come on his radio program and talk about the upcoming conference. She said, "No." When I related this to Mike, he asked me to come on his show and talk about Medjugorje and the conference. I agreed to talk about Medjugorje but I told him I knew nothing about the conference.

The night of the radio show, I was driving home after work to try to catch some sleep before driving back to KDKA and Mike's show. Totally exhausted from my hectic speaking schedule the past few days, I was falling asleep at the wheel. I turned on the air-conditioner full blast, opened all the windows, blared the radio and sang my way home to keep awake.

Once home, in bed, I prayed to Jesus, "Lord, I know it's within Your power to give me some kind of super-sleep for the next hour so I can be awake enough to drive back to Pittsburgh for the radio show. Please Lord, give me that rest." Bam! I was out!

An hour later I awoke . . . paralyzed! I couldn't move any part of my body, not even my arms or legs. I was terrified. Realizing something supernatural was going on, but not knowing whether it was good or evil, I instantly reminded myself, "Whoa! Who do I work for? I work for Jesus Christ." I said, "Jesus, if this is You, let Your will be done. Satan, if this is you, I command you to leave in the name of Jesus Christ!" Electricity began to work its way back and forth through my feet, then my legs, up my body, through my hands and arms . . . back and forth, all the way to the top of my head. Then it quit. Instantly forgetting what had just happened to me, my initial reaction was that of being upset because I was awake too soon and couldn't fall back to sleep. I was more awake than ever in my life! I got up, showered and went to work on the computer until it was time to leave for the station. I was not the least bit tired and sang all the way to Pittsburgh, religious songs, of course.

The program was delayed because of a hockey game, and I had to wait an additional hour and a half to get on the show. But when the show started, everything went as planned. For the most part the program dealt with Medjugorje. Mike did ask me about the Pittsburgh conference and all I said was that it was happening that weekend and it was an event no one should miss.

During a break, Mike explained to me that although all went well so far, I should prepare myself for the next segment because he was going to have to ask me some tough questions about Medjugorje. I said to him, "Hey, if you want to ask me something tough, ask me about Bishop Zanic and how he doesn't believe the apparitions are taking place." He sighed and said, "That's what I was going to ask you!" Mike ended up asking me about the Bishop but it wasn't the blockbuster he hoped it would be. I explained how all authority was removed from Bishop Zanic by the Vatican on rendering any judgement on Medjugorje. Mike related to me after the show that several times while I was telling my story, he got goose bumps and said, "Maybe someday I might go to Medjugorje. I'd like to invite you back sometime." After agreeing to come back, I left for home.

On the way home, not tired at all, I sang some more songs, this time along with one of my "Glory and Praise" tapes. About 2:00 am I went bouncing into the house, still feeling better and more awake than ever in my life. Walking into the bedroom, still singing, I awoke my wife. Mary asked what was the matter with me, singing like that in the middle of the night. She asked why I was so happy. It was then that it hit me. Instantly, I realized what the Lord had accomplished in me. It all came back to me and it was very vivid, being paralyzed, the electricity and how awake I became because of it. The Lord had rejuvinated me. It seems that God will give you anything you need, if you give Him your life. I was in awe!

That morning I was off to the conference. Earlier in the week I asked Maryann if I could pass out my Medjugorje flyers at the conference. There was some concern about how many would be distributed. Her decision was that only 500 flyers could be given out, which bothered me. Out of 5,000 people attending, only one out of ten people would get a flyer. I guess a lot of people badgered Maryann about putting literature out and maybe she saw it as a problem. Now, I had the videotapes in my car and boy, would I have liked to have given them out at the conference. But if Maryann didn't want the flyers distributed, surely she wouldn't want the tapes given out.

At the lunch break, I got ten tapes from the car and put them in my briefcase; then went to Wendy's for a bite to eat. I don't know how the information was getting out about my having tapes of my talk to distribute, but someone at Wendy's yelled across the restaurant, "Hey Tom, I understand you have a copy of your talk on videotape. Could I get one of those?"

I yelled back, "Sure." Probably everyone in the whole place heard me when I said, "I have some with me, but I hoped to give them to people from out of town. If you see me later, I'll give you one."

Someone piped up, "I'm from out of town! I'll take one." Someone else yelled, "I'll take one," and again . . . "I'll take one." Before I knew it, all ten were gone. I had to go to the car to get more. I had conversations with some of the people who asked for the tapes, and it never really registered who was who or where they were from. I had no idea how many different States the tapes went to but the conversion story of Tom Rutkoski was leaving Pittsburgh on its own.

About two or three weeks later I got a call from a man named Joe Schroer. He was from Louisville, Kentucky and he told me he watched the videotape and enjoyed it very much. He inquired if I would come to Louisville and tell my story. I said, "Sure, I'll come." He said he was going to work toward that end and try to set up a date.

I forgot about my conversation with Joe, but unbeknownst to me, there he was back in Louisville, still trying to arrange for me to come to speak. However, he was running into difficulty trying to show the tape to folks down there. No one seemed interested. He couldn't even get them to watch it.

There was a Medjugorje retreat in Louisville one day, and folks were watching tapes about Medjugorje. When no one was looking, Joe took the one tape out and put mine in. The way he tells the story, people started to gather around the TV and ask, "who is this guy?" The crowd got bigger and bigger. During my witness I had tears in my eyes and it seems that a lot of the people watching the tape got tears in their eyes. They wanted to know where the tape came from. Joe finally spoke up and told them that this was the tape he'd been trying to show them.

Shortly afterward, I received a phone call from a woman named Debbie Womack. She explained to me that Joe brought a tape to their mini-conference and everybody was excited about my story. Would I come to Louisville and tell it? Immediately I replied, "Yes." She asked, "What does it take to get you here?" "Simply send me a ticket and find me a place to stay," I responded. She asked about my fee. "Who could ever charge for talking about God? There's no fee," I told her. Debbie made arrangements for me to come to Louisville in November, 1990.

This is when I learned how far ahead of me Jesus Christ was working and laying down plans. About a month before this invitation, I succumbed to a great deal of persuasive invitations by a priest named Father Ron Lengwin, the Communications Director for the diocese of Pittsburgh. Fr. Ron had a radio show on KDKA radio, and I would see him occasionally as he passed through the television side of the station. He saw me frequently, at daily Mass at St. Mary's Church, in downtown Pittsburgh, and knew that I took my religion seriously. So he assumed that I might want to help the diocese. He approached me and said, "Tom, we're going to start a little video program in the diocese. The Bishop is going to do a half-hour show and I wondered if you would be interested in volunteering as a cameraman? We sure could use your expertise." I said, "No, no . . . I'm so busy, I couldn't possibly fit that in." He said, "It wouldn't be a lot of time. We're going to do it on Saturday from 8:30 a.m. until about noon, but not every Saturday."

That took it from a "No, no," to an emphatic "NO!" Saturday morning was when I went to the men's prayer group at St. Ferdinand church. I wasn't about to give up that precious time in front of the tabernacle for anybody.

The things I learned there were tremendous. Well, Fr. Ron didn't let the matter drop. He approached me a second time and a third time and the last time just a few days before their first shoot.

Father Ron pleaded, "Tom, we're in a terrible bind. I know that you already said you can't do this, but if you could just help us out this one Saturday, I'd really appreciate it. I'm sure the Bishop would appreciate it also."

Well the tone of his voice seemed so urgent I had to feel some kind of compassion for the Church's problem. Trying not to be selfish, maybe I could give a little of my time to the diocese. Would it hurt so much if I missed one Saturday at the men's prayer group? "Okay, Father, I'll be there Saturday," I responded.

Their shoot that Saturday was in a small, cramped studio. The equipment, especially the tripods, were somewhat less sophisticated than what I normally used. My main problem was with the tripods themselves. It was hard to get steady shots with that equipment but there I was, trying to do my best with what was available. Just one Saturday and it would be over. That was the first time I ever met Bishop Wuerl. We were introduced and I felt an instant rapport the first time we shook hands.

Each show was broken into three segments. Our job was to do the first segments of five shows. This first part that we did was the teaching segment. When the process of videotaping the Bishop started, I soon found out how hard it is to pay attention to camera work, listen to the Bishop and still pray. With little time to spare, my every free moment was used to say the Rosary. Listening to the sincere and profound words coming from Bishop Wuerl, well it went right to my heart. It was impossible to do anything but listen. I knew Jesus was using him because the words were so perfectly placed.

I don't know if anybody noticed, but tears were running down my face. My only explanation to you about how powerful this experience was for me, is to tell you that it completely altered my decision about working on the show. I offered my services to the Bishop and Father Ron. If I didn't have a speaking engagement on a Saturday, I would be there. While taping the Bishop's show, I could learn directly from him. The Shepherd of our diocese could teach me as I performed a service for the Church. That overwhelmed me.

While working several Saturdays on the videotaping, a thought occurred to me. Was there anything I was saying in my talk that could be offensive to the Catholic Church? I didn't see how that could be, since it seemed to change people's lives in such a positive manner. I asked the Bishop to review a tape of my talk, and he did. The Bishop sent me a letter saying, "Tom, in the past few weeks I've had a chance to view your presentation on Medjugorje. You present the story so well that my only concern now is that you might edge me out of my niche on the teaching of Christ."

With his gentle humor, the Bishop was saying that he enjoyed it! Although he wasn't giving it an imprimatur, he found nothing contradictory in it. In essence, his message was, "Go ahead, tell your story."

Going to Louisville to tell my story in the churches, seemed to be a certainty. However, some questions to Debbie were raised about who I was. It was brought to the attention of Archbishop Kelly of Louisville. He wanted to know more about Tom Rutkoski before he would allow me to come and speak in any of his churches. So Debbie called me back and asked if I could give the Archbishop an explanation of my talk.

What better testimony could I give the Archbishop than explaining the work that I do for Bishop Wuerl, along with the Bishop's letter of approval. After receiving that, Archbishop Kelly permitted me to come to the Louisville area to speak. So you can see now, how the Lord was laying His plan for my future.

Debbie asked me how many churches I would like to have her set up for speaking engagements. I said, "Get one north of the city, one south, one east and one west. We can put the Sign of the Cross over Louisville and my conversion story would be all over the area at the same time." She said, " Are you sure? Other speakers who come here only speak at one place. Are you really willing to speak at that many?" "Debbie," I said, "I'm not coming to socialize, I'm coming to evangelize."

And that's exactly what I went there to do, evangelize. How I loved doing it! Just the thought of going on the road with this story was so exciting and very fulfilling. The knowledge that Jesus loved me so much that He would allow me to give of myself even more deeply than I had been, was truly rewarding! Following Jesus certainly didn't seem like I was carrying a cross!

Off to Louisville. It was wonderful meeting Debbie and seeing Joe Schroer for the second time. Now I realized who it was that took my video tape that day at Wendys in

Pittsburgh, and accomplished so much through it. May God bless you, Joe.

At the first talk I let the audience know that it was Joe who made my being there possible. That surprised a lot of people. I think that there were many who didn't think Joe looked the part. At the second talk, Debbie said her hands felt hot and she was wondering if she could lay them on my head and pray for me. This sounded strange to me and made me feel really uncomfortable, but I said "I don't care, go ahead." She laid her hand on my head and said a few words. I couldn't hear what she was saying and it was time for me to go up in front of this group and talk, so I didn't have time to ask her. After the presentation Debbie said she had been given a message by the Lord and it was for me. She read it:

"You are My true disciple, My beloved son, My precious one, chosen to bring My message of Mercy and the fruits of My Holy Spirit to all the world. I love you, My chosen son. Your responsibility is a great one, the one to shatter the shackles that are holding My people bound. My grace is poured forth upon you and all those you reach with My Message of Peace. Be humble. Be holy. Be true. You shine forth My light to more lives than even you can imagine. I have placed you in the depths of My Sacred Heart. You are to be the image of My Love to all you meet. You are precious. You are pure. You are mine. I love you, Thomas."

As the words left Debbie's mouth they by-passed my ears and went straight to my heart and soul. I again was rendered to tears. For the first time this message made me realize the magnitude of my conversion and the responsibility that came with it. Several of us went to a grotto built for the Blessed Mother located in front of the church. We knelt and said the Sorrowful Mysteries. This was the most powerful Rosary I can remember saying. We were all filled with the Holy Spirit. The words of meditation that came to me at each mystery, flowed from my heart and rendered us all to tears.

Saturday afternoon, we went to Mass at the Cathedral. After Mass, Debbie asked me if I ever had the Blessing of the Blessed Mother. I said, "No, I haven't. I've heard of that Blessing but I've never met anyone who was given it." Supposedly, there was an apparition in Medjugorje and Our Lady blessed the group during the apparition and said that She wanted each of them to take it home and start spreading it. It's called "A Blessing to Save the World". Each person who received it could pass it on to others; the more you use it, the more powerful it becomes. It could be as simple as saying, "May you have the blessing of the Blessed Mother," or it could be included with a prayer. You could lay your hands on people and pray that way. Or you could see someone walking down the street that you didn't even know and in your heart you could say, "I give you the blessing of the Blessed Mother." Whenever you did it, that person would be blessed and it would aid them in their conversion. So Debbie laid her hand on my head again and said, "I bless you with the Blessing of the Blessed Mother and may you pass it on." I can't say I felt anything. It didn't seem to change me any at that time.

The next afternoon on Sunday, I don't know whether it was before the talk or after the talk at the church that Debbie approached me with the idea of blessing everybody in the church with Mary's blessing. I said," Oh, my no! Who am I to go around blessing people? I just give my talk."

Debbie said, "The idea of this blessing is to pass it on to others and what better way to pass it on than to give it to all of these people!" She explained you can only bless one person at a time. "The Blessed Mother says it's like a hug; you can only hug one person at a time. We could invite everyone to come up and you could give each person the blessing."

I balked at the idea, but somehow Debbie convinced me to do it. At the end of the talk I told the people that there was a special blessing, and explained how it worked. Anyone who would like to receive it, could come up and I would give them this gift from the Blessed Mother.

I was astounded to see just about everybody in the church get up and come forward. Then the process started. I laid my hand on the first person's head, and said out loud, "May you have the Blessing of the Blessed Mother, and may you pass it on."

One person after another came forward and I would lay my hand on their head and say the blessing, repeatedly, for each person. After repeating the blessing for so many people, it became almost monotonous. I spoke to the group out loud saying, "I'm going to say this blessing in the silence of my heart, but know that when I lay my hand on your head, and then take it off again, you will have the Blessing of the Blessed Mother and you will be able to pass it on."

When I started praying the blessing silently, I became like a little child inside. I had observed two priests doing this very same thing, Father Jozo from Medjugorje, and Father Svetozar who traveled through the United States giving Life in the Spirit seminars. When each of these priests laid their hands on the people, some of them would fall to the ground. I know when Fr. Svetozar came to our church for a five-day seminar, I went up for the blessing five times, and five times I found myself on the floor, resting in a gentle peace. It's known as "resting in the spirit". Now as I continued to say these words in my heart, asking the Blessed Mother to bless these people, I began to experiment with words; "May you have the Blessing of the Blessed Mother; may you pass it on. May the power of the Holy Spirit come upon you."

I started to try all the holy words I could conjure up in my mind. What were the powerful words that those pious priests used to make people become "slain in the spirit"? Holy word, after holy word, combination after combination, I interjected with absolutely no effect. I started to talk to Jesus, saying, "What is it, Lord, that these men have in their lives that I haven't. I've given you everything I have. I've even offered you my job, and you asked me not to do that. What is it that I could give you so as to be entrusted with a gift like those holy men? I see changes in so many lives after their blessing." Then these words came to my mind, *"Father, I want it."*

I laid my hand on the next person's head, a middle-aged man, and I said, "May you have the Blessing of the Blessed Mother and may you pass it on. May the power of the Holy Spirit come upon you." Then, I repeated those words, "Father, I want it." And the man started toward the floor! I was so stunned that it was happening through me. I reached out and grabbed him before he hit the floor, before he might get hurt. He looked at me and said, "What do you have in your hands?" The thought was going through my mind . . . What did I ask for! Now that I have it, what is it? More people came up and were affected by the words of the Blessing.

I was in Louisville for several reasons; the greatest one was to convince two prayer groups there to unify, to align themselves in a peaceful manner, because there was some strife between them. Hopefully, they would be willing to come under the umbrella of Gospa Missions and work with us. The people seemed at peace with the idea, and they were quite in awe of what was happening with this Blessing. I knew that this group was going to become a special part of Gospa Missions. After the Blessing was completed, we knelt down and sang songs of praise before the tabernacle to our Lord in thanksgiving for all we had experienced this wonderful night. I left Louisville feeling that God had just taken over another part of my life; that He was going to use me in other ways.

When I returned from Kentucky, my first talk was in Homestead, Pa., the very next day. At the end of the presentation, I explained that some very unusual things had happened to me in Louisville. Through touch and the Blessed Mother's Blessing, they could have the gift of the Holy Spirit, allowing God to work in them in a truly powerful way. That was the beginning of a wonderful addition to the talks and everyone seemed anxious to receive Our Lady's gift and that of the Holy Spirit.

Upon my invitation, people came forward. The first man stood in front of me. My eyes were closed as I reached for his head to give him the Blessing. I wondered if the Blessing could possibly be as powerful as it was in Louisville. I was embarrased because I couldn't find his head. The Blessing was just as powerful; he was already on the ground. I told the Lord, "Let's go!" It was euphoric. Many were, "slain in the spirit" during the Blessing. However, I wondered what the problem was with those that were not slain.

The Lord stopped me for a moment to correct this very big error. He said, *"Thomas, you're judging these people. You think the ones on the ground are blessed and the ones that remain standing are not. You are judging and you are wrong. Know this also, Thomas, you have nothing to do with this Blessing other than being an instrument to accomplish it. Your yes, your willingness in allowing me to use you is good, but the Spirit is the power. Don't judge, simply love."*

Sounds easy, don't judge. I still wondered what was wrong. The number of individuals that ended on the floor from the Blessing became fewer and fewer at each presentation until, one day, no one went out in the Spirit. I was devastated! Did I do something wrong and the Lord was taking the gift away? I was partially right. The Lord wasn't taking the gift away, but I was doing something wrong by judging and the Lord wanted it stopped. I told you I was a slow learner.

After most of the people had left the presentation that night, a woman came up to me and said, "Mr. Rutkoski, when I came here tonight I was in such pain, but when you laid your hand on my head it all went away. Thank you." "Don't thank me, thank God. I can't take pain away," I responded. Then Jesus spoke to me again. *"Tell me, Thomas, is she not blessed?"* I think it was at that point I understood. If that was a healing, as far as I know, that was when this new dimension to the Blessing was added. Many people started to claim healings after that. They ranged from simple to profound. Many miracles abounded everywhere I went, but the greatest of all were the spiritual conversions.

Now you see, if I would have tried to remain in control of this conversion story, it would be known only to a few, maybe just in Pittsburgh. It took the efforts of someone like Chuck Cleaveland to tell me that this story didn't belong to me, it belonged to anyone who would listen to it; that it just might be the catalyst to further their conversion. Thank you Chuck! And God bless you!

Chapter 11

The Fruits

Gospa Missions continued to grow and has blossomed into as many as seven offices in six States. On Christmas Eve, December 24, 1990 the Federal government officially recognized Gospa Missions as a non-profit foundation. What a Christmas present! As funds came in we would open new offices. Louisville, Kentucky was the first and that office was opened by Debbie Womack. The second was in Boston, Massachusetts and opened by Suzanne Syska, then Julie Zackrisson in Charlottesville, Virginia; Kevin Loughery in Whately, Mass.; Marianne Berkemeier in Jackson, Michigan; and the latest office was opened by Geralyn Jaskey in San Diego, California.

Each new office receives a computer to dispense the Blessed Mother's Messages and also other equipment to fill the needs of that area. The equipment remains at each location as long as the service is provided to the community in compliance with Gospa Mission standards.

It all started with Medjugorje pilgrimages, including helping the poor to get there, dispensing Our Lady's Messages and my speaking engagements. Then we added pilgrimages to other shrines, an annual retreat on the farm at Gospa Missions headquarters in Evans City, a newsletter, Marian Conferences, and fund and clothing drives for war refugees of what was once Yugoslavia. Most recently, Gospa Missions gave Father Jozo $10,000.00 in cash, during his first visit to the States, to help those refugees.

The involvement varies at each office, but is always on a volunteer basis. No one at Gospa Missions draws a salary. Each office that is added, each person that volunteers, or any conversion that is caused by the activity of all of us involved, is the fruit of Medjugorje.

The miracles mentioned so far in this book are just the tip of the iceberg. They were placed in each chapter where they are, only because I remembered specifically when and where they happened. The following is a collection of events that happened, but cannot be specifically placed chronologically. They are presented to you to further enhance your awareness that God really does exist and He is still working in and through man today, as much as ever, if not more. They all are the fruits of Medjugorje. All the supernatural events are true and many can be substantiated by witnesses and others by facts and documents. Only a few cannot, like the one following. You will have to take my word for this one. Fortunately, it is one of the least significant.

A Lesson in Humility

I never was a humble person. I explained to you in Chapter four that I would race from city to city while on vacation, just to add yet another famous place to my list and come home and brag about it. Then in Chapter six, I mentioned an incident with Marija where after our interview, she extended her hand to shake mine good-bye and I bent to kiss her hand. She instantly snapped her hand back. I explained how I was left there, kissing the wind. I was so embarrassed and I didn't understand why she did that. I found out, after the Lord gave me the gift of healing, the position Marija was in. After a talk and during a blessing, a person felt moved to take my hand and attempted to kiss it. I instantly snapped my hand back. I can only imagine that this was a fruit of Medjugorje, a type of humility. For in jerking my hand back, I realized that the person was trying to attribute this powerful evening to me and the Lord had already explained that it had very little to do with me. Now I know that Marija, in pulling her hand back, wasn't trying to embarrass me, she was simply trying to be humble and keep things in perspective.

The Pheasant

I was going out the driveway one day and pulled up to the gate. Getting out of the car, I saw a rooster pheasant standing on my left about ten inches from my foot. I looked down at him, he looked up at me, and I said, "Well, look at you! I haven't seen one of you guys around here in a long time!" The pheasant population had been diminishing on the farm for years so I was really shocked to see one and he stood right by my foot. A thought came to me and I said, "Tell you what, Lord, there have been so few pheasants on this farm. If You find a mate for this little guy, I'll never shoot another pheasant as long as I live." The rooster just walked away and I got in my car and continued on my way.

The next day I was at the gate again and looked down to see that same rooster, only this time he had a mate with him! I said, "Well, I guess we got a promise to keep here with the Lord. Hope you two have a very good time together and let's see some young ones." They waddled off into the brush.

Several months had passed. I was coming down the driveway toward my house. Suddenly, I had to put on my brakes. There in front of my car, were a rooster pheasant, a hen pheasant and a whole string of little ones just waddling right down the middle of the road. To try to get them out of the way, I beeped the horn but they just continued right down the middle until the rooster cackled a couple of times. Then they wandered off into the brush.

It seems everything I pray about, even this rooster and this hen, comes to be. Summer passed, Fall came and it was hunting season again but I was busy doing the work of the Blessed Mother. This would be the first time in my life I would miss hunting season.

Returning home from work one day, I saw a rooster pheasant in the field. The old hunting instinct came back; the excitement, the thrill of the hunt. The adrenaline started flowing. Running to the house, I got my shotgun, then to the garage to grab a handful of shells. I dashed out to the field and raised my shotgun. I was all ready to squeeze the trigger and have pheasant for dinner that night. Just the second before I pulled the trigger, that voice in my head said, *"I thought you weren't going to shoot any more pheasants."*

I backed off that trigger and popped those shells out of that gun so fast! Returning the gun to the house I said, "You're right, Lord, I just forgot." That little pheasant didn't know how close he came to being on a plate. He's still enjoying the farm because of my promise to the Lord.

God sends Lorraine

It needs to be known that I wasn't the only person to quit a job to serve the Lord and Blessed Mother through Gospa Missions. The following was also an answer to prayer.

With all the help that did come and as thankful as I was for it, again, it was insufficient. Since I was the only one to staff the home office, there was a big void when I was away on speaking engagements. The requests for talks came from all over the country and other countries as well. Because I was away from the office, at times for a week or more, the work really piled up.

I prayed, "Jesus, would it be possible to send someone to work here full time?" In just two days, Lorraine Mutschler arrived. She is a woman who had been on pilgrimage with me and had sponsored a speaking engagement at her church. When she came to my house to deliver a prayer group list, I honestly couldn't even remember her first name, that's how little we knew each other. While at my house, Lorraine said, "I've been thinking about this for some time and wondered, would it be okay if I quit my job and came here to work for you?" Laughing, I answered, "I've been expecting you," and welcomed her aboard.

My prayer was for full-time help, Lorraine's intention was to come part-time, a few hours a week. But we never discussed it. The end result is, Lorraine is here sometimes six days a week, as many as ten hours a day. Some part-time job! Now *Lorraine* has to be careful what I pray for.

Why was Lorraine quitting her job? She heard my witness and was so deeply moved by it, she went to Medjugorje. Half of her family of twelve was converted back to Mass, the rosary and the sacraments because they saw how the Blessed Mother had changed Lorraine. The astounding thing is, Lorraine and her children, through their conversion, are living Mary's message, and causing many conversions in others because they are willing to share. That is how the Blessed Mother's plan works.

Gold Rosaries

On my second trip to Medjugorje someone asked me about rosaries turning gold. I responded, "I don't know anything about rosaries turning gold other than people showing them to me." Just then, I pulled my rosary out of my pocket to show that mine was still silver. It seemed unusually warm and by the time my hand was extended to show the rosary to those gathered around, the metal had become hot! It was astonishing. My rosary was turning gold right in front of our eyes. People shouted, "Look, they're changing now!" And they started to pass them around. By the time I got them back, they were beautifully transformed. The links for the Hail Marys were gold, but the Our Father links were only gold on the edges and not on the flat part.

By this time, others were getting out their rosaries to see if theirs could have possibly changed. It was like a chain reaction. One after the other shouted, "Mine are gold!" "So are mine!" In ten minutes time, twenty rosaries had changed! We were gathered below Apparition Hill and about to load onto our bus when this happened. On the bus, I related to the rest of the group what had just occurred. We found out that more people's rosaries had changed.

One in particular sticks in my mind. Dave Sisk had brought a rosary with him that was a family heirloom. For almost a century, these rosaries were silver, now they were gold. Dave had some concern about what to tell his family about what happened to the silver rosary. Was he to tell them that the Mother of God changed them? I guess we all have to find our own way of explaining the supernatural events that happened in our lives because of Medjugorje. This is my way. Dave surely found his.

One of the more profound changes in me and believe me there have been many, happened when I gave that rosary away. A gift like that from God could be given to another person and maybe inspire them to tell others, "Look, this rosary turned gold for a man!" Telling the story creates an excitement within them and maybe it would play a part in their conversion. Wouldn't you think that I would have carried that rosary with me until I died? But when the time came to part with it, amazingly, it was the easiest thing in the world to do. It was only a short time after, my next rosary turned gold. I thought that rosaries turned gold only in Medjugorje, but it happens anywhere. Mothers are like that!

I got an invitation to speak at my parish, St. Ferdinand Church, and that made me feel particularly good. Two things made it a memorable evening. Dorothy Ziccardi, a parishioner, called out as I was answering questions, "Look, my rosaries turned gold, just now!" Seeing the rosary, now golden, I explained that was the kind of confirmation Mary gives us to affirm this is all true.

That never happened at a talk before. Subsequently, several people have approached me to ask the Lord to give them a sign for one reason or another. I generally respond with, "You ask Him." Inevitably they say, "God listens to *your* prayers." Then I say, "God will listen to anyone's prayers if they truly follow His will. Do you have a pair of rosaries on you?" They will show them to me. I inquire, "What color were they before you asked for a sign?"

"Silver," they respond. I ask, "What color are they now?" With a look of astonishment, they yell, "They're gold!" I simply say as I walk away, "God loves you."

After the woman told me about the gold rosaries a second thing happened. The pastor didn't agree with my telling the audience that I always asked the Lord for permission before going to communion. "What if people don't go because of thinking that way?" Father Ken asked. I responded, "What if they are going to communion and they are in mortal sin? The Blessed Mother says many are doing that and causing great harm to their souls! I feel I am led by the Holy Spirit to say this. Why don't you ask the Lord if this is good or bad. He talks to you, doesn't He?" Father Ken's response was, "Yes, He does. I'll ask."

The next day Father stopped me after Mass and said, "I received confirmation on what we talked about. It's okay for you to keep telling everyone that you ask permission to go to communion." Amen!

Medjugorje Cross Spins

Father Ken Oldenski went on a pilgrimage to Medjugorje with us. Rita Claus was there also, and several other people were present at this particular miracle. When they were coming down Apparition Hill, folks were looking over toward Krizevac mountain and what they saw amazed them. The cross was spinning around. Some people said it completely disappeared off the mountain. I can remember Father Ken turning to Rita Klaus and starting to say, "Is that . . . " and he never got the words out of his mouth before Rita cut him off saying, "Yes, it is Father. The cross is spinning."

Cross Spewing Red

John Rabick and I were in front of St. James church in Medjugorje. We walked around to the left side of the church and looked up. I was astounded at what I saw. On top of Krizevac mountain an enormous red light was shooting out of the top of the cross, making a perfect arc over the top. Most of the miracles in Medjugorje, I took fairly calmly, but this time I shouted out, "Look at the cross! Look at the cross!" Possibly other people saw it, too. Sometimes miracles happen that way in Medjugorje. Some see them and some don't. The red reminded me of a gigantic fireworks display, except this wasn't fire, it was some kind of very intense light. But how could that be? It was broad daylight!

Paul Ruggieri

The circumstances that determine which people would go to Medjugorje or not go, always amaze me. One specific instance stands out well. At KDKA TV they were escorting a new employee around whose name is Paul Ruggieri. While I was in the building that day, editing a news feature for a show called, KD-Country, the door slid open. A management person introduced me to the young man standing beside him. "Tom, this is Paul Ruggieri." I looked up at Paul and said, "Did you ever hear of Medjugorje?" He said, "Medja what?" I said, "Medjugorje! Come back later and I'll tell you about it."

Those were the first words Paul Ruggieri ever heard from my mouth. Paul did come back and I told him the story, many stories. He came back time and time again, any chance he had, to hear more. He got so excited that he decided he and his wife and his mother were all going to go to Medjugorje. Several months prior to our leaving, Paul called me, and with a great deal of sadness in his voice said, "We can't go to Medjugorje." I asked him why not. Paul explained, "They just diagnosed my mother with terminal cancer and the doctors only give her a short time to live."

"Why would that stop you from going?" I said. "You and your wife go. When you get back your mother will be alright." He said, "Are you serious?" I repeated, "Go, and when you come back, your mother will be fine." Paul did go. I've never seen a man get so spiritually involved in anything in my life. Paul took to Medjugorje like a fish takes to water.

The most miraculous thing about the whole trip was when he returned from Medjugorje, his mother was free of cancer. I don't even know what made me tell him to go and that his mother would be alright when he came home . . . the words just came out of my mouth. And they came true! If we could only convince the whole world to believe what the power of prayer can do.

Father John

One day a priest named Father John Bauer called me. He said, "Tom, I'd like you to pray for my church." I asked him why he would ask me to pray for his church. He said, "I know who you are, and what you're doing, and it would be a good thing if you would pray for my church." That seemed highly unusual, that a priest would call *me* and ask for my prayers! But I was willing to pray for anyone, anywhere, anytime. So I told him, I would not only pray for his church, but would rally those I knew who prayed fervently, to pray for his church. Father John thanked me and extended an invitation for me to visit him.

He explained that he had many problems at his church. People were fighting because the diocese was thinking of closing the school there. He wanted to talk about that and visit with me.

I drove to Washington, Pa., to Immaculate Conception Church, and talked with Father John. We were discussing the problems at his parish when he asked me to come to his residence and look at some Icons he owned. Several Icons were hanging on the wall. He made a very strange request. He said, "Hold your hands in front of the Icons, close your eyes and tell me what you see." I wasn't a stranger to unusual happenings at this point, so I agreed, but was uncomfortable about doing it.

The first Icon was a picture of the Blessed Mother from the waist up looking from left to right. What I saw, when I closed my eyes and held my hands up in front of it, was the Blessed Mother looking from right to left. The Icon was blackened and there were tears running down Mary's face. I was shocked at what I saw, to say the least. When I told Father John what I had seen, he asked me to check the other Icons.

At each Icon, when I closed my eyes and held my hands up in front of it, internally I saw something different from what was there. Turning to the next wall, I started to cry profusely. There was a picture of the Blessed Mother, standing with a legion of angels around her. This immediately made me recall the first time I had said the "Hail Holy Queen" prayer from memory. At that time, there was an explosion of a celebration in my head. I could physically feel and hear people rejoicing at my accomplishment! (It's very difficult for me to memorize things.)

Well, when I looked at this picture, the Lord said, *"These are the ones who cheered for you when you said the Hail Holy Queen for the first time."* It was impossible to hold back the tears. Father John asked me what was wrong. I said, "I want that picture!" He said, "You can't have that picture, someone gave it to me as a present." I pleaded, "I really *need* to have that picture!" And I told him the story. Father said, "Maybe we can find another for you." Well, I never did get a copy of the picture. Father John, if you're reading this book, I remind you again, because I've never seen another one like it.

Father John and I finished our chat and he asked me if I would come to the church and speak sometime. I agreed and then left.

On my way back home I passed the Washington Mall. There was a restaurant there that my wife and I favored, The Twenty-first Amendment. They serve a wonderful lobster dinner. My rationale was, since I'd been working so hard, I was entitled to a good dinner. The menu listed the lobster dinner at 'market price'. I was never reluctant about market prices before, but this time I asked and was told the price was $30.00! I said, "How much is the spaghetti?" The waitress said, "$3.95." "I'll take it," I said.

Before I was finished with my dinner, the Lord said, *"Go back. Go back."* "Go back where?" I asked. He said, *"Go back to the church."* I hesitated, "I just left there, there's nothing to do there." Again, the Lord said, *"Go back!"* I wasn't about to argue with the Lord. So not knowing why, I left the Mall and turned back for Immaculate Conception Church.

When I arrived, people were filing into the school for a meeting. There were some very angry people. I followed the crowd in and sat down on a radiator below a window. A man stepped up in front of the group and the meeting started. The man yelled out, "Does Bishop Wuerl own this church?" And the group yelled, "NO!" "Does Father John own this church?" "NO!" everyone shouted.

I started to tremble inside not knowing why the Lord wanted me here or what He was going to do. There was a crucifix on the wall on the left side of the room. I hurried to stand underneath the crucifix, feeling safer there. The crowd continued expressing how upset they were about the prospect of their Catholic school closing. The chairman finished by asking for suggestions from the people. One at a time they expressed why they thought this was an awful thing.

When the meeting seemed to be winding down, they asked if anyone else wanted to say something, and my hand shot up. Believe me, I had no intentions of raising my hand! I was thinking inside, Lord, what are we doing? I started to speak, "If my church in Evans City was closing, how many people here would come up and help me?" Only one hand out of a hundred was raised. I said, "Well, I'm here to help you." And everybody started to cheer. I cautioned them, "I don't think you'll want to cheer once you hear what I have to say."

I walked up to the front of the room and said, "You folks didn't even start this meeting with a prayer, and without prayer you can solve nothing. You started off by shouting that Bishop Wuerl doesn't own this church. You're right, Bishop Wuerl doesn't own this church. Then you shouted that Father John doesn't own the church. You're right. Father John doesn't own this church. This church belongs to Jesus Christ. And anything you ever gave Him, you took back tonight. Would anybody like to pray now?"

Almost everybody bowed their head. We prayed together for a while. Then I explained to them that the solution to their problem could be accomplished through prayer. "If you live your life the way the Lord wants you to, and pray the way He wants you to, prayers get answered. That's how you solve this problem." When I was finished, I walked past that crucifix on the wall, and oh, how I wanted to kiss the feet of Jesus, but it was too high. So I kissed my fingers and touched them to the feet of Jesus. As soon as I did that, my hand came down, with my finger pointing at the group and my mouth said, "I'll be back." My every action that evening seemed to be taken over by the Lord. The whole thing seemed straight out of John the Baptist. Usually when I speak, it's from my heart and very passive. This was bold.

A teenager followed me outside and remarked, "Mr. Rutkoski, that's the first time anybody said anything that made sense here. Thanks for coming."

"I'll tell you what, young lady. Your parents have forgotten how to be the role models for you children. So maybe you should gather your friends together and be the role models for your parents. Start praying about your school and show the adults that a solution can come about through prayer." She smiled and said, "I'll do that." She ran off and I drove home.

Subsequently, I went down to Immaculate Conception Church and gave my presentation two or three times. Once, my friend George Wilson was with me and we presented Father John with the Pieta Prayer Book and the booklet on the Divine Mercy devotion. Father John began the Divine Mercy devotion in his church and in his satellite church down the road.

There was a great conversion at Immaculate Conception and a prayer group started. The beautiful Icon of the Blessed Mother was hung in the Church. It was just so overwhelming, to me and everyone involved, to see that great conversion of the entire parish. The miraculous turnaround of the people of Immaculate Conception Church came about, through intercessory prayer, through the prayer books and devotions, and I'm certain through Father John's great desire to see his church healed of their anger. All played a part in this great spiritual reversal. And it wasn't a slow process, it happened rather quickly.

Bob Kocur

I mentioned earlier about my meeting the Kocurs, Bob and Dorothy. They went on a couple of trips with us, and shortly after the second, Bob got involved with Gospa Missions. He was helping us with computer information. Bob's heart was in it, but he was losing his strength for some reason. Then he started getting very ill. It turned out to be acute leukemia. I don't think I ever prayed so hard for anybody in my entire life. Every day I would pray for Bob Kocur. Soon he was hospitalized and I would go to see him. I'd gather with his family and we'd lay hands on Bob and pray, but he seemed to be getting worse instead of better. All attempts to reverse the progress of his illness, either medically or spiritually, were failing. I expected through prayer, that he would be healed; there was no question in my mind.

One day while I was at the hospital visiting Bob, I found out that several other people I knew were there and I started making the rounds, visiting. My best friend from high school days, John Fediaczko, was a patient, as was his mother, who was like a second mom to me. I couldn't find her. The woman in the bed that had her name on it didn't seem to be Mrs. Fediaczko, so I went out to look on the door again. The name on the door was hers, but most certainly there was a mistake here somewhere. I went to the nurses' station and told them there had to be some mistake; the woman in the bed wasn't Mrs. Fediaczkco.

The nurse explained to me that it was, and that she'd been very, very ill. I asked to see the medical records so I could check the address and see if it was the same Mrs. Fediaczko. It was. I went back into the room in awe of how different this woman looked because she was so ill. Just then her son, Gordon walked in, confirming that it was her. I said a stupid thing just then; the words just came out. "Gordon, your mother looks awful."

It was a dumb thing to say, but she looked so bad. She opened her eyes a little bit and I asked her if it was alright if I prayed for her. She shook her head slightly in agreement. I prayed to God that he would make her better. Then I went to visit for awhile with my friends, John and Bob.

The next day I came back again and made my rounds. This time, when I went to see Mrs. Fediaczko, she looked a little bit better. When I walked over to her, she recognized me. She said, "Oh, Tommy, it's so good to see you. Would you help me to sit up?" She sat up for a while. I said, "I came to pray for you, Mrs. Fediaczko, is that alright?" She said, "Of course." So I laid my hand on her head and asked the Lord to make her better and we talked awhile. Now she looked like the Mrs. Fediaczko I knew. I told her I'd return after visiting a couple of others friends in the hospital.

When I stopped back, she was sitting up in a chair and eating real food. I remember someone saying to me the first day I saw her that she was too ill to leave the hospital, and that she would pass away right there in that bed. At the time I said, "Don't be so sure." It's not that her life was prolonged forever . . . but it showed that through prayer things could change. She looked like herself again, and she did end up going home. She didn't last a long time, but we have to understand God's will.

That last day I was in her room praying for her, a little voice came from behind the curtain on the other side of the room. "Mister, mister, would you come here and pray for me?" I walked over to the bed. I knew the woman must have been from India, because of the red dot in the middle of her forehead. She was a beautiful woman. She looked up at me with big brown eyes, and said, "It's sad that I never thought about God until someone told me that I was about to die." She had acute leukemia also. I used the same words. I said, "Don't be so sure. Let's ask Jesus Christ to help you." I laid my hand on her head and I prayed to Jesus to make her well.

I left that day and came back a day or two later to find Bob Kocur's bed empty. The nurse came by and asked if I was looking for Mr. Kocur. I said, "Yes." She said, "He passed away last night."

I was devastated. The intensity of my prayers was greater than on any other occasion. I never rallied around one person more in my life, and he was gone. I couldn't understand. Since I was in the hospital, I figured I'd go down to see Mrs. Fediaczko and that's when I found out she'd gone home. I peeked around the corner to see if the woman from India was there . . . she was, but she was asleep. So I just stayed by her bed for a moment to say a prayer for her. While I was praying, she woke up. She started saying, "Thank you, thank you, thank you." I said, "What are you thanking me for?" She said, **"I don't have leukemia anymore!"**

A miraculous cure. A person that I didn't even know and prayed for, a terminal patient, reversed in a day, but my friend, Bob Kocur, was dead. I asked the Lord why, and He explained it to me this way. *"Thomas, you have to understand the Father's will. It was God's will that Bob die. The woman from India was just to let you know it was possible; that one could be that sick and through intercessory prayer, could be made well."* So I guess we should always pray like Jesus prayed in the garden, *"Father take this cup from me, but if it be Your will, let Your will be done."*

The Picture on the Cover

This is the way the cover picture came into being. I knew that there were many supernatural pictures taken by various people. One picture, in particular, was taken by a friend of mine, Joseph Hooker. Joseph's picture, which he had taken in Medjugorje, was a cloud in the shape of a man from the waist up. It took no imagination to see that it was a man and possibly Jesus, the Good Shepherd. That picture impressed me so much that I said to the Lord, "I'm a photographer, why can't I take a picture like that?" Miracle envy? Maybe it was a seed that the Lord planted, because several months later in early June, 1991, I asked the Lord for yet another sign. The messages I was hearing at that time made me wonder again if these were really from the Lord. At times, Satan tried to imitate the Lord in an attempt to dupe me. So this time I was more specific than I had ever been with my request. "If this is really you, Jesus, I want a sign in the sky that I can photograph." (The thought of "asking" slipped my mind.)

Later that June, I was preparing to depart for what would be my last trip to Medjugorje before the war in Yugoslavia. As I was leaving the house the Lord said, "Take your camera with you." My intention was not to take it with me, but I succumbed to His request.

On pilgrimage the Lord asked me to carry the camera with me. Two times He asked me where the camera was. I had forgotten it, and the Lord told me to go get it. That must have been a lesson in obedience, for now that I had my camera with me, images started to appear and disappear in the sky so quickly that I didn't have time to take pictures of them. I saw men's faces and lambs among other things.

Many times on Pilgrimages I could close my eyes and see images and once I saw a gold escalator with people coming down from Heaven. Ironically, my friend, Toby Gaines, saw the same thing except the people were going up to Heaven confirming that it was not my imagination. But the images in the clouds were a first for me. Unfortunately, because I was so slow in obeying the Lord, I left Medjugorje with no supernatural pictures.

If only I had as much patience with others as the Lord had with me. Right at the time when I was wondering what the cover for this book would be, it happened! At approximately 3:00 p.m., on Aug. 5, 1991, I was digging potatoes in my garden. (Legend has it that my last name, Rutkoski, in Polish means "potato digger". I don't know if that is really true or not, but someone once told me that.) This was my first time digging potatoes. For some reason, my attention was drawn to the sky. I was shocked to see the Blessed Mother's image in the clouds above my barn.

I ran into the house to get my camera. I returned and took three pictures, then put the camera back in the house. I half expected the image to be gone when I went back outside, but it was not! Now, more amazing than before, the Blessed Mother was holding baby Jesus in Her arms. I ran back into the house to get the camera again, and took four more pictures. The image stayed in the sky for hours.

Fortunately, I had a good zoom lens on the camera and was able to capture some good close-ups. In the largest picture you can clearly see baby Jesus in Mary's arms, the Cross, the Eternal Father, the Holy Spirit and many peoples' faces. Many people who had seen the picture called to tell me that they saw my face in the clouds. I asked Jesus, "Lord, people keep telling me that this is my face in the picture. Who is it?" Jesus answered, *"It is you, Thomas."* What a Gift! I knew instantly that this was to be the cover for my book.

Retreat at Farm

Annually we have a retreat at my farm that includes speakers, fifteen decades of the rosary, Mass and a healing service. If two occurrences in a row is a pattern, then there is a pattern developing. Because, both years that we had the retreat, there has been a miraculous healing.

Geralyn Jaskey had such a severe allergy to wine that she couldn't even use wine vinegar on her salad. While on pilgrimage in Medjugorje during September, 1990, Geralyn was slain in the spirit after being blessed at Father Jozo's church. That evening she went up on Krizevac mountain, and an internal voice told her, *"You may now have wine."* With a leap of faith she was elated to take her first taste of the Blood of Christ during the outdoor Mass at the Gospa Missions retreat a week later. From that day on Geralyn never again experienced her life-threatening allergy.

Marianne Berkemeier, who runs our Jackson, Michigan office, came to the 1991 retreat with her family, including her twelve-year old asthmatic son, Michael. Michael was scheduled to report to a specialist in Minnesota several days after the retreat to try to find a remedy to alleviate some of his suffering. At the end of the day, while the healing service was taking place, Michael explained to his mother that he was having trouble breathing and had to go to the car to get his inhaler. His mother said, "No, Michael, go up for the Blessing first." Michael obeyed his mother's direction and came forward for the Blessing. No more asthma! He never had to go see that specialist. How can I explain how Marianne felt? It's best expressed by the words she used, "God has blessed my son, and our family; and we wish to praise Him and thank Him for all eternity."

My Wife Mary

A question frequently asked of me during my speaking engagements, is "How does your wife react to all of this?" It is by the grace of God that Mary, my wife, is able to deal with the 180 degree change in my life. There has been a positive effect in her life also. Mary was away from her faith, as was I, and has returned to Mass every Sunday. Although she neither understands nor believes all that has happened to me, at times she is very supportive. Because of Medjugorje, the one greatest single change in our combined lives is the validation of our marriage in the Catholic Church, on my birthday, August 4, 1990. Our ability to handle any strife that comes into our life is now done in a more peaceful manner.

A Great Message

While in Jackson, Michigan speaking, I went to Mass on May 17, 1991. The church sanctuary caught my attention. It was semicircular and surrounded by statues of the twelve Apostles. I looked at Saint John and said to Jesus, "I want to be able to love you the way Saint John loves you." Later in the afternoon I received a fax from my friend, Debbie, in Louisville, Kentucky. She received this message for me from the Lord. Debbie had no way of knowing my prayer. The message ended with scripture, Tobit 9, " The Money Recovered." At that particular time I suffered much anxiety over a great financial problem with Yugoslav Airlines, to the point that I was getting hives.

Be steadfast and strong. My time is at hand and I need you, My precious son, to dispense My Words as few others can. There are many souls who ache to know and hear of My Mercy - who will tell them? Only a select few are willing to risk ridicule, persecution and even death to make known My plans. You have been chosen for the feat. You are confident in My Will in your life and I have blessed that confidence with peace in your heart. You are beloved, just as

My disciple John was beloved to Me. So many souls are searching for Me in their own minds but they have not discovered that I dwell in their hearts. Tell them, Thomas, that they must know Me and come to the Father through Me: for if they do not they will perish. They must not seal their fate towards damnation but towards everlasting Love with the Father in Heaven. I have called and cannot continue for much longer. The challenge is set before you, will you now accept this cup which I offer you? I know that you love Me. Do not tarry, the road is long, the wind is stilled. The calm is an omen.

Heed My Words, Chosen One, for in them many will find hope for their salvation. All the ends of the earth will know that I AM Jesus Christ, Savior, Redeemer, Lord. They remain stubborn in their wicked ways and false hope set by the traps of the evil one. Be precise - have courage - I shall not abandon you to them but shall keep you ever protected in My Sacred Heart and in the folds of My Mother's Immaculate Heart. Bring hope to the weary, bring My Peace to the world for it does not know My Peace. Steadfast and true, My beloved son, always close at My side until the day of the Feast when we shall be united as One. I give you My Strength and My Love. Be always Mine. As the Father has sent Me so now I send you. Thank you for your desire to serve Me.

Only days after returning home the great financial problem was solved.

Here's the greatest miracle of all. Before Jesus spoke to me on that boat, I would have been so skeptical about all of this. It would have been laughable to me. Now here I am trying to convince *you* that all of this is true.

Even after my conversion started, I found it all hard to believe.

Please, just try to understand that *God* does these things! The last thing I want is for you to think I'm someone special, because I'm not. This can happen to anyone who really tries. I cringe when people say to me, "You're so good." Jesus was accurate when He said, *"Nobody is good but God."* We're vicious at times with our tongues, more dangerous than a man with a gun, because the damage is much greater. The gun only wounds the flesh, the tongue wounds the soul and the heart.

So if there's one thought I'd like to leave with you in this chapter, it would be this: look back at all these little miracles, all the things that God gives us to aid in our daily conversions of the heart. He gives them to us because He loves us. God sees the effort we are making to change our lives and He, great Father that He is, wants to reward and encourage. That encouragement creates in me an understanding and perseverance in trials, because I know now that God *really exists* and I try harder and harder to be what He wants me to be. The end result of His patience and persistence with me is that I want others, YOU, to work hard at defeating Satan and even harder at pleasing God!

Chapter 12

Apostles Of Light

Previously I mentioned to you about the greatest decision of my entire life, that of quitting my job and going on the road for Jesus. When I did, my Bishop called me into his office and said, "Tom, when I first heard that you quit your job to evangelize, I thought it a mistake. But then I re-evaluated my thinking and came to the conclusion that is exactly what the Apostles did; so how could that be wrong?" He congratulated and blessed me. On the road I went to any place that would let me speak and tell my story. Where they wouldn't let me speak in their churches, I spoke in their halls and city parks.

Does that make me an apostle of light, an "Apostle of the Last Days"? Well, I am certainly trying to be brighter than I was before and I do believe we are in the end times. Whatever I am, let God decide; let His Will be done. I have recently consecrated my life to the Blessed Mother through the Saint Louis de Montfort consecration. I lay my life at Her feet to be transformed through Her Immaculate Heart into something pleasing to Her Son.

What is it God is calling me to? Perfection! He is calling all of us to Perfection! We are to get the plank out of our own eyes and then work to help others as the Lord draws us to His Perfection. Why is the world in such darkness? There are not enough people stepping forth to be light, Apostles of Light.

The song that the pilgrim group sang on top of the mountain in Medjugorje my first night there, explains why I can see in and through this darkness. "I once was lost and now am found, was blind and now I see." The previous eleven chapters tell of the enormous amount of grace the Lord poured upon me, to get me to accept this gift that He wanted me to have, the grace to develop this new sight. It is here in these last pages that I will tell you what it is that I see with this new sight.

In the first chapter I told you I promised to take you full circle as the Lord did with me. This is the circle. Before my conversion I justified all the wrong-doing in my life. If someone stole from me, I would steal from them. If someone hurt me, I would hurt them back. My motto was, 'it's only fair'. This book doesn't elaborate on *all* the wrong in my life, so don't be too quick to say, "You weren't that bad." I *was* that bad, but it's not necessary to get into all of the gory details. This is not a soap opera.

Now for the other half of the circle (and thank you, God, for this new insight). What was it that Jesus said to me about the right-of-way problem when I said, 'You don't understand Lord'? His reply was, *"No, Thomas, you don't understand, you are supposed to turn your cheek seventy times seven."* Who among us does that? If we all lived by this rule, our light would be infinitely brighter. Before, I never turned my cheek; now at least I try. With this new sight I now see how wrong my attitude was.

It's clearer to me now how Satan works his almost imperceptible influence. He has our lifetime to destroy us and uses every means at his disposal. When I point out separately each little deception that Satan works, some people think I am making a mountain out of a molehill.

That's what he wants us to think. Put all of his deceptions together and you can see through the extent of the evil he has successfully planted in the world.

When I was a child you couldn't say the word "damn" on television; now you can watch the sex-act. Day by day, no one notices the subtle changes. The Blessed Mother commented on the miserable state of the world in one of Her messages when She said, *"What was wrong is now right and what was right is now wrong."* How's that? Forty years ago abortions were a secret sin and small in number. Now, in public clinics, 2,000,000 babies a year are slaughtered in America alone and half of our population thinks it is okay to do that. At your next family reunion, try to get everyone to say the rosary together. Or the next time you leave your boss's office say, "May God bless you." It is almost always socially unacceptable and people will consider you strange.

The job of the "apostles of the last days" is to witness by their lives, the reality that God exists. The world proclaims that He exists, just like I proclaimed His existence before 1987, with my mouth rather than with my life.

We all make anti-God decisions everyday and are oblivious to the fact that they are anti-God. God, in His love has given the earth's inhabitants everything we need. There is enough for everyone and no one should ever go to bed hungry. But we, and in particular people like me, became over-consumers. The decisions to buy a bigger house than we need, a car costing too much or buying pleasure items like big boats, while people starve to death, says to God, "I don't believe in you." That may be the ultimate injustice. Some day we will stand before God and have to justify our every action.

Mary, Our Mother, if you believe in Her, said in Medjugorje, *"I come to tell you that God exists."* Why would we need Her to tell us that? Because God loves us so much, He wants to let us know that we are way off track and need to change directions. The Blessed Mother delivers this message: *"Go to Mass every day, say fifteen decades of the rosary every day, fast on bread and water Wednesdays and Fridays, go to confession once a month and have conversion of the heart every day."* Those who live this life send a message back to God: "We know you exist." Living the messages as you have read, can bring about great miracles. Prayers get answered, and as Our Lady says, *"By praying you can stop wars."*

The killing of human life, as in Yugoslavia or the killing of defenseless babies in the womb, can be stopped. First we have to stop the spiritual war in our churches and unite in our prayer.

We need to mend our differences and realize the truth of the "One Bread, One Body" teaching. Yes, Jesus died once and for all, but that does not mean that everyone will be saved. It is not as simple as saying, "Jesus Christ is my Savior." Some preachers teach that Scripture alone is the way; that is only a half-truth. Study the scriptures after serious fasting and praying for discernment; then ask God what the truth is. He made one teaching emphatically clear. So much so, that many of Christ's disciples left him when He explained, *"Unless you eat My Body and drink My Blood, you have no life in you."*

"Can't you understand?" These are the words Jesus Christ spoke to me on my boat in August of 1987. The same words He wants spoken by me now. The next several paragraphs came into being this way. I was working on chapter five and the Lord said, *"Go to the last chapter, chapter twelve and type what I tell you."* At that time, I didn't even know that the book would have twelve chapters. I did as I was instructed. The message is for all of us.

"Can't you understand the absolute necessity of the Eucharist in your lives? That it is truly the Body and Blood, Soul and divinity of Jesus Christ? The miracles surrounding the Eucharist are astounding. Teresa Neuman lived on <u>just the Eucharist</u> for years. It is documented, in several instances, that at Mass when the Priest broke the Eucharist it bled real blood and turned into real flesh. Angels, in apparitions, have presented the Eucharist to seers in Garabandal."

The Lord Jesus Christ has given me a mandate to tell the world that salvation comes from Jesus Christ, through His "bride", His Holy Catholic Church. There are saints whose bodies do not deteriorate as proof of their holiness. This testifies to the truth that the one, holy, Catholic and apostolic Church, under the spiritual leadership of the Pope is the true Church.

All other churches came from a fight, an argument that brought division. That division, through pride, caused an organization to be formed that others call a "church". Twenty-two thousand different denominations exist! That is impossible because Christ has only one "bride", and His house is not divided, His children are. Those children need converted back to the Universal Faith, the Catholic Church, the Church that Jesus Christ started when He said to Peter, *"On this rock I will build My church <u>and the gates of</u>*

said to Peter, *"On this rock I will build My church and the gates of hell will not prevail against it."* He, who dares to say the gates of hell have prevailed against the Catholic Church, calls Jesus Christ a liar. It is not that other religions don't have some or even most of the truth; it is just that they don't have *all* of the truth, the most important truth. Only a Catholic priest has the power to make the Sign of the Cross over bread and wine and change them into the Living Body and Blood of Jesus Christ.

Most Catholics do not understand the responsibility that comes with being a Catholic. The Lord explained this to me, *"A person would have to be a fool to think one only needs to receive Jesus Christ once a year, once a month or once a week. You cannot do battle with Satan every day, without Jesus Christ every day, and you **are** doing battle with Satan **every day!**"*

The beauty of the Catholic faith is that it acknowledges that salvation lies only in God's hands. This faith teaches us also that God, in His infinite mercy, takes into account what is in a person's heart. Therefore the possibility exists for Baptism of Desire. Can it bring one into the realm of salvation? Only God knows. Baptism of Desire can occur when a person lives a good life, follows God's laws and loves God and his neighbor, but does not know the true Church. This person, if he really understood that the Catholic Church was the one true Church and it was here alone that they could receive the Body and Blood of Christ, they would join. If this person should die after living such a life, God alone has the final gift of Mercy at His discretion. However, not taking full advantage of all that God offers is saying to Him, "I can make it on less. I don't need all these gifts." That's playing with fire.

The Catholic Church has been placed on the chopping block so many times. Too often men wielding swords of heresy have hacked away at this Bride of Christ. Their tongues are two-edged swords. They claim to represent Christ but these wolves in sheep's clothing are blinded by Satan. Using God's name for their own ends, they convince many to follow them, never understanding their own blindness. When they explain passages in the Bible, many times they distort them. So as not to disclose their fraud, they conveniently never mention the verse, *"Unless you eat My Body and drink My Blood, you cannot have life within you."* Let's take a look at several teachings in Scripture that help us to understand this passage about "eating the lamb".

Exodus 12:3-32. "Tell the whole community of Israel that on the tenth day of this month each man is to take a lamb for his family, one for each household. {4} If any household is too small for a whole lamb, they must share one with their nearest neighbor, having taken into account the number of people there are. You are to determine the amount of lamb needed in accordance with what each person will eat. {5} The animals you choose must be year-old males without defect, and you may take them from the sheep or the goats. {6} Take care of them until the fourteenth day of the month, when all the people of the community of Israel must slaughter them at twilight. {7} Then they are to take some of the blood and put it on the sides and tops of the doorframes of the houses where they eat the lambs. {8} That same night they are to eat the meat roasted over the fire, along with bitter herbs, and bread made without yeast. {9} Do not eat the meat raw or cooked in water, but roast it over the fire--head, legs and inner parts. {10} Do not leave any of it till morning; if some is left till morning, you must burn it. {11} This is how you are to eat it: with your cloak tucked into your belt, your sandals on your feet and your staff in your hand.

Eat it in haste; it is the Lord's Passover. {12} "On that same night I will pass through Egypt and strike down every first-born, both men and animals, and I will bring judgment on all the gods of Egypt. I am the LORD. {13} The blood will be a sign for you on the houses where you are; and when I see the blood, I will pass over you. No destructive plague will touch you when I strike Egypt. {14} "This is a day you are to commemorate; for the generations to come you shall celebrate it as a festival to the LORD, a lasting ordinance. {15} For seven days you are to eat bread made without yeast. On the first day remove the yeast from your houses, for whoever eats anything with yeast in it from the first day through the seventh must be cut off from Israel.

Numbers 9:11-14 They are to celebrate it on the four-teenth day of the second month at twilight. They are to eat the lamb, together with unleavened bread and bitter herbs. {12} They must not leave any of it till morning or break any of its bones. When they celebrate the Passover, they must fol-low all the regulations. {13} But if a man who is ceremonial-ly clean and not on a journey fails to celebrate the Passover, that person must be cut off from his people because he did not present the Lord's offering at the appointed time. That man will bear the consequences of his sin. {14} "'An alien living among you who wants to celebrate the Lord's Pas-sover must do so in accordance with its rules and regu-lations. You must have the same regulations for the alien and the native-born.'"

John 6:48-69. I am the bread of life. {49} Your fore-fathers ate the manna in the desert, yet they died. {50} But here is the bread that comes down from heaven, which a man may eat and not die. {51} I am the living bread that came down from heaven. If anyone eats of this bread, he will live forever. This bread is my flesh, which I will give for the life of the world." {52} Then the Jews began to argue sharply among themselves, "How can this man give us his flesh to eat?" {53} Jesus said to them, "I tell you the truth, unless you eat the flesh of the Son of Man and drink his blood, you have no life in you. {54} Whoever eats my flesh and drinks my blood has eternal life, and I will raise him up at the last day. {55} For my flesh is real food and my blood is real drink. {56} Whoever eats my flesh and drinks my blood remains in me, and I in him. {57} Just as the living Father sent me and I live because of the Father, so the one who feeds on me will live because of me. {58} This is the bread that came down from heaven. Your forefathers ate manna and died, but he who feeds on this bread will live forever." {59} He said this while teaching in the synagogue in Capernaum. {60} On hearing it, many of his disciples said, "This is a hard teaching. Who can accept it?" {61} Aware that his disciples were grumbling about this, Jesus said to them, "Does this offend you? {62} What if you see the Son of Man ascend to where He was before! {63} The Spirit gives life; the flesh counts for nothing. The words I have spoken to you are spirit and they are life. {64} Yet there are some of you who do not believe." For Jesus had known from the beginning which of them did not believe and who would betray him. {65} He went on to say, "This is why I told you that no one can come to me unless the Father has enabled him." {66} From this time many of his disciples turned back and no longer followed him. {67} "You do not want to leave too, do you?" Jesus asked the Twelve. {68} Simon Peter answered him, "Lord, to whom shall we go? You have the words of eternal life. {69} We believe and know that you are the Holy One of God."

The observation I make in connecting these passages is: God is telling us that when He instructs us what to do with the lamb and we do not obey, we will suffer the consequences. He wants total obedience. I don't want to suffer the consequences He's talking about! Do you?

We need to understand the 'wolves in sheep's clothing' passage. Matthew 7:15 *"Watch out for the false prophets. They come to you in sheep's clothing, but inwardly they are ferocious wolves."* Look at what the wolves have done. They have taken the one true teaching and confused it. I present this to all my non-catholic brothers and sisters. May God grant you the grace of understanding.

One church is the true Church and that Church always has the Chair of Peter to lead it. The others are in violation of Holy Scripture. The Lord's teaching is explicit in Matthew :13 *"Do not separate the wheat from the weeds."*

Matthew 13:25-43 "But while everyone was sleeping, his enemy came and sowed weeds among the wheat, and went away. {26} When the wheat sprouted and formed heads, then the weeds also appeared. {27} The owner's servants came to him and said, 'Sir, didn't you sow good seed in your field? ***Where then did the weeds come from?'*** *{28} '''An enemy did this,' he replied.* ***"The servants asked him, 'Do you want us to go and pull them up?' {29} 'No,' he answered, 'because while you are pulling the weeds, you may root up the wheat with them. {30} Let both grow together until the harvest. At that time I will tell the harvesters: First collect the weeds and tie them in bundles to be burned; then gather the wheat and bring it into my barn.'"***

{36} Then He left the crowd and went into the house. His disciples came to Him and said, "Explain to us the parable of the weeds in the field." {37} He answered, ***"The one who sowed the good seed is the Son of Man. {38} The***

field is the world, and the good seed stands for the sons of the kingdom. The weeds are the sons of the evil one, {39} and the enemy who sows them is the devil. The harvest is the end of the age, and the harvesters are angels. {40} "As the weeds are pulled up and burned in the fire, so it will be at the end of the age. {41} The Son of Man will send out His angels, and they will weed out of His kingdom everything that causes sin and all who do evil. {42} They will throw them into the fiery furnace, where there will be weeping and gnashing of teeth. {43} Then the righteous will shine like the sun in the kingdom of their Father. He who has ears, let him hear.

How is it then, that a man could come along and say to any group, "let's gather our wheat and leave these weeds," and anyone would listen to him? That is to say, how could anyone ever say, "Let's go and start our own church with a new doctrine." And again that's playing with fire!

The chart on the next page shows some of the splits from the first and true Church. It tells the story of how many times the wolves convinced their followers to follow them into great apostasy. Every one who did so is in violation of the above scripture! Not only are these wolves scattering the flock, they are claiming to be the "truth" as they do it. If you have followed them, reevaluate! How can anyone follow them after reading the book of Matthew? How can you not want to investigate more seriously the first Church? *"He who has ears, let him hear."*

We, in our individual lives, do not have the time it takes to come to a full understanding of what Christ's teachings are. All that Jesus Christ is leading us to and all the wisdom He gave us is in the Bible and pertains to our

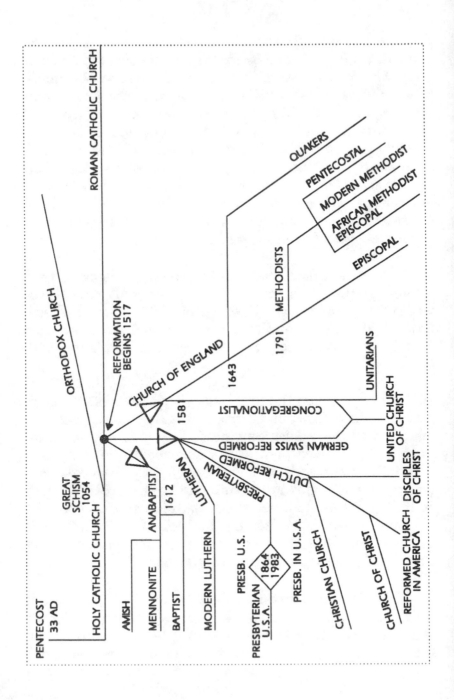

daily lives. It would be foolish, as Christians, to think that we could live our faith without the guidance of the Magisterium of the Church; without the truth of Christ given to us through His Vicar on earth, the Pope. We'd be an army without a general; a corporation without a board of directors; a nation without a president.

One can see the results by opening the Yellow Pages and looking under churches. Depending on the size of your city, using for example, New York, there are thousands and thousands of churches listed. Different doctrines, different church laws and teachings, all proclaim to tell the "truth" about Jesus Christ. With teachings so diverse, so opposed, how can they all be the true teachings of Jesus Christ? This is illogical and impossible. One church says, "The bread, after consecration, becomes the Eucharist, the Body of Christ." Another church says, "No, it only *represents* the body." One has to be a false teaching. One church believes that Jesus Christ is God. Another believes He is the Son of God, but not really God. One church believes in the Father, Son, and the Holy Spirit, three Persons in one God. This is not taught in other churches. They don't believe in the Holy Trinity. All of them cannot be right.

To my Catholic brothers and sisters, I ask you this. If you are not living the messages that the Mother of God is delivering to earth because you don't believe it is She, what if you are wrong? What if this really is the Blessed Mother? Wouldn't your disbelief then be spiritually disastrous? But if you lived Her messages by going to Mass every day, saying the Rosary daily and fasting to support God's plan, what could it hurt? If you don't live the messages, you possibly turn your back on God. If you do, it is a win-win situation. The worst that could happen is that you'd become a better person.

God is calling us to the Eucharist. I offer to you my last revelation of this writing. The Lord's explanation of the "woman at the well."

Februrary 13, 1992, 9:30a.m.: I was sleeping latet this day. Two days before, after speaking at a church that was many hours away, I arrived home late and was very tired. The previous night, I had worked late on our finances trying to find a $45 imbalance. For two nights in a row, my bedtime was after 1:00 am. The alarm was set for 7:30 a.m. so I could attend Mass. Having difficulty trying to sleep, I got up to get a drink of water. I felt rather ill with a headache and queasy stomach. This was caused from my fasting the day before and was a regular occurrence on fast days. When my headaches turn to migraines, at times, I will take aspirin. This time I took not only aspirin but some Tums because the pain caused a lot of stomach acid. I returned to bed and glanced at the clock. It was already 5:30 a.m. so there was only two hours to sleep. Feeling as I did, it was difficult to sleep. I grasped for my rosary. When I have difficulty sleeping, I pray the rosary and fall asleep. I said, "Blessed Mother, please help me to sleep." I started the rosary and was out like a light. The alarm went off at 7:30 a.m. shattering what little sleep I had. The thought ran through my mind, "Maybe I could skip Mass this one day." Tonight was going to be another late night. The thought only lasted a second when I realized "who" was trying to influence me. I instantly decided to get up and get ready for Mass. It was then that the Lord spoke. *"Rest, there will be a mass this afternoon at the home for the elderly."* I knew that to be true. This Mass took place only on Thursdays. "Oh thank you!" I said to the

Lord. I turned off the alarm and fell like a piece of lead back onto the bed. The next thing I knew, the Lord spoke to me again.

"Thomas, when I was at the well with the woman what did I tell her?"

The Lord was referring to, John 4:5-14. *So he came to a town in Samaria called Sychar, near the plot of ground Jacob had given to his son, Joseph. {6} Jacob's well was there, and Jesus, tired as he was from the journey, sat down by the well. It was about the sixth hour. {7} When a Samaritan woman came to draw water, Jesus said to her, "Will you give me a drink?" {8} (His disciples had gone into the town to buy food.) {9} The Samaritan woman said to him, "You are a Jew and I am a Samaritan woman. How can you ask me for a drink?" (For Jews do not associate with Samaritans.) {10} Jesus answered her, "If you knew the gift of God and who it is that asks you for a drink, you would have asked him and he would have given you living water." {11} "Sir," the woman said, "you have nothing to draw with and the well is deep. Where can you get this living water? {12} Are you greater than our father, Jacob, who gave us the well and drank from it himself, as did also his sons and his flocks and herds?" {13} Jesus answered, "Everyone who drinks this water will be thirsty again, {14} but whoever drinks the water I give him will never thirst. Indeed, the water I give him will become in him a spring of water welling up to eternal life."*

I thought about what the Lord asked and replied, "You said that You would give her living water to drink. If she drank this water, she would live forever." *"What was she doing at the well?"* "She was getting water." *"How often did she come to the well?"* "It must have been everyday." *"Why?"* "Because we need water every day." *"Why do you need water every day?"* "If we don't drink water every day, we could die." *"Why are you so ill?"* "Because I fasted yesterday and when I fast, sometimes I get ill." *"Why do you get ill?"* "I guess it's because I've deprived my body of something it needs and it's sending a signal to me." *"How does this apply to the woman at the well?"* It became so apparent to me, the lesson that was being taught here. Don't feed your earthly body every day and you'll not only realize the bad effects, but you will suffer them also and you will do anything to correct the situation. "Here You were telling the woman at the well that You would give her the living water that she might live forever. This all is a direct parallel; don't eat or drink physically and you will die. Don't eat or drink spiritually and you will die." *"Exactly, Thomas. People can't understand the damage they are doing to their souls by not feeding their souls every day. You can't live forever if you don't eat every day. Get up and write this down."*

I glanced at the clock and it was 9:30 a.m. I said, "I have to say my morning prayers before I write it down." The Lord replied, *"Say your prayers afterwards. Go and write it down."* Again it was clear to me precisely why He was telling me to do it now. I reflected back to the statement He made to me before, *"Get up Thomas and write this down. You forget too easily."* So I got up and wrote it down.

Now it makes me wonder why I didn't write everything down. Jesus Christ has said so many beautiful things to me. If I would have just written all of them down you could have shared *all* the words and it might have helped you more. Analyzing myself, I realize how many corners I have cut. If I hadn't been so lazy, and had written down more details, you could understand more clearly. For that I apologize to you.

I feel like Job when I speak to someone about what the Lord says to me and they doubt or consider me a liar.

Job 31:35-40 ("Oh, that I had someone to hear me! I sign now my defense--let the Almighty answer me; let my accuser put his indictment in writing. {36} Surely I would wear it on my shoulder, I would put it on like a crown. {37} I would give him an account of my every step; like a prince I would approach him.)-- {38} "if my land cries out against me and all its furrows are wet with tears, {39} if I have devoured its yield without payment or broken the spirit of its tenants, {40} then let briers come up instead of wheat and weeds instead of barley."

That is exactly how I feel and if I am not producing good fruit then let God be my Judge.

To my non-catholic brothers and sisters, I just ask you to consider this. How is it then that you can celebrate the special days of famous people, for instance in America: Washington's birthday, Lincoln's birthday, etc., and not set aside a single day to honor the Woman who gave birth to Our Savior Jesus Christ. In the Magnificat (Luke 1:49) She says, "All generations will call Me Blessed." She is the new Ark of the Covenant, the new Eve. To simply discard the perfect container in which Jesus Christ was delivered and think that is not offensive to God is indeed foolish.

To my brothers and sisters, the religious, to the shepherds, I offer you the words of Jonah:

*Jonah :3 Then the word of the LORD came to Jonah
a second time: {2} "Go to the great city of Nineveh and proclaim to it the message I give you." {3} Jonah obeyed the
word of the LORD and went to Nineveh. Now Nineveh was a
very important city--a visit required three days. {4} On the
first day, Jonah started into the city. He proclaimed: "Forty
more days and Nineveh will be overturned." {5} The Nine-
vites believed GOD. They declared a fast, and all of them,
from the greatest to the least, put on sackcloth. {6} When the
news reached the king of Nineveh, he rose from his throne,
took off his royal robes, covered himself with sackcloth and
sat down in the dust. {7} Then he issued a proclamation in
Nineveh: "By the decree of the king and his nobles: Do not let
any man or beast, herd or flock, taste anything; do not let
them eat or drink. {8} But let man and beast be covered with
sackcloth. Let everyone call urgently on God. Let them give
up their evil ways and their violence. {9} Who knows? GOD
may yet relent and with compassion turn from his fierce anger so that we will not perish." {10} When GOD saw what
they did and how they turned from their evil ways, he had
compassion and did not bring upon them the destruction he
had threatened.*

If Jonah came today and said, "*"Forty more days and
Nineveh,* (Pittsburgh, Cleveland, wherever) *will be overturned"*, destroyed, **would your flock get into sack cloth or
would they perish?** Or is Jonah already here?

In reality, does it matter who the messenger is, Jonah, the Blessed Mother, you or me? There are so many reported supernatural events happening now. God allows
these to happen because of His great love for us.

With millions of abortions, wars, drug abuse, pro-
miscuous sex, and total selfishness, the world has never

been darker, or more evil! In many of the messages from Our Blessed Mother, Our Lady speaks of chastisements that are coming and some that are already here. Most people do not want to hear of chastisements and say it is not a message of peace and love, so it can't be Our Lady. The Blessed Mother gives us advance warning of these chastisements so that we might change as they did in Nineveh. This is love of the greatest kind; a Mother protecting Her children.

What matters is, are we ready? Not for the great chastisements that may come, because the world deserves them, but for the truck that might slam into your car when you round the next bend; the next heart attack. Are you ready _now_?

We come to the end of my story, but not really the end because every day is a new start, a new chapter. I will pray for you every day for the rest of my life and I ask that you do the same for me. If I am the instrument of a blessing, I give you the Blessing of the Blessed Mother and may the power of the Holy Spirit come upon you. As tears roll down my cheeks now, I pray this writing will help you in your faith journey. The following are words of wisdom from Our Lady. Let the Journey began with Her.

Medjugorje Message

Our Lady's Message for March 25, 1992. _"Dear Children, Today as never before, I invite you to live my messages and to put them into practice in your life. I have come to you to help you and, therefore, I invite you to change your life because you have taken a path of misery, a path of ruin._

When I told you, "Convert, pray, fast, be reconciled", you took these messages superficially. You started to live them and then you stopped because it was difficult for you. Know, dear children, when something is good, you have to persevere in the good and not think, "God does not see me, He is not listening, He is not helping."

And so, you have gone away from God and from me because of your miserable interests. I wanted to create of you an Oasis of Peace, Love and Goodness. God wanted you with your love and with His help to do miracles and thus give an example.

Therefore, here's what I say to you, "Satan is playing with you and with your souls and I cannot help you because you are far from my heart." Therefore, pray, live my messages, and then you will see the miracles of God's Love in your everyday life. Thank you for responding to my call."

Arizona Messages

Message from Our Lady of the Americas. May 2, 1992. *"My Dear Children, To those of you who have heard My call and answer it and are now helping Me with your prayers, I thank you greatly. I thank those of you who are here with Me on this evening as we gather to pray for the salvation of men in the world.*

I have come to the world to call all My children to return to God, to seek a life of goodness and of holiness. Many have heard My call, have made a sincere effort to change, but still continue to struggle with true commitment in following the path to God.

You continue to concern yourselves and worry too much about your own personal needs and comforts and barely see the concerns and worries of the world around you. You see the devastation of humanity yet you continue to focus on yourselves, your physical comfort and well-being. My children, when are you going to understand what I am here to tell you? Are your eyes so intent on yourselves that you are incapable of focusing on the signs that are occurring around you?

My call to you has turned from a whisper to a loud voice, trying to warn you, to force you to take notice of what is going on around you. I am calling you from many parts of the world to ask you to return your lives to God, to the goodness and holiness of who He is, for He is your only salvation. As the world crumbles around you, you still continue to ignore it. How long is your blindness going to continue? As long as your eyes continue to focus on yourselves and refuse to focus on the world's needs you will continue to walk the path of destruction and chaos.

On this day I plead with you to pray harder than ever to turn your lives to God's love and through that love begin to love each other. Begin today, immediately, to love each other - to reach out to each other in respect and dignity. If you do not, you will surely destroy each other. Turn your focus from yourselves to the external, to the world that is in such need of God's love, for God's love for you and your love for Him is the only way to your salvation. I love you and thank you for listening to My words. Message given in the house of, Mr. Reyes Maria Ruiz 30 East Cody Dr. Phoenix, Arizona. 85040

Message From Our Lady of the Americas, May 16, 1992. *"My Dear Children, I thank all of those who have committed to prayer for the salvation of mankind. It is on those of you who have heard My cry and answered that I put my trust. It is your prayers and love that have helped to open many hearts to God and that will continue to help Me as I call out to all My children throughout the world.*

I come to call out to all, in love, hoping that all mankind will hear Me in these times of trouble in the world. I make My voice ever stronger as I speak through many to try to touch as many as possible. Our Lord has never been so evident as He reaches out to all humanity in His mercy and love. Many have heard Our call of love and many have not. Many more will hear Our call of love and answer, and others will not.

But you must be assured that our Lord will continue to send abundant graces in these times of need. The world is desperately in need of God's love and Our Lord will never fail you. As evil escalates its attempt to destroy, so does our Lord escalate the abundance of graces to assist mankind in its struggle to victory over this evil.

Those of you who have opened your hearts to My call and to God's love must never fear the power of evil, for you are made strong through the power of God's love in you. All forces of darkness will not and cannot overpower you, for God's strength in you is immensely more powerful. If you have turned your lives over to God, asked Him to live in you through His Holy Spirit, you need not fear to walk strong in love, faith and hope. You will be able to walk firmly in faith spreading God's love to all. Remember that God's love is reflected through kindness, patience, forgiveness and hope. His abundant flow of graces will shine through you, especially in these times of darkness, but you must be open to receive them. Pray, My faithful ones, that all mankind will open their hearts to receive these graces. I love you and thank you for listening to My words."

Message given from the house of: Mr. Reyes Maria Ruiz, 30 East Cody Dr., Phoenix, Arizona 85040

Glory be to the Father, and to the Son, and to the Holy Spirit: as it was in the beginning, is now, and ever shall be, world without end. Amen.

Epilogue

In any religious endeavor one should always pray for confirmation. I believe confirmation has come for this writing. On the day before printing and just in time to include in this book, the 1991 supplement to Father Gobbi's book, "To The Priests, Our Lady's Beloved Sons" was mailed to those in The Marian Movement of Priests. The book is a chronological listing of the messages Father receives from the Blessed Mother. This year's supplement includes the message I claim as confirmation, "Apostles of the Last Times."

"Today you are celebrating the liturgical memorial of my Immaculate Heart. This is your feast, my beloved ones and children consecrated to me.

You have been chosen by me and called to form part of my victorious cohort. You form part of my estate. I have a great design upon you. This design of mine has been revealed to you in every detail. It must now appear to the Church and to humanity in all its splendor, because these are the times of your maturity and of your public witness.

Show yourselves to all as my consecrated ones, as **The Apostles of These Last Times.**

As **apostles of the last times,** *you must announce with courage all the truths of the Catholic faith; proclaim the Gospel with force; and resolutely unmask the dangerous heresies which disguise themselves with truth in order to* *better deceive minds and thus lead astray from the truth a great number of my children.*

*As **apostles of the last times**, you must withstand with the strength of little ones the proud force of the great and the learned. who, seduced by a false science and by vain glory, have torn to pieces the Gospel of Jesus, by propounding an interpretation of it which is rationalistic, humanistic, and entirely erroneous. The times foretold by Saint Paul have come, times when many announce false and strange doctrines and thus they go running after these fables and stray away from the truth of the Gospel.*

*As **apostles of the last times**, you must follow Jesus along the road of disdain for the world and for yourselves, of humility, of prayer, of poverty, of silence, of mortification, of charity and of a more profound union with God. You are unknown and despised by the world and by those who surround you; you are often obstructed, marginalized and persecuted, because this suffering is necessary for the fecundity of your very mission.*

*As **apostles of the last times**, you must now illuminate the earth with the light of Christ. Show yourselves to all as my children, because I am always with you. Let the faith be the light which illuminates you, in these days of apostasy and of great darkness and in these times of such a vast infidelity, let it be zeal alone for the glory of my Son ,Jesus which consumes you.*

*As **apostles of the last times**, there befalls you the duty of carrying out the second evangelization, so much asked for by my Pope, John Paul II. Evangelize the Church, which has strayed from the Spirit of Christ and has allowed itself to be seduced by the spirit of the world, which has*

B

penetrated it deeply and has pervaded it entirely. Evange-lize humanity which has again become pagan, after almost two thousand years since the first announcement of the Gos-pel. Evangelize all men, who have become victims of errors, of evil, and of sin and who let themselves be swept away by the impetus wind of all the false ideologies. Evangelize the peoples and the nations of the earth, immersed in the dark-ness of the practical denial of God, as they prostrate them-selves in the worship of pleasure, of money, of power, of pride and of impurity.

Your times have come and I have formed you during these years, so that you may be able to give now your strong witness as faithful disciples of Jesus, even to the shedding of your very own blood.

*When from every part of the earth, all of you, my chil-dren, will give this witness, as **apostles of the last times,** then my Immaculate Heart will have its greatest triumph."*

A second confirmation came when the I.S.B.N. num-ber, the universal book numbering system located on the back cover, was assigned to this book and the last three dig-its were 7-7-7. This number is described in Holy Scriptures as Heavens number.

On the next page you will read a poem that the Lord placed on my heart. The message contained in it, I believe, will explain what *Apostles of the Last Days* is all about.

C

AUTUMN

It starts with a leaf turning, one here, one there.
Then a whole tree turning, winter's coming, beware!

Nature displaying beauty, beyond compare.
With her autumn palette, she paints with a flair.

To warn us, to guide us, she nudges beware.
Winter's coming, winter's coming, you must prepare!

Brilliant summer's flowers, will soon deplete.
The ants and the bees, will also retreat.

The animals all know it, even the small.
We have a name for it, we call it fall.

In this grace period, of grand color release.
Before winter's grip, it brings us some peace.

Leaves in cool breeze, they dance and they sway.
Winter's coming, winter's coming, no time for delay.

So cut up your pumpkin, and do what you do.
Stack up your firewood, and clean out your flue.

But if you grant me this moment, I have words for the wise.
The reds and the yellows are just a disguise.

So don't stand by idly, and stare at the trees.
Take Mother's warning , you can learn from the leaves.

We all must surrender, and fall to the ground.
That's nature's way, for new life to be found.

Winter's coming, winter's coming, you better prepare!
That's Mother's nature, and truly is fair.

An Invitation

I invite you to become a part of Gospa Missions, (Our Lady's Missions). You can do this in many ways. You can support a message computer in your area to dispense the Blessed Mother's messages. You can subscribe to our newsletter which will keep you abreast of our many projects and we ask that you encourage others to do the same. You can help to arrange pilgrimages or to set up speaking engagements in your area. I will gladly come to tell my story for no charge except for my travel expenses. Being a member of Call 10 is the simplest way to participate. Call 10 is a phone tree designed to spread important religious information quickly. If you are interested in serving the Blessed Mother through Gospa Missions and need further explanation of any of these projects, please contact us at the home office.

A donation of $20.00 is requested for this book by all who read it, even if it was simply lent to you. It is our desire to get it in as many hands as possible and your donation will help to do that. I now give them away at the talks and ask folks to send a donation based on what they received from it. All proceeds go to spread the Blessed Mother's messages, to help the poor, and to keep Gospa Missions alive. Reduced donations are always accepted if a person can not afford $20.00 and it can and will be sent free to those who can afford nothing. Donations to Gospa Missions are tax deductible.

For a complete list of all items available through Gospa Missions call 412 - 538 - 5700 and 538 - 3513 or write to me:

Thomas Rutkoski
Gospa Missions
200 Wilderness Trail
Evans City, PA 16033